Praise for *A Curious Curriculum*

This is a powerful, hard-hitting book about how we ensure that the curriculum truly ...spires curiosity and challenge in primary-aged learners. Alongside beautiful illustrations and inspiring stories of practice, there is a strong undercurrent that cuts across complacency. With dialogic pedagogy at the heart, this text seeks to explore how the highest standards can be achieved within and through foundation subjects – standards that can never be achieved via formulaic lessons. The authentic wisdom of these authors really packs a punch. Not to be missed.

> Dame Alison Peacock, DL, Chief Executive, Chartered College of Teaching

An intelligent, honest and practical account of a multi-academy trust's journey to create an authentically rich and progressive curriculum. Claire Banks and Mick Waters present a compelling vision for a preferred future for primary school provision.

> Kevin Butlin, Director of Education, Plymouth CAST Multi-Academy Trust

A Curious Curriculum is likely to be an enormous asset to all in primary who (using the authors' own words) seek to be 'well informed, well read and thoughtfully discerning ... careful to distinguish between trends, fads and genuine new answers to perennial questions' in relation to the curriculum. This approach is to be admired for the whole curriculum and in particular for foundation subjects – which are so often the poor relative. I particularly like that the whole process of collaboratively applying this approach to create a truly owned curious curriculum that has both depth and breadth is analysed in a way that does not claim to create a model that can be 'lifted and shifted' into different contexts. Rather, what arises from the analysis is a set of principles and ways of working that can be applied and owned in a range of ways.

> Professor Sam Twiselton, OBE, Director of Sheffield Institute of Education, Sheffield Hallam University

The focus on curriculum development and its position at the core of school improvement is one of the golden threads of what makes for a strong and sustainable trust. When a trust is set up, it is done so with the core aim of creating better educational opportunities for children than were possible before. That was the deal! This brilliant book, from a trust I know well and have huge respect for, traces the development of curriculum thinking from the perspective of the trust, seen through the eyes of the schools. This book does not tell people what to include in a curriculum. Why would it? Instead, it is a case study in leading change. How to take people with you. How to communicate intent. How to create expectations of what will happen in different classrooms where the ownership of the trust curriculum is with the teacher and not the trust itself. The more our most credible practitioners can share with the wider sector, the better. This book adds to the growing library of must-read books. I loved it.

> Sir David Carter, former National Schools Commissioner, Director of Carter Leadership Consultancy

There is so much in this book that I wish I had written, and even more that I am glad I have read. I will go back to it again and again and will look forward to every visit.

> David Cameron, The Real David Cameron Ltd

This compelling narrative unveils the journey of a collaborative endeavour that is steeped in a commitment to an ecology of learning and flourishing. Claire and Mick provide an honest and insightful account of how the trust has been able to foster and nurture a curriculum that provides an equity of provision and opportunity for all children. With practical tips and key questions underpinned by an informed and inspired philosophy of education, this book is a crucial read for all pragmatic educators who are interested in planning for the unpredictable and cultivating joy.

> Vikki Pendry, CEO, The Curriculum Foundation

A Curious Curriculum doesn't offer an off-the-shelf solution (although QR codes link directly to resources for readers), but rather a lively buffet of what a curriculum could be – for those brave enough, and curious enough, to try.

> Judith Schafer, Director, One Cumbria Teaching School Hub

A really interesting read that will help schools navigating their important journey in developing and evaluating their curriculum. It highlights the importance of the thought behind individual curriculums and provides a structured way to reach the desired outcome, learning from this trust's experience.

> Mrs J. Heaton, OBE, CEO, Northern Lights Learning Trust

Crafting a school curriculum that is rich in engaging learning experiences should be a priority for every school, yet it is a complex task fraught with challenges. *A Curious Curriculum* describes the journey undertaken by a school trust to bring teaching communities together to construct the foundations of a school curriculum that is engaging, motivational and wholly relevant to the present and future world in which our young people live. At the same time, it provides other schools with a framework to allow them to reflect on their own practice and inspires them with practical tools to reimagine a school curriculum that places high-quality learning at its heart. Thank you, Claire and Mick, for a compelling and uplifting read that will benefit educators around the world.

Daniel Jones, Chief Education Officer, Globeducate

Refreshing in its honesty and humility, *A Curious Curriculum* is a comprehensive resource for any school or trust leader looking to improve their curriculum. Rightly proud of Olympus Trust's curious curriculum, the authors nevertheless do not present it as a blueprint for others to follow, rather as evidence of the depth of thinking and planning that characterise their approach to the foundation subjects. The real value of this book is in how it describes one trust's journey in navigating the snakes and ladders of curriculum development. Readers are invited not to 'drag and drop' the curious curriculum developed at Olympus, but to learn from how it was done, what worked and what was difficult. It was a joy and an education to see beneath the bonnet of such a considered and coherent approach to curriculum.

Dr Kate Chhatwal, OBE, Chief Executive, Challenge Partners

I encourage all educators to read this book! Filled with a sense of joy, it has put learning at the centre for all. It will empower you to wonder, explore and become forward-thinking leaders. This book exemplifies the journey of a trust that has understood that if you want innovative learners, you need innovative educators/facilitators. Ultimately, innovation is not about a skill set, it's about a mindset, and to develop this mindset takes planning, sampling and, most importantly, talking about learning. Claire and Mick guide the way with great models, questions and exemplars that will help any educator to critically assess where they are on the journey. I am left with the curiosity to take a deeper look at the curriculum models in our trust. I particularly love how the development takes into consideration how the curriculum will be experienced by the child by using 'through the eyes of the child' in the planning.

Sarah Finch, CEO, Marches Academy Trust

Wherever you are on your curriculum journey, I highly recommend this book. Through the eyes of the children, it charts the long-term journey Olympus Trust has taken to ensure that the foundation subjects are taught as well as English and maths. It provides a practical walkthrough with real examples of their rich and engaging process, reminding us of the importance of sharing the 'why' behind all decision-making. This is not an off-the-shelf answer for your curriculum. It will inspire you to think and have rich discussions about how your curriculum and pedagogy are interwoven to ensure children are equipped with the best opportunities to flourish and thrive.

Narinder Gill, School Improvement Director, Elevate Multi-Academy Trust,
author of *Creating Change in Urban Settings*

The Curious Curriculum is a must-read for anyone with a passion for a values-driven, child-centred approach to teaching and learning. Claire and Mick brilliantly articulate the interconnection between a philosophy of education, inclusive pedagogical principles and deep subject knowledge. Claire and Mick place great sensitivity on the context of individual schools and the autonomy of practitioners.

Claire Shaw, Diocesan Director of Education

This is so much more than a book on developing a great foundation curriculum! It is a book about effective change management, about leadership behaviours, culture and practice, underpinned by an honest narrative sharing all the benefits of hindsight. The 'through the eyes of the child' perspective reminds us all that we should never get distracted from this. I feel inspired!

Mrs Claire Savory, Director of Academies, Gloucestershire Learning Alliance

A Curious Curriculum

Teaching foundation subjects well

Claire Banks and Mick Waters

Crown House Publishing Limited
www.crownhouse.co.uk

First published by

Crown House Publishing Limited
Crown Buildings, Bancyfelin, Carmarthen, Wales, SA33 5ND, UK
www.crownhouse.co.uk

and

Crown House Publishing Company LLC
PO Box 2223, Williston, VT 05495, USA
www.crownhousepublishing.com

British Library Cataloguing-in-Publication Data

A catalogue entry for this book is available from the British Library.

Print ISBN 978-178583643-5
Mobi ISBN 978-178583649-7
ePub ISBN 978-178583650-3
ePDF ISBN 97-8178583651-0

LCCN 2022936629

Printed and bound in the UK by
Gomer, Llandysul, Ceredigion

This book is an appreciation of the professionalism and commitment of head teachers and the community of schools in the Olympus Academy Trust. Their efforts have enriched learning and enhanced the life chances of children in our schools.

Foreword

It is odd that in some quarters there is talk about the curriculum as though it is a 'new thing'. Yet, there has always been a curriculum, even before the national curriculum, and even before it became a focus in the quality of education judgement in the latest inspection framework. What is new, however, is the attention being paid to the quality of what is being offered to pupils, particularly in the foundation subjects. While English and mathematics have been well served in terms of resources, thinking and planning – and with good reason – the same cannot be said for the other subjects. What has characterised the planning and delivery of the foundation subjects in many, but not all, parts of the sector, is that they are something to be 'covered', in the form of activities for pupils to do rather than worthwhile areas of exploration.

The reasons for the foundation subjects being poor relations in terms of curriculum thinking and realisation are understandable: pressures of time, absence of resources and lack of knowledge about where to find good materials. But, with the sector now focused on levelling up the wider curriculum beyond the core, many of us have realised that this is about more than tarting up plans or refreshing a bought-in scheme. It is more complicated than that, and there is work to be done over the long term.

We talk about making sure the curriculum is coherent for our pupils, but is our approach to thinking about and planning that curriculum also coherent? Is there a shared meaning beyond the catchy headlines? If we are going to get better at this, we need to begin by taking a wider view and looking at and interrogating examples from other contexts. *A Curious Curriculum* provides a missing link in the literature on how to make this aspect of school provision actually work on the ground.

We might have all the values statements in the world, but are we doing the gritty work of making sure that the curriculum is working for every child, every day, in every classroom? It is never a blame game, but why is it so common to find that schools are downloading generic stand-alone lesson plans and then wondering why the pupils don't know, aren't able to talk about or do something with what they have been given? This is because we have often slipped into a hand-to-mouth approach, as Banks and Waters call it, to curriculum delivery. In these cases, it means that the provision of a task or an activity becomes more important than whether the pupils have learned anything.

It struck me as I read this book that the three categories of student teachers identified by Professor Sam Twiselton[1] might be applied to curriculum leadership: *task managers* who view their main role as being very product orientated, concerned with completing the task rather than developing the learning; *curriculum deliverers*, where there is more explicit reference to learning, but this is conceived within the restrictions of an externally given curriculum and where curriculum coverage frequently trumps learning; and, finally, *concept and skill builders*, where there is a focus on proficiency and deep learning.

---

1   S. Twiselton, V. Randall and S. Lane, Developing Effective Teachers: Perspectives and Approaches, *Impact: Journal of the Chartered College of Teaching* (summer 2018). Available at: https://my.chartered.college/impact_article/developing-effective-teachers-perspectives-and-approaches.

What we have in this terrific book is the account of one trust setting out to think about, talk about and attempt to realise what an honest, ambitious provision might look like. At Olympus Academy, a cross-phase trust with eleven schools, this work is led by Claire Banks, director of education, with support from Professor Mick Waters (lucky them). It is full of provocations and bold statements, which help us to move from task managers to concept and skill builders. The authors explain how the trust has answered these questions, why they established 'narrative' curriculum plans, which is a genius idea, and give us examples of what this looks like in their context. It is this concrete, exemplar work that will be a real boon to the profession.

There are several important threads in *A Curious Curriculum*. One relates to reappraising what counts as valuable work: when presented with the 'products' of pupils' learning, can we really say that they have learned something when all they have done is fill in the gaps or coloured a worksheet, when instead they might be presenting at an exhibition?

Another notable thread is a proper focus on the curriculum as it is experienced through the eyes of a child. We are likely to know that we are on the right track if we hear pupils talking about their work being complicated, that what they are learning is making them wonder and that the questions help them to understand bigger, wider ideas.

A further thread is that this sort of work is fundamentally about problem-solving: solving problems is complex and occasionally frustrating but also exhilarating when things go well. This is much more rewarding than the pursuit of silver bullets and quick fixes.

To shift the perspective from 'What am I doing as a teacher?' to 'What are my pupils learning?' needs sensitive and purposeful engagement to get to the heart of the matter. In *A Curious Curriculum*, Banks and Waters describe how they went about this: the setbacks, the insights, the doubts and, above all, the growing ownership by all involved in this important work. We need to stop thinking that this element of provision can be completed quickly. It can't. It is slow, deliberate, purposeful work, and it will always be work in progress. What the authors have also shown in this book is that it can also be great fun!

Mary Myatt

ACKNOWLEDGEMENTS

Claire Banks and Mick Waters may have written this book but they have simply told the story. In truth, the story has been written by the teachers and children in our schools, supported by colleagues within Olympus Academy Trust. As with all organisations, some of the head teachers and teachers have moved elsewhere and some are newer to our community. Their names may only be listed here but their contribution to our book is significant.

- Bradley Stoke Community School: Sharon Clark, head of primary phase, working with Vicky Williams and Natasha Beech as curriculum leads.

- Callicroft Primary Academy: Lucy Lang, head teacher, working with Camilla Oscroft as deputy head and Rachel Wagstaff as curriculum lead. Richard Clark was the previous head teacher who retired in April 2022.

- Charborough Road Primary School: Matt Lankester, head teacher, working with Claire Jones as deputy head and James Davolls, early years lead.

- Filton Hill Primary School: Ian Oake, head teacher, working with Sara Malik, deputy head, and Emma Escott, curriculum lead. Kirsten Lemming was the previous head teacher who retired in August 2021.

- Meadowbrook Primary School: Nicola Bailey, head teacher, working alongside Laura Walker as deputy head and curriculum lead.

- Stoke Lodge Primary School: Will Ferris, head teacher, working alongside Sarah Reeves as deputy head and curriculum lead.

- Dave Baker: CEO, Olympus Academy Trust.

- Sarah Gardner: executive assistant, Olympus Academy Trust.

- Kate Sheldon: trustee, Olympus Academy Trust.

- Richard Sloan: previous chair of trustees, Olympus Academy Trust.

- Jen Wathan: teaching and learning lead, Olympus Academy Trust.

- Sarah Williams: chair of trustees, Olympus Academy Trust.

We owe a huge debt to those who have helped us to bring this book to the reader. As well as the contributors listed above, we would like to thank Mary Myatt, an accomplished author and recognised authority on curriculum practice in schools, for offering to write our foreword. Alistair Bryce-Clegg's work has informed our parallel work in the early years phase, and Rob Carpenter at Inspire Partnership supported our early enquiries into development. We are grateful for the assistance of Patrice Baldwin, chair of the Council for Subject Associations.

The graphic work in our trust publications, and much of it in the book, has been developed by Rob Wilson from FortyFour Creative. Many of the photographs in the book and on the accompanying web platform have been produced by Richard Clark, Blue Apple Education and Richard McDonough. Jen Wathan has, as always, been a valued support to us in the work we have done with schools, as well as helping us to collate examples of illustrative material. We are indebted to Amarjot Butcher who has helped us with the organisation and management of producing the book. Lastly, the team at Crown House has been a source of support and advice throughout, particularly our editors, Daniel Bowen and Emma Tuck. We are grateful to them all.

CONTENTS

PART THREE:

Introduction: a curriculum built on a good foundation

Why we have written this book

We want to help teachers enjoy teaching some of the foundation subjects well, and, in doing so, see children in primary schools become intrigued by their world and set on a path to success in school and beyond. Knowing that schools grapple with the challenge of curriculum design and the teaching that accompanies it, we wanted to share our experience of developing foundation subjects in the hope that a description of our work and the thinking behind it would be of use to schools elsewhere. This is a book that tries to support head teachers and curriculum coordinators by showing practice, exploring the thinking behind it and describing the process of securing consistent benefits for all children. It tells the story of the development of entwined curriculum and pedagogy in some of the foundation subjects.

Over the course of five years, we have worked together with a group of head teachers, teachers and teaching assistants to help them make a positive difference to children's learning experiences. The schools involved are now proud of their professional work in this area. We know that every school sets out to teach well and ensure good learning outcomes for its children. Every school also sets out at some point to define, reshape and redefine its curriculum. In this book, we explore how our schools have managed to both design an appropriate curriculum and teach it.

Children experience and enjoy the learning we plan. In our schools, it is provided as a Curious Curriculum. Both of these words have Latin roots. Curriculum means 'course', in the sense of a route to be followed. We also wanted our children to build their sense of being eager to learn and know – the Latin meaning for the word 'curious'. Curriculum also means 'speculation or intent' – our ambitions. Our Curious Curriculum is a course that leads children to the learning ambitions we have for them.

Who we are and how this story began

Five years ago, Claire had recently been appointed to support the work of all primary schools in the Olympus Academy Trust to the benefit of every child. She had many years of experience as a head teacher in an inner-city primary school in Bristol and was building working relationships with the schools in the trust: the head teachers, teaching and other staff, children and wider communities. A common thread for all the schools was concern about the effectiveness of curriculum, partly as a result of revision of the national curriculum in 2013[1] and partly due to the natural commitment of most staff in primary schools to enjoy the best of learning with and for children.

The community of head teachers signed up to a programme of curriculum development to unfold over the next year or two. Claire decided that it would be useful to have some advice and support from a source external to the trust and turned to Mick.

Mick had been around the educational block a few times in various roles from schools to local authority to a national role as director of

---

1   Department for Education, National Curriculum (14 October 2013, updated 16 July 2014). Available at: https://www.gov.uk/government/collections/national-curriculum.

curriculum at the then Qualifications and Curriculum Authority. Mick's experience in supporting schools in different parts of the country and beyond had been utilised by Claire in her previous school, and she asked him again to lead an initial staff development day about the curriculum at the start of a school year, followed by intermittent school-based support over the course of the next twelve months. At the time, Mick remarked that it would take longer than that, and they discussed the premise that curriculum has to be linked with pedagogy to make progress.

Mick has spent about ten days a year supporting the trust, working in schools, contributing to their conferences and workshops, and doing detailed work with head teachers or curriculum lead groups. His role has been to provide the necessary spur, to throw a new pebble in the pond, to hold a mirror up to what was being achieved. Over the five years we describe, Mick spent a total of about thirty days with the schools prior to the COVID-19 lockdowns, supplemented by time spent producing documents, being in touch and talking on the phone to Claire. During lockdown he Zoomed in periodically.

Where Mick has floated in, Claire has been submerged, helping the schools to develop on a day-by-day basis. Naturally, there is the ongoing big agenda linked to supporting schools in seeking continuous improvement, checking progress, helping with all manner of urgencies, and looking after individuals and schools when problems crop up – the agenda that anyone in a leadership position would recognise. Alongside this, she has also done the hard bits: supporting people's efforts, reminding them of agreements, checking understanding, organising meetings, insisting that things get done, confronting occasional shortcomings, and endlessly recognising effort and achievement.

Although Claire and Mick have an unbalanced partnership, both agree that the crucial work in developing our curriculum story successfully has been done by the teachers, teaching assistants and head teachers day after day in the schools. Nothing that has been achieved could have been achieved without their commitment and willingness to keep pushing the boundaries of practice. At times it has been exhilarating, at times frustrating and at times sheer graft. What it has been is a story of continuous improvement, children's achievement and professional worth.

What this book tries to do

A book can only ever accomplish so much. There are libraries of books on curriculum theory and rationale. This is a book about some of the foundation subjects – those subjects that primary schools often teach through a themed or topic approach. Much of the focus is on the teaching of history, geography and science, of which there has been much consideration about where knowledge fits in; there is less specific reference to music or PE. We have also covered design and technology (DT) and art and design, two areas that are often challenging for teachers in primary schools.

As the book is about the foundation subjects, it addresses the prospect of organising learning into themes that bring the subject disciplines together under 'big ideas'. But it is not a book that rejects the discrete teaching of some aspects of some subject disciplines. Nor do we shy away from giving examples of where mathematics and English can be strengthened through good work in foundation subjects or used to strengthen the wider subject knowledge of the children. As Mary Myatt comments, we are not a trust that has sidelined the wider curriculum;[2] indeed, this book is about exactly the opposite. We stress that our teaching must avoid the superficial and trivial and must be rooted in extending and challenging children.

---

2   M. Myatt, *The Curriculum: Gallimaufry to Coherence* (Woodbridge: John Catt Educational, 2018), p. 24.

This is a book about how we can teach some aspects of the broader curriculum and do it at depth - and teach it well.

Many books deal with curriculum design by relating curriculum theory to the content that schools need to include, through requirement or philosophy. Other books offer schools a curriculum plan to ensure coverage and depth. Yet more books explore pedagogy or assessment. Our book tries to explain how we made decisions on the 'what' of curriculum and then ensured that everyone understood the reasons for those decisions - the 'why' of the work we do. This is vital for the adults in the school, of course, but also for the parents and, most importantly, the children.

We then go on to set out some of the tactics we have used to overcome challenges and make successes become routine. Part Two is almost a collection of insights, linked to research, which would support consideration of many aspects of school leadership. We take the general principles and explore how schools can make them work in their own circumstances.

We needed our staff to make the curriculum their own. We wanted teachers to commit to a curriculum for their children - a curriculum that mattered for their community rather than one that was simply packaged for them to deliver. What we call our Curious Curriculum is work in progress, and always will be. That is the thing about learning and teaching: we should keep exploring new territory and pushing the boundaries in the quest for continuous improvement.

We deal with both the big picture and the detail, addressing intellectual concepts and how they are best explored, and delve into the ways that teachers can organise and manage specific and detailed aspects of classroom life to ensure success. At times, we focus on global issues that affect our world today and our children's futures, such as sustainability, economy, identity and technology. At other times, we find ourselves discussing how to help children to fold paper, use scissors or mix paint.

This book is essentially our own dialogue about the development of the Curious Curriculum – how we approached the work and how we got it done. It is not a model curriculum that can be uprooted and planted in any school, but we hope that the discussions, explanations, assertions, asides and advice will resonate with you as you relate the circumstances to your own school setting. We have spent many hours over the last five years discussing the complicated world that is the school and the best way to enable those closest to the children to take another step towards the effectiveness that every teacher wants to feel.

This is not a 'certain' book with a straightforward solution or a 'must do' sequence of actions. We offer our experience with professional humility, inviting readers to use what makes sense for your own school at the time you need it. We both learned long ago that the application of a formula is rarely effective in teaching.

Because we do not believe in off-the-shelf solutions, we have not included our whole curriculum plan, but we have included many sections to exemplify what we do cover.

This book paints a picture of how we developed the Curious Curriculum over time and, importantly, how it will continue to develop. We all know that curriculum doesn't stand still. It evolves and adjusts to new developments in thinking and research, to new understandings about learning, and to our own growing professional competence and confidence.

We wanted everyone involved to engage deeply rather than be expected to 'deliver'. We wanted them to exercise responsibility over the work they do, collaborate over curriculum design and innovate to push the boundaries of pedagogy. We wanted them to be professionally curious about just how good learning could be and aim for excellence.

Why investing in our teachers and other staff matters

The story of curriculum is paved with good intentions. So many nations, schools and teachers set out to provide coherent teaching with good learning outcomes, and then find a gap between the planned curriculum and what the child experiences.

The first challenge facing schools is to make sense of the many and competing demands in terms of what children should be taught. In England, on top of a national curriculum (which, of course, is not required of academies) and guidance from government sits a whole range of imperatives: some are local expectations, some are traditional to the school, some are interpretations of the accountability framework and some are aspects that are 'on message' at the time. Often, when schools have organised all this into policies and charts, they breathe a sigh of relief – until next time. There is an intrinsic fascination with trying to sort out learning journeys for children, coupled with a recognisable frustration that outcomes often fall short of managerial expectations.

The second challenge schools face is how to interpret curriculum expectations in terms of how they are taught. The recognition that variability within schools is a key problem has led to leaders being urged to secure consistency, which in turn has brought about many of the compliance-focused developments of recent years. Performance management and target-setting have resulted in lesson observations and the emergence of 'good lesson' templates to ensure that teachers include the essential features.

More recently, some trusts and schools have started to provide scripted lessons, quality assured by leadership. The main problem with a scripted lesson, of course, is that the children need to know the script or there is a risk that the lesson will go off course. The same blueprint was behind the provision of textbooks and workbooks fifty years ago.

They were eventually phased out because the professionalism of the teacher was being factored out and learning would not work in the same way for all aspects of a subject discipline. The other reason textbooks faded away is that children vary so much that the blueprint very quickly fails to work with a significant proportion, and the teacher is left grappling with a different problem. It is vital, therefore, that teachers understand fully the thinking behind the curriculum they provide and learn how to make it work with all their learners.

All of this has now come into sharp relief because the inspection framework has changed to include a focus on the curriculum.[3] This is not a book about how to keep inspectors happy, although inspectors have been very positive about developments in the trust's schools in respect of the Curious Curriculum. This book is built on first principles – of doing right by every child – on the premise that accountability begins there.

The curriculum comes alive at the point when it meets the child. It is only then that it informs, clarifies, reassures, intrigues and amazes as it unveils new areas of learning and builds on what is already in place. Until that point, the curriculum is an abstract; it is what the government or the school expects all children to be offered.

We have written this book jointly, so you might detect differences in style at times. Some of our writing is business-like and functional. At times, there is a narrative describing a series of steps or events. At other times, the writing is lyrical or quizzical. This reflects the sorts of dialogues we have had over time as we have grappled with our developing agenda. We have organised, managed, structured and recorded our development, and we have puzzled, wondered, researched and laughed. We hope this is reflected in our writing.

---

3   Ofsted, Education Inspection Framework (14 May 2019; updated 23 July 2021). Available at: https://www.gov.uk/government/publications/education-inspection-framework/education-inspection-framework.

This book tells our story. You might want to dwell on some parts and dig into the detail. We visit some points more than once in different contexts because that is what teaching is like. We have alluded to research and background reading that you may wish to explore further. You might want to delve into our connected website (www.crownhouse.co.uk/curious-curriculum), using the QR codes, and explore some of our resources as a stimulus for your own work. We have included some photographs, though anyone in a school will understand the need for caution around images of children. It is not an instruction manual. We would love you to be curious, to be fascinated by learning and to be stimulated by the professional excitement of seeing children truly engage with it. We hope that you enjoy our Curious Curriculum adventure – and then enjoy your own.

Is the Curious Curriculum based on a particular theory?

Our curriculum development takes account of theoretical perspectives but, crucially, it is not wedded to any particular school of thought. Theoretical perspectives evolve over time as they are informed and influenced by research.

Our starting point is to be well informed, well read and thoughtfully discerning. We are careful to distinguish between trends, fads and genuine new answers to perennial questions. Too often, novel approaches sweep through schooling based on new rhetoric and become dogma and unquestioned practice. Both of us try to couple our insight from the education discourse with which we engage with the insights we have gained, and continue to gain, from our constant involvement with schools, classrooms and teachers. In this book, we have referred to some sources of further reading that might be useful in explaining or delving deeper into our thinking; at times, we have expanded on the rationale or justification.

From time to time in schooling, particular authors or voices urging change or specific approaches become prominent and are quoted constantly. Ten years ago, politicians leant on the work of E. D. Hirsch to validate their position and today many schools cite Mary Myatt or Barak Rosenshine as justification of their approach. Of course, most authors, particularly when writing about curriculum theory, refer to, add to and summarise the theories of others; so, someone like Myatt, rather than introducing new research, is trying to help readers to appreciate the implications for their practice.

Within curriculum and pedagogy, there is rarely any groundbreaking practice. For instance, the arrival of technology did not change pedagogy that much as it allowed itself to be modified to be accommodated in classrooms. The much-vaunted introduction of synthetic phonics (later known as applied phonics) was built on the reawakening of traditional practices. Rosenshine's principles of instruction were first expounded in the 1980s but only took hold in England nearly forty years later.

Few classroom developments are researched in depth. Most good research on curriculum or pedagogy needs to be long term; one example of this would be the work of Robin Alexander on dialogic pedagogy.[4] This is high-level classroom-based research which has developed enhanced classroom processes proven by rigorous evaluation and analysis. Our work on the Curious Curriculum is informed by dialogic pedagogy without being driven by it.

University research rarely gains prominence in schools, so in recent years the Education Endowment Foundation has become a reference point for the efficacy of practice. Similarly, the Chartered College of Teaching is encouraging action-centred research and disseminating the results. We encourage teachers to make

---

4   R. Alexander, *Towards Dialogic Teaching: Rethinking Classroom Talk* (New York: Dorchester Publishing Company, 2008).

discerning use of the findings promoted by these organisations, as well as considering the emerging practices in curriculum and pedagogy from other nations, regions and continents, such as Wales, Scandinavia and Asia.

What matters, particularly in a school community or group of schools in a trust, is a shared philosophy for education. Can we articulate our views on childhood and learning? Do we agree on how children should be treated and how they should encounter learning? Are we clear on the teacher's role? Are we clear on what constitutes success in our schools? Can we use new thinking to inform and improve our practice?

A brief history of curriculum and pedagogy in primary schools in England

Before we begin our story, it might be helpful to sketch out the background to the way in which curriculum and pedagogy have evolved over time. Few things are new in education and many debates are very old. Whenever a school sets out to update, renew, change or develop its practice, it does so as another step on a long professional pathway. So it was with us as we sought to build a shared outlook with a group of people who had very different starting points and histories in the world of teaching.

It is hard to imagine that until relatively recently teachers could make their own decisions about what they taught and how they taught it. It was widely assumed that children's ability was fixed, and the professional ability or contribution of teachers went largely unquestioned.

For a long while after the Second World War, most primary schools would follow a fairly common curriculum, mainly drawn from textbooks that children would work through with teacher guidance. The three Rs of reading, writing and arithmetic would fill most of the morning and afternoons would include geography, history and physical education. There was some science but it was generally undeveloped and often masqueraded as 'nature study' lessons. Most primary children experienced arts and crafts, including needlework, weaving, drawing, painting, pastels, clay and lino printing. Music was also present in the majority of schools with children singing and having an opportunity to play percussion instruments regularly.

Gradually, advocates of what came to be seen as progressive methodology began to question this tradition. Most of the change was in terms of pedagogy, with some teachers organising children into mixed-ability groups or allowing them to discover as opposed to being instructed. Such approaches were fuelled by the work of Jean Piaget, who described the stages of development through which children need to travel and questioned whether the school system enabled or constrained that development.[5]

Some teachers began to use their time more flexibly, shifting to an integrated day (or curriculum), and others began to work with colleagues on team teaching – sharing expertise and teaching loads. Publishers sensed a growing market and began to produce individualised programmes, usually focused on work cards that children could manage and progress through at their own rate. There was a heavy emphasis on the display of children's work on classroom walls as the children stopped using exercise books for all their recording and teachers encouraged a range of responses to the stimulus of cross-curriculum themes and topics. Architects designing new schools also sensed the mood and designed modern buildings to enable these approaches, which were open plan to allow flexibility. Teachers who appeared forward-looking often secured promotion and, in turn, encouraged their staff to embrace the new order and

---

5   See S. McLeod, Piaget's Stages of Cognitive Development: Background and Key Concepts of Piaget's Theory, *Simply Psychology* (7 December 2020). Available at: https://www.simplypsychology.org/piaget.html.

practices. This shift of emphasis reached a crescendo in 1968 with the publication of the Plowden Report, which urged primary schools to adapt and see their role as guiding children through learning with a broad and practical curriculum experience.[6]

The problem was that the effectiveness of the new, more 'progressive' practices was variable, although probably no more variable than 'traditional' practices. The traditional practices were at least understood by most adults, since they had experienced them themselves as children. (Even if they had achieved poorly at school, they had learned that schools got it right and that underachievement was their own fault or destiny.) Many in the profession were reluctant to adopt the new approaches: in the new open-plan schools, some teachers created makeshift classrooms using furniture (and sometimes children's bags!) to build 'walls', so they could continue with formal, didactic lessons.

In the early 1970s, the rearguard action against progressivism gained pace with the publication of what were called the Black Papers,[7] which set out to cast doubt on the shift from traditional approaches. The tensions reached fever pitch in 1976 with the publication of the Auld Report on the failures at William Tyndale Primary School in London,[8] which were portrayed by many as the natural outcome of the progressive approach. In the same year, Neville Bennett's study of thirty-two primary schools in Lancashire appeared to indicate that traditional teaching styles led to greater pupil progress than

---

6   B. Plowden, *Children and their Primary Schools* [Plowden Report] (London: HMSO, 1967). Available at: http://www.educationengland.org.uk/documents/plowden/plowden1967-1. html.

7   See https://www.oxfordreference.com/view/10.1093/oi/authority.201108030955 10219.

8   R. Auld and Inner London Education Authority, *The William Tyndale Junior and Infants Schools: Report of the Public Inquiry* [Auld Report] (London: Inner London Education Authority, 1976). See also J. Davis, The Inner London Education Authority and the William Tyndale Junior School Affair, 1974–1976, *Oxford Review of Education*, 28(2/3) (2002), 275–298.

progressive methods.[9] While the findings were disputed, not least by Bennett himself who said that he had struggled to find a school not using traditional approaches, the book played into the hands of the sceptics. In October 1976, the then prime minister, Jim Callaghan, made a watershed speech at Ruskin College calling for a Great Education Debate to bring consensus.[10]

Callaghan's speech brought to an end a period of optimism and trust in schools (and other public services) that had existed since the war and began an age of doubt and distrust during which the arguments continued. In 1978, a report produced by Her Majesty's Inspectorate (HMI) urged a balanced approach using didactic alongside discovery approaches,[11] and HMI began publishing regular discussion documents on aspects of the curriculum to encourage debate and careful development of improved pedagogy.[12] However, as the economy changed and families moved to different parts of the country for work, the variability of schooling became increasingly apparent to parents. Different expectations on children were exposed and parents witnessed the diverse routines and practices in schools. Issues such as children studying the Romans, for example, more than once because of a move of school began to be seen evidence of a lack of coordination.

In 1988, the secretary of state, Kenneth Baker, brought in the Education Reform Act 1988 which began a process of centralising

9   N. Bennett, *Teaching Styles and Pupil Progress* (London: Open Books, 1976).

10 J. Callaghan, A Rational Debate Based on the Facts. Speech delivered at Ruskin College, Oxford (18 October 1976). Available at: http://www.educationengland.org.uk/documents/speeches/1976ruskin.html.

11 Department of Education and Science, *Primary Education in England: A Survey by HM Inspectors of Schools* (London: HMSO, 1978). Available at: http://www.educationengland.org.uk/documents/hmi-primary/hmi-primary.html.

12 Department of Education and Science, *Curriculum Matters. An HMI Series* (London: HMSO, 1984–1989). Available at: http://www.educationengland.org.uk/documents/hmi-curricmatters/index.html.

the school system.[13] It included arrangements for a national curriculum, which came into force in 1990. The national curriculum organised the primary phase into Key Stages 1 and 2 and structured learning by subjects with attainment targets. The Act did not specify approaches to teaching but it did bring in Standardised Attainment Tasks (SATs), which would help teachers and parents to find out how well their children were performing compared with average expectations.

In 1992, the government established the Office for Standards in Education, Children's Services and Skills (Ofsted). The first inspection framework had a significant focus on whether schools were 'covering' the national curriculum. The National Curriculum Council and Qualifications and Curriculum Authority, which was replaced by the Office of Qualifications and Examinations Regulation (Ofqual) and the Qualifications and Curriculum Development Agency, produced guidance on how best to teach the new curriculum,[14] and the official endorsement meant that many schools resorted to using this in the face of inspection.

A relatively uniform curriculum began to appear across the country, although teachers complained that there was too much content and the recently created Ofsted inspections made them feel vulnerable, so the government commissioned the Dearing Review in 1994 to slim down the content.[15] At the same time, data from the early SATs suggested that schools' performance in English, mathematics and science was variable. As computers began to make the management of data more adept, it became apparent that this variability was not predictable entirely by virtue of home background. This led Ofsted to conclude that teaching was a key variable, and therefore the

---

13 See https://www.legislation.gov.uk/ukpga/1988/40/contents.

14 See https://www.qca.org.uk.

15 R. Dearing, *The National Curriculum and its Assessment: Final Report* [Dearing Review] (London: School Curriculum and Assessment Authority, 1994). Available at: http://www.educationengland.org.uk/documents/dearing1994/dearing1994.html.

inspection framework was changed to place less focus on curriculum and more on teaching quality.

In 1997, the Blair government swept to power with the promise of raising school standards; among their flagship programmes were the National Strategies for literacy and numeracy.[16] For the first time, central government was recommending pedagogic approaches through the literacy and numeracy hours, which balanced teacher direction of learning with whole-class and group work as well as including some practical work in each one-hour lesson. The rise in standards was credited largely to improved teaching, but the high-stakes accountability of league tables and inspection led to widespread concerns that the curriculum was being narrowed. The government attempted to counter this with the publication in 2003 of *Excellence and Enjoyment*, which urged schools to spread excellent teaching across the range of children's curriculum experiences.[17]

This was followed later the same year by the publication of a new strategy in response to the tragic death of a child and growing concerns about childhood: *Every Child Matters*.[18] The initiative was generally embraced by schools. The five outcomes – being healthy, staying safe, enjoying and achieving, making a positive contribution and achieving economic well-being – appealed to teachers and answered many of the concerns about the narrowing down of the curriculum.

---

16 Department for Education, *National Strategies 1997–2011: A Brief Summary of the Impact and Effectiveness of the National Strategies* (2011). Available at: https://assets.publishing. service.gov.uk/government/uploads/system/uploads/attachment_data/file/175408/DFE-00032-2011.pdf.

17 Department for Education and Skills, *Excellence and Enjoyment: A Strategy for Primary Schools* (Nottingham: DfES, 2003). Available at: http://dera.ioe.ac.uk/id/eprint/4817.

18 HM Treasury, *Every Child Matters* (Norwich: TSO, 2003). Available at: https://www.gov.uk/ government/publications/every-child-matters.

The Rose Review of the primary national curriculum began in 2008.[19] It proposed a rounded school experience with six areas of learning (as opposed to subject divisions), which met the expectation of Every Child Matters within schooling. However, just before its approval in 2010, a general election was called and the draft bill was not supported by all parties and did not pass into legislation.

The reason for this became clear when the new Conservative government implemented plans for education which included a review of the whole national curriculum. Michael Gove, as education minister, championed a return to a traditional curriculum, which was strong in subject knowledge and facts and not encumbered by what he saw as fripperies – for example, directly referenced aspects of personal and social education or sustainability.

Almost as soon as this new curriculum was enacted in 2013, the call for supplements to it began, such as the demand for character education to go alongside the curriculum. At the same time, concerns about terrorism led to the introduction of fundamental British values, and high-profile cases of children being groomed sexually resulted in renewed expectations around relationships and sex education – a casualty of Michael Gove's reforms.

Those reforms also included the establishment of academies and the formation of multi-academy trusts. Schools that were deemed successful were invited to become academies, and one of the promised autonomies was release from the imposed national curriculum. Schools that failed inspection were required to become academies under the control of what were seen as successful schools. Many trusts began to develop a 'house style' for their curriculum offer and, in turn, their expectations for teaching. Those schools that chose to stay autonomous within their local authority showed more

---

19 J. Rose, *Independent Review of the Primary Curriculum: Final Report* [Rose Review] (Nottingham: Department for Children, Schools and Families, 2009). Available at: http://www.educationengland.org.uk/documents/pdfs/2009-IRPC-final-report.pdf.

variability within their approaches, yet all were constrained to a greater or lesser degree by their inspection standing.

In 2019, Ofsted published a new inspection framework with a renewed focus on curriculum; it asked schools to focus on 'intent', 'implementation' and 'impact'. Her Majesty's Chief Inspector (HMCI) Amanda Spielman recognised that inspection had, in part, brought out a narrowing of the curriculum and set in train a focus on a more rounded experience with depth in subject experience across the curriculum. Schools addressed the intent aspect with vigour, appreciating what they saw as Ofsted's change of direction and, once again, responding to the accountability agenda.

In 2020, the COVID-19 pandemic affected pedagogy in a more immediate way than any development in the history of schooling. Homeschooling forced teachers to use technology in ways that had been possible for some time but largely sidestepped. Homeschooling also brought teachers out of their classrooms, albeit virtually, to teach before an audience, which increased parents' awareness of curriculum expectations.

Today, we have variability in curriculum and pedagogy but within a narrower range than previously. Some trusts and schools go as far as providing scripted and resourced lessons for teachers, while others guard jealously their 'imaginative', 'creative' or 'whole-child' approaches. The former are often seen by the latter as traditionalists, and the latter by the former as sentimentalists. Ironically, where the latter used to be seen as progressive, that mantle now falls to the former, who often see the latter as 'old-fashioned'. While that sounds complicated, it sums up the vehement polarity that exists in the pedagogy of English schooling.

Why this history matters when introducing the book

Schools are intensely personal places. The teaching profession deals with the unpredictability of growing young people rather than the predictability of programmable machines. Most of us know that there are few guarantees in the classroom. The best planned learning experience can founder on a change in the weather or the mood of just one child; meanwhile, productive learning can be ignited unexpectedly by the children's reaction to something that sparks their interest. What we can do is try to make our teaching as effective as possible, and the starting point is an agreement on what we need to teach (our curriculum) and how we will teach it (our pedagogy). These are affected by our experiences of teaching and leadership.

A school's approach is hugely influenced by its head teacher and, partly depending on their career stage, they will have had different baselines for their thinking on curriculum and pedagogy. Of course, their educational philosophy will also be guided by their reading, conferences they have attended, courses of study they have followed, people they have met, places they have worked and their own school days. While some head teachers can be almost carbon-dated in the way their approach matches their career start, most have developed a personal set of beliefs.

Teachers are shaped by their head teachers and the outlook of the schools in which they have worked, as well as their period of teacher education and training. A teacher who entered the profession during the last twenty years will have been trained in approaches to pedagogy that are teacher directed, emphasising mathematics and English with little exposure to the foundation curriculum. Within any school, each teacher will bring different perspectives and understandings to their work. They might collaborate on agreed policies and standardised practices, but the extent to which they do so will rely on their conviction and subscription to the school's values, aims and ambitions.

Our book is all about the effort to encourage a group of professionals to develop practice based on a shared belief and purpose rather than imposing a set of expectations. The development of curriculum and pedagogy is an ongoing story full of intrigue, complexity, personalities and drama. Understanding that development over time – how today's issues have arisen – is an essential aspect of taking it forward. We need to harmonise the expertise of people with varying experiences and outlooks to the benefit of our children.

PART ONE

The essential features of the Curious Curriculum

It is probably best to start with a disclaimer. This part is the equivalent of reading the last pages of a whodunnit first. So, for those of you who bought this book in order to discover the structure and organisation of our curriculum, here it is. For those of you who want to know about the journey, the rationale, the pitfalls and failures along the way, the rest of the book shouldn't disappoint. That isn't to say that the curriculum we have designed is not significant; it is simply to say that a curriculum is never really finished. The most interesting part of our story is that it is still unfolding.

We will begin with a description of what our Curious Curriculum is, what teachers within our schools are expected to teach and what our children are expected to learn. We will explain the features of the curriculum with diagrams and examples.

We believe there is a coherent logic to the architecture and various elements that fit together to achieve our ambitions. When you reach the end of Part One, you might be thinking that you could adopt this as a package and use it as it is in your own school, or you might be seeing aspects that you could use within your current working curriculum. For some, there will be a sense of 'What's new?' as most of the elements in the Curious Curriculum are being used in some school somewhere – little is truly new.

We fully appreciate all of that. Schools are at different places in their development, although for the last couple of years many have been both trying to think through their intent and, as a result of the pandemic, grappling with a curriculum that needs to be channelled through remote and school-based approaches. Now, most schools have settled on their intent and are working out how to implement it – which is when the Curious Curriculum structure will be most helpful as a model, guide or mirror. For schools at the point of starting afresh, it might be the case of picking up a near blueprint, although we would advise caution on that. For others, there might be helpful solutions to niggling problems. For others again, it might help the curriculum fog to clear and accelerate pre-existing plans.

This part is a scene-setter. Once we have explained what the Curious Curriculum is, we can tell the fascinating story of how it evolved and how we overcame many of the challenges that lots of schools face when moving from the grand plan to implementation.

CHAPTER 1

What is the Curious Curriculum?

The Curious Curriculum is an approach to teaching foundation subjects well. We organise most learning into themes, although some learning is discrete and we are clear that subject disciplines shouldn't be shoehorned into them. The curriculum does not include much PE, languages, music or RE, which have their own sequences of learning. It does include the content of the national curriculum, which we supplement with the United Nations Sustainable Development Goals (or SDGs) and our focus on developing global citizens.[1]

Teachers are expected to follow the curriculum and work with others who teach the same year groups in order to share ideas and economise on work and effort, but they are not restrained by a list of content, an expected or standard timetable, or the format of lessons. We want our teachers to be imaginative and to respond to the children they teach as well as to particular circumstances, environments or events. We would also like our teachers to address certain principles, and so, to help them with that, we provide some clear expectations, which we continue to address together, to lift quality, enjoyment and standards as our Curious Curriculum unfolds.

---

1 See https://sdgs.un.org/goals.

Teachers work from a set of documents – handbooks, if you will – that outline the clear rationale and expectation of our curriculum. These documents guide us towards new learning and better provision, setting out the educational philosophy and pedagogical principles behind our curriculum. Of course, the success of it all depends on head teachers, teachers and teaching assistants – and, of course, the children themselves. At the same time, they all need a structure to work from and guide their efforts. That is our Curious Curriculum.

Described in this way, we could simply produce a copy of the curriculum documents and let you get on with it. We too have sat in conferences and workshops where someone from a school has talked with enthusiasm about their own curriculum and presented some extracts. However, we know that back in school afterwards, others who try to replicate the development will encounter unforeseen difficulties. We also know that there are some excellent published curriculum approaches available, but that when they are implemented in a school it is often not quite as simple as it seemed.

What is the starting point?

The first important point to understand when thinking about curriculum design is the fact that curriculum and pedagogy are interlinked and neither stands alone. Leadership theory usually promotes clarity about 'what' followed by 'how'. This is picked up in school leadership texts and courses, which move us from vision to curriculum to pedagogy as consecutive steps. Before we can decide on a curriculum design, we must first recognise that it will be entwined and interconnected with educational philosophy, pedagogy and subject knowledge. The current debate about the relative importance of curriculum content leaves schools constantly adjusting to revised demands and seeking pedagogy that will

Figure 1.1. Our pedagogic principles

achieve them. When determining what subject content will be taught, and in which year group, we are making values-driven decisions.[2]

Our curriculum starts not with determining content but with our values: *collaboration*, *excellence* and *opportunity* run through everything we do as a group of schools. It is these values that informed our pedagogical principles – what we believe our schools should offer the children who attend them. This is partly because the starting point for our school leaders needs to be children's outcomes in the widest sense, and partly because we want to be clear on a structure or framework within which we can test our decisions and choices.

---

2   M. Young, A Knowledge-Led Curriculum: Pitfalls and Possibilities, *Impact*, 4 (autumn 2018). Available at: https://discovery.ucl.ac.uk/id/eprint/10060317/1/Young_FINAL.pdf.

Our pedagogical principles (see Figure 1.1) are our litmus test on whether we are being true to our values. They help us to sieve through the vast weight of potential curriculum content and approaches that are available. They are our collective moral compass, which enable us to see through government initiatives, Ofsted frameworks and other media and parent-driven pressures that land on the metaphorical doorstep of every head teacher in the country.

The framework consists of eight agreed principles that our group of schools holds as our collective truth. These are our guiding drivers when making decisions and choices about what is important to us and what, in a world where we can be blindsided by government initiatives, keeps us focused and concentrated on the things we have decided are the most important as a lens through which to view our work. Through these principles, we agreed seven statements that are at the core of our educational beliefs:

1. We set high expectations and provide opportunities for all children to achieve, responding to any learning needs.

2. We offer learning experiences and environments that inspire children to question the world around them, develop their ideas and grow as lifelong learners.

3. We develop local, national and global knowledge and understanding by providing enriching experiences, developing global citizenship, celebrating diversity and creating cultural capital.

4. We commit to providing consistently high-quality education based on current academic research and pedagogical principles.

5. We are proactive in removing barriers to learning through early identification, effective intervention, improvement through partnership and raising aspirations.

6. We provide a rich multisensory environment that promotes, celebrates and provokes learning and reflects the importance of aesthetics and beauty.

7. Through a holistic approach, we ensure the development of our learners' physical, social and emotional well-being. This will support their resilience and future life chances.

We imagine that as you read these statements you will be wondering, 'What's new?' If we were to collect together examples from any ten schools across the country, we would probably find similar ambitions, words and phrases. Our challenge to ourselves was to make these principles the start, middle and end of our work – our constant watchwords.

How do we make the curriculum coherent?

We identified seven key components that support teachers to make links between the many elements that constitute a curriculum and to understand how teaching well is about connections. There are many elements that we could have included, but these seven essentials provided a comprehensive starting point to see the curriculum in the round.

When we talk about our curriculum we mean:

1. The importance of the learning environment.

2. The philosophy behind the sequence of teaching English and mathematics.

3. Our philosophy of the early years foundation stage.

4. The importance of understanding metacognition and self-regulation.

5. Purposeful foundation subject teaching and learning.

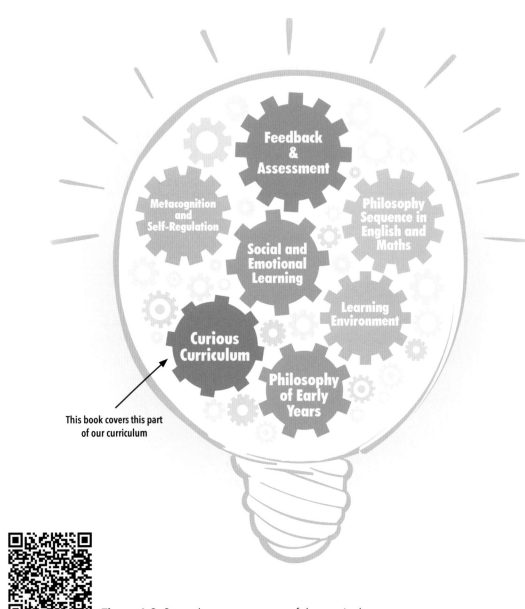

Figure 1.2. Seven key components of the curriculum

6. How we develop and support social and emotional learning.

7. Why we need high aspirations, and the importance of feedback and assessment.

To give these components visual impact, we illustrate it as a light bulb switching on learning (see Figure 1.2).

The fifth component on our list, the purposeful teaching and learning of foundation subjects, developed into our Curious Curriculum and is the focus of this book. Each of the seven areas above overlaps with the other six to create quality in our curriculum, which enables us to meet a set of principles that we have agreed on together.

What about the early years?

Our Curious Curriculum encompasses all of the primary key stages, including the early years foundation stage (EYFS). In the reception year, like most EYFS settings, we embark on a play-based curriculum, offering a mix of child-initiated and adult-led learning opportunities – but always taking into account the interests and needs of the children. The curriculum across the EYFS is based on the principles of *Development Matters*, which focuses on the aspects of a 'unique child', 'positive relationships' and 'enabling environments', leading to 'learning and development'.[3] Recently, due to the revised EYFS curriculum guidance from the Department for Education,[4] we have decided to move towards Birth to 5 Matters as our non-statutory guidance.[5] With support from educational consultant Alistair Bryce-Clegg, we have been revisiting and refreshing our provision across

---

3   Department for Education, *Development Matters: Non-Statutory Curriculum Guidance for the Early Years Foundation Stage* (2020, rev. July 2021). Available at: https://www.gov.uk/government/publications/development-matters--2.

4   Department for Education, Early Years Foundation Stage (EYFS) Statutory Framework (March 2021). Available at: https://www.gov.uk/government/publications/early-years-foundation-stage-.

5   See https://birthto5matters.org.uk.

the year group, with a new nursery provision opening in one of our schools.[6]

It was an excellent time to revisit our principles of providing play-based opportunities to learn with a focus on engagement and curiosity. Play enables children to experience learning in a meaningful and purposeful way, allowing them to develop the skills needed to become effective learners. Ensuring opportunities for children to develop creative and critical thinking is a key element of our provision. It will enable them to foster good learning attitudes that will build the foundations for the rest of their journey through education. We do not set themes across EYFS year groups, however, and instead focus on the gap and strength analysis to plan our environment in order to develop knowledge and skills in our youngest children.

While this book does not focus on the early years curriculum, we feel it is important to share how our EYFS provision provides the springboard for our Curious Curriculum. The effective characteristics of learning in the early years are the fundamentals of learning: playing and exploring, active understanding, creating and thinking critically. These run through everything we do in our EYFS provision, with a focus on how children learn as well as on what they learn. Our Curious Curriculum aims to build on the same attention to detail in Years 1–6.

The model outlined here covers all aspects of a broad and balanced curriculum; we have chosen to share specifically our design for teaching our foundation subject disciplines well. Our experience tells us that, for a whole range of reasons, some schools have distorted children's learning with lip service being paid to some subject disciplines. Our principles could not allow us to let that happen, although it was a real possibility and one that we had to work hard to avoid.

---

6   Alistair Bryce-Clegg is an established educational consultant specialising in the education of children in the early years – see https://abcdoes.com.

THEORY OF EVOLUTION

- Evolution is the process by which changes in plants and animals happen over time. It is a process of slow change and development

- Evolution, in biology, is a theory that the differences between modern plants and animals are the result of changes that happened by a natural process over a very long time

- INHERITANCE - Biological inheritance is a process where an offspring cell or organism acquires or becomes predisposed to characteristics of its parent cell or organism. Variations that are exhibited by individuals can mount up and cause a species to evolve through inheritance.

VOCABULARY

Adaptation – The process of change so that an organism or species can become better suited to their environment

Body fossil – Preserved remains of the body of the actual animal or plant itself

Breeding – The mating and production of offspring by animals

Environment – The surroundings or conditions in which a person, animal, or plant lives

Evolution – The process by which different kinds of living organism are believed to have developed from earlier forms during the history of the earth

Fossil – The remains or impression of a prehistoric plant or animal embedded in rock and preserved

Inherit – To gain a quality, characteristic or predisposition genetically from a parent or ancestor

Offspring – A person's child or children/ an animal's young

Reproduction – The production of offspring by a sexual or asexual process

Selective breeding – The process by which humans use animal breeding and plant breeding to develop selective characteristics by choosing particular animals and plants

Trace fossil – Indirect evidence of life in the past such as the footprints, tracks, burrows, borings and waste left behind by animals

- Species
- Evolution
- Natural selection
- Theory of Evolution
- Organism
- Generation
- Classification
- Naturalist

What are the key features of the Curious Curriculum?

The Curious Curriculum is carefully designed to engage children as active participants in their learning journey. We believe that children are at their most successful when their imagination is stimulated, their curiosity is heightened and their learning makes links to their lives and the wider world – what John Hattie and Gregory Donoghue call the learning outcome that moves from 'surface' to 'deep' to 'transfer', allowing children to go beyond the knowledge given and to relate and transfer these ideas effectively on their own.[7]

Our Curious Curriculum builds on these early years experiences. It is a framework that develops creativity, critical thinking and discovery, while ensuring a clear focus on the intellectual concepts being taught and the knowledge needed to understand those concepts. Mary Myatt has written about the importance of concepts in bringing coherence to a curriculum and making learning efficient.[8]

That is it! We believe that if the Curious Curriculum does its job, and the other six components in our light bulb support the curriculum to be as effective as possible, then we will meet our curriculum principles. So, our Curious Curriculum is not the whole curriculum, although it influences and is influenced by the whole curriculum. In the foundation subject disciplines, we expect children to build and use knowledge, to develop and deploy skills, to practise and improve positive characteristics and personal qualities.

---

7   J. Hattie and G. Donoghue, Learning Strategies: A Synthesis and Conceptual Model, *Npj Science of Learning*, 1 (2016). Available at: http://www.nature.com/articles/npjscilearn201613.

8   M. Myatt, *Back on Track: Fewer Things, Greater Depth* (Woodbridge: John Catt Educational, 2020), p. 89.

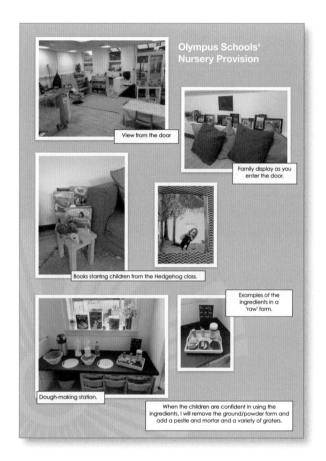

Olympus Schools'
Nursery Provision

View from the door

Family display as you enter the door.

Books starring children from the Hedgehog class.

Examples of the ingredients in a 'raw' form.

Dough-making station.

When the children are confident in using the ingredients, I will remove the ground/powder form and add a pestle and mortar and a variety of graters.

If that is the essence of our Curious Curriculum, the rest of this part of our book is about how it is structured, what is in it and how it works. We have briefly explained our rationale – the logic that matters to us. All schools do this. What we explain next is how our Curious Curriculum unfolds – the logic we apply. We then describe how it unfolded – the way the logic worked in practice, the assumptions, problems and successes. We also apply that wonderful tool called hindsight, which, if only we'd had it at the beginning, would have been very helpful.

What is important is that, from agreeing a rationale, we have focused on quality throughout. That is exactly what the principles are about: how we give each child a quality education.

How do teachers get from big principles and ideas into the detail?

What flows from our principles are decisions about planning, which lead to the experiences we anticipate and what approaches to teaching will ensure that the experience is embedded. The next sub-layer adds further detail: planning needs design as well as detail, the experience is where learning meets the child and teaching takes us into issues of pedagogy. Macro pedagogy includes school-wide influences on success – the things an individual cannot control or is not expected to do: timetable, room allocations, resources, distribution of exercise books. Micro pedagogy could be seen as the teacher's organisational repertoire: the range of teaching methods they can manage, their versatility and agility.

Are we specific about what children need to learn?

We are specific in outline and we provide a structure, but teachers have the scope to interpret and extend. We call this our intent for subject disciplines, which we express through key learning intentions (KLIs). Structured around the national curriculum, our Curious Curriculum takes what children need to learn within a key stage and, progressively and systematically, divides it into year groups, focusing on subject discipline, subject intent and depth of understanding and knowledge.

Our drive for equity of provision and opportunity for all children and staff drives our desire to align learning continuity across the trust. Our KLIs were inspired by Ron Berger's *An Ethic of Excellence*[9] and the moral purpose to ensure that the same high expectations should be placed on all learners in all year groups and in all schools. The

---

9   R. Berger, *An Ethic of Excellence: Building a Culture of Craftsmanship with Students* (Portsmouth, NH: Heinemann, 2003).

KLIs are a set of explanatory documents for each subject that clearly summarise what needs to be taught in which year group and which skill should support the embedding of which piece of knowledge. The principal idea behind the KLIs was to make sure that if you were a class teacher in Year 5, for example, you would know what to teach in art with respect to drawing, painting or sculpture. We asked ourselves the question: how would you know you were not reteaching areas that had already been taught? Or, worse still, missing huge areas of the curriculum (because, to be honest, it is too messy and difficult to teach)? The KLIs help schools and teachers to design the progression, sequencing and development of learning in each subject area across the year groups and ensure they know the standards expected. Based on the national curriculum, the KLIs systematically show the building of substantive and disciplinary knowledge, and how this can be applied and understood in each year group.

The structure of the KLIs involves:

- Learning about … – knowledge (substantive knowledge).

- Learning to … – skills (disciplinary knowledge).

- Learning through … – understanding/application (interdisciplinary knowledge).

With Tier 2 and Tier 3 vocabulary mapped into key stages, this helps to ensure a clear schematic progression across our year groups and then schools. Teachers are free to meet the KLIs in any order and either within the Curious Curriculum theme or in a discrete lesson. The choice is theirs.

We have included some examples of our KLIs.

The first is from our science knowledge KLI:

Learning about... (Knowledge)

BIOLOGY	YEAR 1	YEAR 2	YEAR 3	YEAR 4
Plants	Identify and name a variety of common wild and garden plants, including deciduous and evergreen trees. Identify and describe the basic structure of a variety of common flowering plants, including trees.	Observe and describe how seeds and bulbs grow into mature plants Find out and describe how plants need water, light and a suitable temperature to grow and stay healthy.	Identify and describe the functions of different parts of flowering plants: roots, stem/trunk, leaves and flowers Explore the requirements of plants for life and growth (air, light, water, nutrients from soil, and room to grow) and how they vary from plant to plant Investigate the way in which water is transported within plants	

This is an example of the art skills KLI:

Learning how to... (Skills)

	YEAR 1	YEAR 2	YEAR 3	YEAR 4	YEAR 5	YEAR 6
Drawing skills	Make marks and lines with a wide range of drawing implements e.g. charcoal, pencil, crayon, chalk pastels, pens etc. Can use appropriate force when using a pencil Can draw shapes in between using objects. Invent new shapes and lines	Order grading of pencil from lightest to darkest Can invent new shapes. Can use a variety of strength with the pencils Control the types of marks made with the range of media; pencils, rubbers, crayons, pastels, felt tips, charcoal, ballpoints, chalk. Experiment with a variety of media; pencils, rubbers, crayons, felt tips, charcoal, ballpoints, chalk	Name, match and draw lines from observations - straight, looped, diagonal, wavy, zig zag, dashed, dotted, horizontal, vertical, spiral Start to use hatching and cross-hatching to add effects to a drawing Experiment with a variety of media; pencils, rubbers, crayons, pastels, felt tips, charcoal, ballpoints chalk Control the types of marks made with the range of media	Experiment with sketching/drawing techniques using a variety of media; pencils, rubbers, crayons, felt tips, pastels, charcoal, ball points, chalk Use a journal/sketch book to collect and develop ideas Use hatching and cross-hatching more confidently when sketching from observations Start to use contour hatching to add effects to a sketch Develop an awareness of composition, scale and proportion in their work	Work from a variety of sources including observation, photographs and digital images Use contour hatching, hatching and cross-hatching more confidently when sketching from observations Start to use stippling to add effects to a sketch Experiment sketching/ drawing techniques using a variety of media; pencils, rubbers, crayons, felt tips, pastels, charcoal, ball points, chalk Begin to work in a sustained and independent way to create a detailed drawing	Begin to use simple perspective in their work using a single focal point and horizon. Have an awareness of how drawings are created –composition, scale and proportion Use different techniques for different purposes Use specific vocabulary (hatching, cross-hatching, contour hatching, stippling, shading) Draw from observation/ imagination for a length of time Manipulate and experiment with the elements of art: line, tone, pattern , texture, form, space, colour and shape.
Painting skills	Explore paintbrushes Choose correct sized paintbrush Explore with watercolours Can create an image using only straight lines	Explore with watercolours and poster paint Mix colours to match a picture Choose correct sized paintbrush Use correct consistency	Explore with watercolours and poster paint Mix colours to match a picture Choose correct sized paintbrush Use correct consistency	Experiment with the effects different paints have on a painting (water colours, poster paints, oil pastels, soft pastels) Blending with watercolours	Experiment with the effects different paints have on a painting (water colours, poster paints, oil pastels, soft pastels) Explore how straight lines can be achieved in	Experiment with the effects different paints have on a painting (water colours) Blending with watercolours Mix and use tints, shades and tones

And this is an example from the geography understanding/
application KLI:

Learning through... (Understanding/Application)

	YEAR 1	YEAR 2	YEAR 3	YEAR 4	YEAR 5
Place studies/ asking geographical questions	Ask and answer questions about places and environments in a near place using basic geographical language. Understand the differences and similarities using basic geographical language to compare with a far place.	Understand why we ask geographical questions about our local area (e.g. where is the warmest part of the school? What kind of houses do most people live in nearby?)	Understand how to use skills and sources of evidence to respond to a range of geographical questions (including far place). Compare the geography of a UK region, a region of a European country and a region in N/S America)	Know how to ask more in-depth geographical questions and how to use them in investigation (e.g. why do most people live in this area? Why do people live near to volcanoes?)	Understand how to go about answering geographical questions through enquiry/investigation work. Understand that enquiry is likely to lead to further questions being required.
Atlas/globe skills, place knowledge	Understand how to use atlases and globes accurately to identify locations of continents and oceans and give basic descriptions.	Understand why there are different sovereign nations within the UK and identify the location on a basic outline map.	Understand how to use atlases, globes and maps accurately to identify and describe the locations of key countries and settlements and major physical features of the UK and the world.	Recognise ways in which capital cities and key physical geographical features such as mountain ranges and locational information can be used for geographical investigation (for near and far place studies).	Understand why it is important to use atlases, globes and maps accurately to pinpoint key locations using grid references and longitude and latitude co-ordinates.
Geographical observations	Understand the importance of using observation skills when visiting a place or environment to identify and state key geographical features. Understand why it is important to identify some local landmarks and famous UK geographical features from images. Describe what is good and bad/liked and disliked about a place or environment.	Understand how to use simple fieldwork and observational skills to recognise how people affect the environment. Describe physical and human features of places. Identify some geographical features of a 'far' place.	Understand how to analyse the geographical characteristics that influence the lives and activities of people living in places near and far. Make basic statements about the geography in different places and the direct effect on people who live there.	Understand how to describe the ways that people seek to improve and sustain environments and explain some ways this is done.	Understand how to describe and explain the ways that physical and human processes can change the features of places. Explain how people can both improve and damage the environment.
Using different forms of data	Identify, interpret and talk about the similarities and differences between places when using photos.	Understand how to use the internet effectively to find out more about places and back up findings from the photos. Describe these findings.	Understand how to and why it is important to use at least two different sources of information to find out about a place (e.g. photos and maps). Describe and explain using appropriate vocabulary to communicate findings.	Understand how to use ICT to present findings, including basic maps to locate.	Understand why it is important to use a range of geographical skills such as numerical, mapped, photos, data collection through observation and measurement to find out about places near and far.
Applying numeracy and literacy in geography	Know why key geographical words are important and use them accurately in sentences. Able to interpret some basic numerical data to identify key geographical features of		Know why it is important to describe places studied using key geographical terminology. Understand how to use basic data to justify some reasons for		

The big advantage of our KLIs is that they demystify the subject discipline content and progression for each teacher in each year group. This ensures that they are all aware of what has been taught before and what will be taught in the following year. We want teachers to focus on bringing the learning to the child through the most effective pedagogy, so we strive to help them think about teaching well rather than producing plans for scrutiny by others.

As you can see, this is not new thinking. Our secondary specialist leaders of education work with us, using the national curriculum and other published progression of skills documents, to derive our KLIs. If we are being honest, after a few years in, we think that some things are possibly in the wrong place and some things are more important than others. However, the key issue is that we have a starting point. We have something to give staff to help them know what went before and what will be coming after.

It is clearly sequenced, progressive, aspirational and balances knowledge, skills, understanding and application, thereby enabling what Daniel Willingham calls 'deep knowledge'.[10] Or what Martin Robinson describes in *Trivium 21c* as a curriculum that balances both the traditional and the progressive in terms of ethos and pedagogy. Children need to have 'a good grasp of the basics, the grammar of a topic. Only then can they become creative, critical citizens fully engaged in the complexities of our communication age, yet also responsive to and knowledgeable of our rich and varied history and culture.'[11]

---

10 D. T. Willingham, *Why Don't Students Like School? A Cognitive Scientist Answers Questions About How the Mind Works and What It Means for the Classroom* (San Francisco, CA: John Wiley & Sons, 2010), p. 150.

11 M. Robinson, *Trivium 21c: Preparing Young People for the Future with Lessons from the Past* (Carmarthen: Independent Thinking Press, 2013), p. 217.

The schools have a point of departure from which to develop their year group curriculum sequences of learning. Each curriculum lead and subject lead is able to ensure not only that coverage is happening but also the acquisition of learning in the appropriate year groups. Each subject and year group then develops a carefully considered version of the KLI with a detailed and specific plan for their own school of what will be taught and when (see Figure 1.3 overleaf).

Quality of outcome is of the utmost importance, but so is the ability of a child to see connections between subject disciplines; this is not about learning and understanding knowledge in isolation. We seek what Fiorella and Mayer call generative knowledge.[12]

The sequencing of national curriculum expectations in the KLIs not only supports teachers' planning, but also enables them to engage with curiosity themselves. Using enquiry questions to punctuate the teaching sequence and enable the ebb and flow of learning is an essential device to engage children as active participants in their studies. Teachers use enquiry questions alongside the KLIs to support the development of both substantive knowledge and the disciplinary concept of the subject being studied. How enquiry questions fit into the planning of the Curious Curriculum is significant; they were a key factor when deciding on the enquiry approach, which fits with our principle of supporting children to be inquisitive and enquiring of the world around them. It also reinforces the seven pedagogic principles described earlier.

 p. 27

---

12 L. Fiorella and R. Mayer, *Learning as a Generative Activity: Eight Learning Strategies That Promote Understanding* (New York: Cambridge University Press, 2015), pp. 6–7.

Figure 1.3. Clear plan for a school

Year 3	Term 1		Term 2	Term 3
Theme Year 3	Growing together		Settlements	
Major/minor focus	SCIENCE Plants		SCIENCE Rocks (discrete)	
Substantive knowledge	Identify and describe the functions of different parts of flowering plants: roots, stem/trunk, leaves and flowers. Explore the requirements of plants for life and growth (air, light, water, nutrients from soil, room to grow) and how they vary from plant to plant. Investigate the way in which water is transported within plants. Explore the part that flowers play in the life cycle of flowering plants, including pollination, seed formation and seed dispersal.		Compare and group together different kinds of rocks on the basis of their appearance and simple physical properties. Describe in simple terms how fossils are formed when things that have lived are trapped within sedimentary rock. Recognise that soils are made from rocks and organic matter.	
Disciplinary knowledge (skills)	**Investigation:** Children will work scientifically by: comparing the effect of different factors on plant growth, e.g. the amount of light or the amount of fertiliser. **Skills focus:** Set up simple practical enquiries, comparative and fair tests. Gather, record, classify and present data in a variety of ways to help in answering questions. Use straightforward scientific evidence to answer questions or to support findings. Use results to draw simple conclusions, make predictions for new values, suggest improvements and raise further questions. Report on findings from enquiries, including oral and written explanations, displays or presentations of results and conclusions.		**Investigation:** Children might work scientifically by: investigating what happens when rocks are rubbed together or what changes occur when they are in water. **Skills focus:** Make systematic and careful observations and, where appropriate, take accurate measurements using standard units using a range of equipment, including thermometers and data loggers. Gather, record, classify and present data in a variety of ways to help in answering questions.	

Term 4	Term 5	Term 6	Term 1
Movement		Our blue planet	

SCIENCE **Animals and humans** **Forces and magnets (discrete)** Identify that animals, including humans, need the right types and amount of nutrition, and that they cannot make their own food: they get nutrition from what they eat. Identify that humans and some other animals have skeletons and muscles for support, protection and movement. Compare how things move on different surfaces. Notice that some forces need contact between two objects, but magnetic forces can act at a distance. Observe how magnets attract or repel each other and attract some materials and not others.		**SCIENCE** **Light (discrete)** Recognise that animals need light in order to see things and that dark is the absence of light. Notice that light is reflected from surfaces. Recognise that light from the sun can be dangerous and that there are ways to protect their eyes. Recognise that shadows are formed when the light from a light source is blocked by an opaque object. Find patterns in the way that the size of shadows change.	
Investigation (animals and humans): Children might work scientifically by: identifying and grouping animals with and without skeletons and observing and comparing their movement; and exploring ideas about what would happen if humans did not have skeletons. **Investigation (forces and magnets):** Children might work scientifically by: exploring the strengths of different magnets and finding a fair way to compare them; and sorting materials into those that are magnetic and those that are not. **Skills focus:** Ask relevant questions and use different types of scientific enquiries to answer them. Set up simple practical enquiries, comparative and fair tests. Use results to draw simple conclusions, make predictions for new values, suggest improvements and raise further questions. Use straightforward scientific evidence to answer questions or to support findings.		**Investigation:** Children will work scientifically by: looking for patterns in what happens to shadows when the light source moves or the distance between the light source and the object changes. **Skills focus:** Ask relevant questions and use different types of scientific enquiries to answer them. Set up simple practical enquiries, comparative and fair tests. Make systematic and careful observations and, where appropriate, take accurate measurements using standard units using a range of equipment, including thermometers and data loggers. Use results to draw simple conclusions, make predictions for new values, suggest improvements and raise further questions. Use straightforward scientific evidence to answer questions or to support findings.	

43

If that is the big picture, what is the expectation on an individual teacher?

What does the Curious Curriculum look like for a teacher? What are the expectations on a teacher in each year group? Our themes are designed to give each child coherent learning throughout their primary school experience, which meets with our principles, supports an agreed approach within schools and ensures connectivity across the trust. At school level, the themes can be tweaked and adapted, and teachers – in discussion with their curriculum leads – can move them around slightly, as long as the reasons are valid and do not interfere with the sequencing of other year groups. Each school and each teacher is responsible for deciding the direction of a theme which will fit into the school's and subject's overall curriculum plan. In essence, the theme is a guide that allows for a coherent structure across the trust, and therefore is a platform for discussion around direction, planning and knowledge within a particular area.

Consequently, our Curious Curriculum places immense importance on the many elements that are essential when children create a schema for new learning. In turn, new learning will grow into rich knowledge and abundant skills that can be retrieved, applied, analysed and reflected on through appropriately developed personal qualities and attributes. The six themes listed below are organised into blocks of half-terms and terms.

- History
- Art
- Geography
- DT
- Music
- Science

For the purpose of this book we divide the year into six terms.[13] Each theme lasts for two terms (or about twelve to fifteen weeks) across two years – for example, children will study Our Blue Planet in term 6/Year 3 and then continue the theme into term 1/Year 4. This is designed to support transition though every stage of the school, and especially within the Year 6/7 transfer to secondary schools within the trust.

The planning design means that teachers need to plan together using the KLIs, being open and transparent about coverage of the curriculum, but also being clear about what has been learned rather than just taught. The themes essentially incorporate the subject disciplines of history, geography, science, art and DT, with English and RE incorporated where they might fit, and mathematics, PE, personal, social, health and economic (PSHE) education, primary foreign languages, music and computing taught separately. Where particular elements of the KLI do not fit with a theme, they are taught discretely.

◀ p. 37

Why not teach them all discretely, we hear you say. Well, we believe that allowing children to see learning linked in this way, driven by quality enquiry questions, not only supports the development of a schema, but also allows them to make significant connections with the world around them.

What themes are there? Is there a chart? Figure 1.4 sets out some of the curriculum themes we use.

 p. 46

---

13 The traditional three-term year has been adapted in many parts of the country, so what we call a term in this book is in many places a half-term.

	Sept-Oct	Nov-Mar	Apr-May	June-July
Year 1	The World Around Me!	I Wonder …	Machines	Wild Things
Year 2	Wild Things	Just Imagine …	How Does It Work?	Growing Together
Year 3	Growing Together	Settlements	Movement	Our Blue Planet
Year 4	Our Blue Planet	Civilisations	Flora and Fauna	Natural Phenomena
Year 5	Natural Phenomena	Who is Shaping Our Future?	Charity	The Whole World in Our Hands
Year 6	The Whole World in Our Hands	Exploration	Bravery	People, Places and Me

Figure 1.4. Curriculum themes

Again, you might be wondering, 'What's new?' Many schools across the country use themes like these which provide a structure and scope for interpretation by individual teachers. However, our Curious Curriculum doesn't just map out the route; it sets expectations linked to the principles we have established for ourselves.

How do we approach content within the themes and maintain the principles?

In any planned period of learning – whether key stage, school year, term, lesson or even a few minutes – quality is essential. We only achieve consistent and coherent quality if teachers work through common thinking in their planning. This means that a teacher is expected to address agreed elements of learning in their planning of a theme. Planning is not simply an intellectual or clerical exercise. We expect teachers to interpret teaching and learning and curriculum content from the viewpoint of the learner – *through the eyes of the child*.

Figure 1.5 shows the elements that are incorporated into each theme in order that sophisticated learning connections can take place. By implication, these essentially start to bring together the curriculum content for each theme alongside the pedagogy. The figure gives an idea of the scope of consideration and some of the joining elements. We have learned that spending a considerable amount of time and effort on each 'box' is well worth it, as well as being productive and enjoyable.

Let's explain these in a bit more detail. While these are elements that the teacher needs to consider in order to arrange content, it is also essential to look through the eyes of the child. Therefore, when expanding the thinking behind each box, we consider: how do children perceive what is offered, demanded and expected?

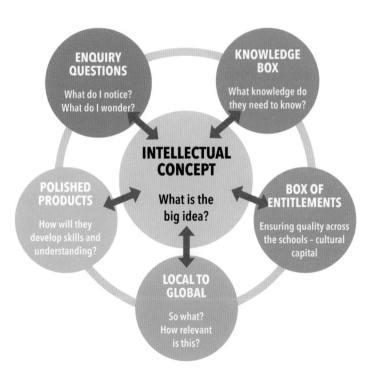

Figure 1.5. Elements that are incorporated into each theme

In any period of learning, we should be seeking to develop the children's intellect. One of the reasons we have schools is to accelerate their intellectual development. Our Curious Curriculum demands that teachers plan for intellectual development by being clear about the 'big idea' to be addressed during the theme. It could be an important concept such as 'civilisation' or a big idea such as 'there is an agreed procedure for carrying out an appendectomy'. The established 'ideas of geometry' have been agreed, for example, but even established ideas can change, such as 'our understanding of the solar system'.

We want our children (and their teachers) to be intrigued by the world. We want them to appreciate the human quest for development – that civilisation has made incredible advances and also calamitous mistakes. We want them to know that new discoveries are being made today and they can be part of that exciting future.

If we are going to do this properly, we need to provide quality experiences and enable conceptual development and, in turn, quality experience will be enhanced by growing intellect.

As we discuss each of the six elements below, we want to consider what they would look like through the eyes of a child. What is it we want those eyes to see? How will we make the learning come alive?

Intellectual concept – what is the big idea?

The teacher needs to ask: what do I want the children to understand by the end of this theme? What wider concept or big idea do I hope the children will have understood using the knowledge and skills taught over this period? The intellectual concept will be an understanding of an idea that has created change or continuity, has resulted in a consequence or significance, and is set in context and chronology. The concept cannot be understood without an essential grounding in specific knowledge, particular vocabulary and a foundational understanding of context and relevance.

We want children to talk with us and each other about what they have discovered and understood, relating one concept with another, linking periods of history with scientific development and being continuously curious: wondering why, wondering why not, thinking 'what if' or 'if only'. We cannot hope to teach all the knowledge they will need, but we can give them the knowledge that will be useful as a prompt for yet more knowledge which, over time, will take them deeper towards specialism or wider towards an eclectic understanding of their world.

Through the eyes of the child ... We need our children to be saying: 'Let me tell you about this big idea ...' or 'I was wondering about ...' or 'What I don't understand is ...' or 'Why do you think ...?'

Knowledge box – what knowledge do they need to know?

Teachers need to ask themselves: what knowledge do the children need to know in order to understand the intellectual concept? How will I cover the KLIs that fit within this theme? What parts of the national curriculum will be covered in this theme? That is, what are the essential pieces of information that a child must know in order to research a bigger idea or understand the intellectual concept in question? This is not just a list of facts that are known but not understood; rather, it is the substantive knowledge that is a given in any discipline. It is the vital link between the knowledge and the subject discipline. Children need to know why we are grappling with scientific understandings, historical accuracy or geographical phenomena. Teachers must make this explicit and link pieces of knowledge together to create intellectual constructs and connections. We need to meet knowledge as a friend to be engaged with, who introduces us to a wider circle, rather than an enemy to be overcome.

Through the eyes of the child … We want our children to be saying: 'Let me tell you all the things I know that help me understand the big idea …' or 'I didn't know …' or 'At last I understand … or at least think I do …'

Box of entitlements – equality across the school and our cultural capital

p. 48

The teacher ensures that all learners receive a broad and diverse range of stimuli and experiences throughout a theme. How can the Sustainable Development Goals be woven throughout the planning? All teachers have a natural or default way of presenting learning, but it is essential to any curriculum design that the daily diet for each year

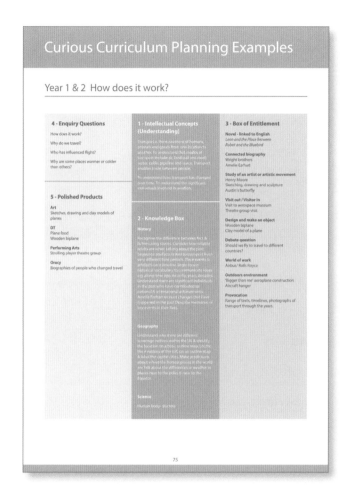

group is varied. How will the learning be linked in a sequential way, progressively developing substantive and disciplinary knowledge through the use of a variety of pedagogical approaches? The use and importance of story within this element of the design is important, as it allows for the child to hook the learning through a narrative constructed over time. Narratives and powerful stories allow learning to be embedded in a schema in the long-term memory.[14]

---

14 C. Counsell, Taking Curriculum Seriously, *Impact: Journal of the Chartered College of Teaching*, 4 (autumn 2018). Available at: https://impact.chartered.college/article/taking-curriculum-seriously.

The sorts of entitlements that we should consider and ensure are experienced over the course of a year or more include:

- A novel – linked to English.

- A biography connected to the knowledge being learned.

- English and maths integration.

- Study of an artist or artistic movement.

 p.165

- Visit out/visitor in.

- Design and make an object.

- Debate a question/topic.

- World of work – how does it connect to our learning?

- Nature and the outdoors.

- Learning environment/learning journey.

- Provocation – how are we using it to stimulate thinking?

These are the sorts of tasks that are regularly incorporated into teachers' planning, but they are more often activity led rather than learning led. We are sometimes tempted to focus on what we as the teacher will do and what we can offer the children as 'good activities' rather than what we want them to learn. The elements we plan need to be intellectually rigorous and demanding. For example, educational visits need to be just that – educational. An opportunity to take history, art, science or mathematics into the real world. A text-rich environment means just that: texts that are of high quality, engaging and challenging, with subject matter that is both intellectually and emotionally simulating; not texts that the children have probably read already, that are below their reading ability when read alone or populist novels that follow a fashion.

Through the eyes of the child ... We should be hearing our children saying: 'We have done lots of different things to understand the big idea in this theme' or 'All the experiences have taught me facts and made me wonder and made me realise ...'

Polished products – what skills and understanding will be developed?

Polished products are the models, maps, diagrams, charts, pictures, posters, presentations, dramas, instrumental pieces, photographs, writing, experiments, structures and debates, for example, that bring learning to life for children. They need to know the purpose and the audience for their learning – and the more immediate and relevant, the better. We want 'work' to be a verb rather than a noun, so the children do the work to produce something that makes a point and advances their own learning. Tim Oates has discussed this in relation to the development of the national curriculum by focusing on what the children are going to achieve through their learning activity.[15]

The teacher will need to consider what skills will be taught and

Polished Products

Teaching sequences give opportunities for the creation of 'Polished Products'.

Ron Berger's 'ethic of excellence' is understood by children and staff and used to build towards the final piece.

Year 2

Year 3

---

15 T. Oates, National Curriculum: Tim Oates on Assessment [video] (22 May 2014). Available at: https://www.youtube.com/watch?v=-q5vrBXFpm0.

developed over this theme in order for the children to produce an extended quality product to exhibit at the end in an exhibition, emporium, museum or exposition. This is our approach. Mary Myatt has written about the importance of quality products and what she calls 'beautiful work'.[16]

The concept behind Ron Berger's ethic of excellence is an essential part of this element of the curriculum design.[17] How do we enable children to produce high-quality products that do not fall into the category of 'traditional' work that is assessed by a teacher or applauded by parents? How can their products be used to stimulate the learning of each other? Does everyone need to produce the same products or can different products take our class to a deeper understanding of concepts and a broader awareness of answers to enquiry questions?

What time is built into the sequence of learning that will allow and enable a child to have the kind, specific and helpful feedback on their work that Berger advocates? How does the progressive, sequential learning journey sustain the deepening of substantive knowledge, while also supporting the child to develop scholarly thinking about the subject discipline they are studying? The idea of developing depth and excellence is not only deeply satisfying but will support teachers to understand the level to which the child understands, knows and is able to talk about their learning.

Allowing children time in the curriculum to refine and polish their work not only shows that it is valued, but also that it takes time to perfect and develop a skill. Opportunities to enable children to make beautiful or functional products takes time. It takes well-planned sequential lessons on the development of the subject at hand. It takes

---

16 Myatt, *The Curriculum*, p. 43.
17 R. Berger, Austin's Butterfly: Building Excellence in Student Work [video], *Models of Excellence – EL Education* (2012). Available at: https://modelsofexcellence.eleducation. org/resources/austins-butterfly.

a range of pedagogy from direct instruction and teacher exposition to purposeful practice. Most of all, it takes a depth of knowledge and commitment from both the child and the teacher to agree to commit to the messy process of becoming 'good' at something. The pride in the face of the child who is able to confidently talk about their polished product and how it relates to their learning is simply magical.

Through the eyes of the child ... When displaying their polished products children should be saying: 'I have realised the importance of being organised and practising skills, so the things I have produced are the best they can be and people want to look at them, read them, watch them or hear them – and be amazed at how well I have done to make my learning really interesting to others.'

Enquiry questions – what do I notice and wonder?

An enquiry question will encourage the children to wonder and notice. It captures their interest and imagination and opens up research opportunities. It shapes the sort of experience they have because it gives them something to delve into in the quest for an answer. The words 'why' and 'how' drive the learning experience towards finding out, observing over time, experimenting, inventing and making; they demand that the teacher plans learning which is engaging, practical and revealing. Children will become deeply involved in a question that has a complex response, and the complexity will grow with the learning maturity of the child. As Christine Counsell says, a good enquiry question may have multiple possible answers but it will have a clear focus.[18]

---

18 C. Counsell, Wrestling with Enquiry Questions: Linking Content and Concept in Medium Term Planning [blog] (2012). Available at: https://andallthatweb.files.wordpress.com/2012/07/wrestling-with-enquiry-questions.pdf.

The enquiry question should be reasonable and there should be some credible research available to answer it. The questions might lead to further questions and develop and explore the children's thinking, concepts and knowledge. The question should support the knowledge that is being presented and the disciplinary elements of the subject. The Historical Association maintains that enquiry questions differ from the pedagogical approach of being enquiry-led: they are a device for teachers to structure coherent sequences of lessons, building knowledge systematically and cumulatively.[19]

The enquiry questions in our Curious Curriculum are structured in order to develop short sequences of learning and to help the child remain interested and engaged.[20] The questions are rooted in curriculum rather than pedagogical enquiry, although the use of a range of pedagogical approaches and teaching strategies is implicit in this curriculum design. The age and stage of a child is also taken into account when considering the best pedagogical approach. We ask: 'What do I want them to learn?' and 'What is the best way for them to learn it?' As Young argues, the difficulty for any curriculum is the balance between basing the curriculum on pedagogic knowledge and developing a curriculum-led pedagogy.[21]

Through the eyes of the child … We should be hearing children saying: 'The question I am trying to answer is complicated. All the things I know are making me wonder – a lot. The questions are enabling me to understand the bigger, wider concepts.'

19 R. Sullivan, DfE Clarifies Reference to Enquiry-Based Learning, *Historical Association* (8 August 2018). Available at: https://www.history.org.uk/ha-news/categories/455/news/3613/dfe-clarifies-reference-to-enquiry-based-learning.

20 D. Cox, Curricular Enquiry Questions in RE – Blog 1, *Missdcoxblog* [blog] (14 May 2020). Available at: https://missdcoxblog.wordpress.com/2020/05/14/curricular-enquiry-questions-in-re-blog-1.

21 Young, A Knowledge-Led Curriculum.

Local to global – how relevant is this to my world and the world around me?

The design of the experiences locates learning in the context of the child's life and local community and also within a national and international dimension. It addresses contemporary issues as well as the big ideas that have shaped the world, sometimes in the context of the child's immediate environment. Teachers should reflect on the community's contribution to the curriculum and think about the relevance to the child and the wider world. The theme should allow for the child to hook the various elements of learning into the local context and the image of world they see around them. The idea that our children are the future scientists, politicians, artists, economists, educationalists, parents and decision-makers of our world is fundamental to the global citizenship element of our design. The Sustainable Development Goals are embedded in our themes and support the concept that children will make connections between their local world and national and global dimensions.

Through the eyes of the child ... We hope our children will be articulating: 'I understand what matters near where I live and how this fits with my country and the world.'

The national curriculum encourages a knowledge-rich approach – can we explore that a bit more?

The role of knowledge has been one of the central curriculum debates in recent years. In order to achieve our principles, we need to ensure that, through their experience in school, children acquire and build the substantive knowledge needed for academic success. Through the careful development and progression of skills in discrete subject disciplines, they should access the disciplinary concepts and knowledge – what Young describes as the power of knowledge.[22] The Curious Curriculum embeds a concept-driven outlook that incorporates both knowledge and skills, using a thematic approach (where appropriate) to support the development of schema or mental structures that learners can use to organise their knowledge. The interdisciplinary element enables children to know when, where and how to use their acquired knowledge – Shavelson et al. call this 'strategic knowledge'[23] – knowledge that is embedded in application and context. A really effective curriculum will be rooted in its own locality and context and will meet the needs of its own learners, while also exposing them to national and global requirements and expectations.

Across our schools, we believe in the importance of the development of substantive disciplinary and interdisciplinary knowledge. We have designed our curriculum to incorporate all three types of knowledge:

1. Substantive knowledge is the knowledge produced by the academic study of a subject discipline. For example, in science this involves concepts that form the underpinning structure of the subject, such as respiration, evolution and the idea of a force.

2. Disciplinary knowledge is the knowledge needed to collect, understand and evaluate scientific evidence – for example, the concept of being a scientist. It is the scientific method, such as changing one variable while keeping everything else the same and seeing what happens.

22 M. Young, The Curriculum. In C. Sealy and T. Bennett (eds), *The ResearchED Guide to the Curriculum: An Evidence-Informed Guide for Teachers* (Woodbridge: John Catt Educational, 2020), pp. 19–29.
23 R. Shavelson, M. A. Ruiz-Primo and E. Wiley, Windows into the Mind, *Higher Education*, 49(4) (2005), 413–430. doi:10.1007/s10734-004-9448-9

3. Interdisciplinary knowledge draws knowledge combining two or more academic disciplines into one activity (e.g. a research project). It is about creating something by thinking across boundaries. Following on from our scientific examples, this might be realising that colour mixing in art is linked to the concept of the spectrum or understanding the scientific principles at play in medieval weaponry as part of historical study.

Figure 1.6 shows how the different types of knowledge are addressed within the planning principles for our themes, as well as the places where we expect the children's growing knowledge to have impact and to be further developed.

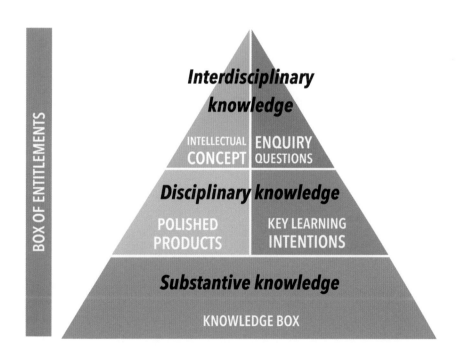

Figure 1.6. Visual representation of how the three types of knowledge are woven through the Curious Curriculum

How do we structure for the development of vocabulary?

It is well documented that the key to success in school, and some would argue in life, is early language acquisition and exposure to an extensive vocabulary. In essence, the quality and amount of contact with a wide range of vocabulary in early childhood and in the formative years of education has a significant correlation with academic success.[24] In light of this, and the fact that disadvantaged children are more likely to have limited vocabulary, our guiding principles focused our attention on how to incorporate the explicit teaching of vocabulary into the curriculum.

This is where our Curious Curriculum links to, supports and develops the expectations of our work in English: teachers need to be cognisant of possibilities all the time. While they are expected to seize on any occasion to expand the children's vocabulary and knowledge, they are also expected to plan deliberate opportunities to teach relevant and appropriate vocabulary. Each theme – indeed, any good planned learning, as Beck et al. argue[25] – will offer the potential for extending vocabulary. We set out to encourage teachers to both deliberately plan opportunities and exploit them as they arise.

Knowledge organisers have become an accepted practice in English schools over the last few years. Developed by Joe Kirby,[26] knowledge organisers can be an example of the type of practice that seeps through the system periodically and becomes ubiquitous before fading again. We decided to use them in our schools as a way of helping the children and their teachers to focus on the key elements of knowledge without allowing bad habits to develop

---

24 A. Quigley, *Closing the Vocabulary Gap* (Abingdon and New York: Routledge, 2018), p. 3.

25 I. Beck, M. McKeown and L. Kucan, *Bringing Words to Life: Robust Vocabulary Instruction* (New York: Guilford Publications, 2013).

26 J. Kirby, Knowledge Organisers, *Pragmatic Reform* [blog] (28 March 2015). Available at: https://pragmaticreform.wordpress.com/2015/03/28/knowledge-organisers.

around them. A well-structured knowledge organiser supports children in understanding the big picture and key concepts, as well as enabling teachers to highlight examples, real-life events and information, along with key vocabulary. This is emphasised by Nimish Lad, who shows how areas of knowledge can be linked across subject disciplines.[27] Combined with the knowledge organiser is an explicit focus on vocabulary. Within the Curious Curriculum, vocabulary is an important element that can be seen in the subject discipline KLIs. This includes Tier 2 words (academic vocabulary needed to understand, read, write and access all subjects) and Tier 3 vocabulary (which Isabel Beck and Margaret McKeown have categorised as subject-specific vocabulary that is specialist within the subject discipline domain[28]). Each of our KLIs contains a list of words which are used by

---

27 N. Lad, *Shimamura's MARGE Model of Learning in Action* (Woodbridge: John Catt Educational, 2021).

28 See O. Sumpter, Using Vocabulary Tiers to Improve Literacy, *Bedrock Learning* [blog] (8 March 2022). Available at: https://bedrocklearning.org/blog/using-vocabulary-tiers-to-improve-literacy.

teachers to plan the vocabulary their children need to learn in order for them to understand the subject content.

Working alongside speech and language therapists, as well as using Word Aware[29] and Vocabulary Ninja,[30] teachers and teaching assistants have been trained to think carefully about not only the Tier 2 and Tier 3 words needed in each theme and subject, but also how they will teach these words and support the children to remember and understand them.

Through the eyes of the child: Children should be talking about language and commenting: 'I know lots of words that help me to articulate my thinking and discuss what I have learned' or 'Knowing lots of vocabulary, its origin and its meaning helps me to learn new unfamiliar words and talk confidently about lots of things.'

How do we use knowledge organisers?

p. 152

p. 58

Alongside the focus on the 'knowledge box', we use knowledge organisers to support teachers and children with the substantive knowledge and disciplinary concepts they need to teach and learn as part of the Curious Curriculum. When planning, teachers research the subjects they are teaching and, using the KLIs, systematise their own knowledge about the theme they will be teaching. As Mark Miller discusses, the use of knowledge organisers needs to be integrated into practice.[31] The teacher's knowledge organiser therefore becomes a teaching resource that enables them to plan, teach and assess well.

---

29 S. Parsons and A. Branagan, *Word Aware 1: Teaching Vocabulary Across the Day, Across the Curriculum* (Abingdon and New York: Routledge, 2013).

30 A. Jennings, *Vocabulary Ninja: Mastering Vocabulary – Activities to Unlock the World of Words* (London: Bloomsbury Education, 2019).

31 M. Miller, Organising Knowledge: The Purpose and Pedagogy of Knowledge Organisers, *Impact: Journal of the Chartered College of Teaching*, 4 (autumn 2018). Available at: https://my.chartered.college/impact_article/organising-knowledge-the-purpose-and-pedagogy-of-knowledge-organisers.

The teachers' knowledge organiser may include specific information for the children as well as background facts, knowledge, concepts or ideas that may simply be for their own use when preparing to teach the subject matter.

The children's knowledge organiser will incorporate the key facts and vocabulary or the information they will need in order to understand the sequence of learning. It should be no more than one or two sides of A4 and should be age appropriate in terms of accessibility. The learning needs to be broken down into small steps and not displayed in blocks of prose. Teachers should include only essential facts and pieces of information – for example, dates and timelines, diagrams, maps or pictures – which should help them to think hard about what they are going to teach.[32] The knowledge organiser is an aid to teaching, not a replacement curriculum.

Through the eyes of the child: We expect children to be saying: 'I can use my knowledge organiser to help me remember the learning I have been taught in class' or 'I can ask someone at home to help me remember the key facts and vocabulary and test me ready for me to use the information in my lessons.'

Getting down to the detail – the narrative

To support teachers' planning, we provide the KLIs and emphasise the fine detail of key vocabulary that should appear in a theme. We also help them to see the big picture over the course of the theme, through what we call a 'narrative'.

The narrative is the story of how we get from the A to Z of the theme, from day one until the end. It is the flow – the sequence detailed in a piece of prose. We want teachers to envision how they will guide the children though the theme and imagine how they will organise some

---

32 Myatt, *The Curriculum*, p. 89.

of the crucial parts along the way. The notion of visualising what it will look like in the classroom can be much more useful than blow-by-blow planning of a one-hour lesson. It helps to shape the sequence, enabling teachers to home in on the parts that are complicated and think about them in detail. Let's face it: teachers don't need to write plans for things they have organised effectively for years. The narrative approach cuts down on workload and means that teachers are planning for themselves rather than to satisfy a managerial procedure.

In effect, a narrative is a written version of the type of conversation a teacher may have with a colleague when they talk about how they will introduce subject content, how they will maintain engagement and how they will ensure that everything that needs to be covered is taught in a coherent, progressive way. The narrative will also identify the prerequisite pieces of information, skills or knowledge. For example, when a class is introduced to a new novel, how will you make sure that you front-load the reading of the text, so the children get hooked and can't wait for the next instalment, rather than routinely drip-feeding the story over many weeks, analysing it to pieces and losing the gist?

The narrative might help a teacher to ensure that the class has the skills to draw and plot a graph before they conduct their scientific research and write up their results. The prerequisites are the skills and knowledge that we all hope children will have mastered as they come to the point when they need to use them. However, they can often become stumbling blocks and create frustration because they were not in place early enough. Teachers then find themselves choosing not to do the science experiment they planned because they have to teach the children how to draw a results table correctly. You get the drift …

There is a progression of study skills that each teacher needs to make sure have been successfully learned across the year and in succeeding years. The narrative helps to plot where the prerequisites might be needed and therefore prompts teachers to cover them in the sequence of learning. The narrative also encourages teachers to think ahead about the different pedagogical approaches they might use, and which ones would be appropriate for which piece of learning. Teachers can use the narrative to tell the story of the children's learning journey, ensuring progression, interconnection and cohesion. As Debra Kidd observes, 'Coherence across the curriculum is easier if … we conceptualise planning as a plait into which we weave the knowledge we need as we go along. This allows us to select content more carefully: do we need it now, later, or not at all?'[33]

Here is part of a narrative for our Year 5 theme 'The Whole World in Our Hands':

> *The theme will begin with an immersion into the sounds of different biomes, which will introduce the children to thinking about how there are different locations around the world. They will revisit their map interpretation skills by looking at a biome map of the world and will begin to make suggestions about which areas might be biomes (practice). This will begin our enquiry question: 'What makes a biome a biome?' (Sustainable Development Goal 15 – Life on Land). After revealing the different biomes (exposition), we will take the opportunity to establish what the children already know about different biomes around the world and allow them to create questions they want to explore. From this point, the children will be split into groups, each one focused on one particular biome, which they will research in order to discover the features that make each biome unique (enquiry). This will include identifying the impact of humans on biomes to address: 'How are biomes changing as a result of human behaviour?' (Sustainable Development Goal 13 – Climate Action). Once they have completed their research, they will combine their efforts in mixed groups, presenting their findings and then making comparisons between different biomes.*

---

33 D. Kidd, *A Curriculum of Hope: As Rich in Humanity as in Knowledge* (Carmarthen: Independent Thinking Press, 2020), p. 45.

Through the eyes of the child: We want to hear the children saying: 'My learning is clear and makes sense. I understand how new knowledge builds on things I have learned before and how this fits together into understanding "big ideas".'

If the narrative helps the teacher to articulate the journey, how do we help the children to do the same?

'Working walls', 'learning walls', 'wonder walls' and 'learning journeys'. These ideas are not new; nearly every primary teacher uses them. But every wall does not always have an explicit rationale for its purpose and structure. Using a learning journey approach to displaying products in the classroom enables teachers to document and track the learning throughout the sequence of the theme. At the end of theme, the wall can be mapped back to the narrative as a form of evaluation, which can help to develop planning effectiveness and the usefulness of the learning journey display itself.

Learning walls should show a range of examples of children's products and in a range of media – a 'studio' feel. Displays should grow as the learning progresses, with examples of work in progress put on show as they happen, not held back to be displayed as a finished product.

We have some clear guidelines to ensure that our wall displays have a consistent quality. Backgrounds are neutral and borders define a space or complement it (without fighting it). The children's efforts, work and creativity should take centre stage. We feature vocabulary as it is used and needed rather than as a wallpaper of words that vanishes into the background. Each school and class teacher adapt and ensure the learning walls are age appropriate and not overly fussy or cluttered.

Our journeys illustrate where the learning fits into the sequence of what is coming next and builds on what is already known. They mirror the narrative and planning teaching structure, but should also be accessible to the children by answering simple questions, such as 'Why this?' and 'Why now?' Learning walls should be used by both the teacher and children as a resource, including learning prompts linked to the key skills that are appropriate to the age and stage of the children. These prompts can be used to support teaching and learning, encouraging the children to engage with their environment and the resources available to them.

Working Walls

Examples of the Working Wall displays that are used to support teaching and learning. These are built up over the two terms.

This approach is grounded in our principle that children have the right to a rich multisensory environment – one that stimulates and provokes learning and reflects the importance of aesthetics and beauty, and one that is well organised, reflects high expectations and standards, and enables learners to develop independence in their learning. At the same time, our multisensory environment is sensitive and reflective, with carefully chosen tones and colours and gentle organisation, rather than an assault on the senses from vibrant colour clashes or harsh materials.

Our rationale is based on various theories, research, concepts and ideas. The relationship between pedagogy and learning spaces is

Olympus Schools' Theme Walls.

Celebrating our 'Curious Curriculum' around our schools.

integral to our approach: we believe first and foremost that the learning environment should be designed to support high-quality interaction and teaching and learning. The Reggio Emilia[34] and Montessori[35] methods have been instrumental in defining our approach. Space, light, colour and form can either enhance and facilitate or impinge and intrude on a child's learning journey. For this reason, they are central to the way that our school environments are planned, which is premised on the belief that environment is 'the third teacher'.[36]

The environment in our schools is by design, not accident. Colour schemes are carefully chosen to be subtle and not to overstimulate. Our schools are not new builds and many were in a poor state previously. However, we regard the environment as a crucial element in our effort to help children learn and we recognise the impact it can have. The dining environment and experience is also designed to value the importance of the preparation and presentation of food and its relationship to learning. We take care when selecting and placing materials in our schools, in the same way that we would in our own homes. Carefully chosen provocations around the school also invite interaction from the children.[37]

Materials and finishes are chosen for their aesthetic and sensory properties. Floors, walls and ceilings are particularly important, so we have paid attention to how these can facilitate and support the children's learning. Uncluttered neutral flooring, subtle muted colour schemes and the use of natural materials (such as hessian) allow the children's learning to be the main focus.

We want our learning environment to reflect our values and to be a vehicle for our pedagogic principles, including our Curious

---

34 See https://www.reggiochildren.it/en/reggio-emilia-approach.

35 See https://www.fundacionmontessori.org/the-montessori-method.htm.

36 See http://www.thethirdteacher.com.

37 S. Durand, Engage Your Early Learners Using Provocations, *Educa* (29 June 2016). Available at: https://www.geteduca.com/blog/engage-early-learners-using-provocations.

Curriculum. These values and principles should be explicit on the walls and tables, not hidden in a policy document on an office shelf. The learning environment serves as a constant reminder to every one of the shared beliefs underpinning our schools.

 p.27

Through the eyes of the child: We should hear our children saying: 'I love my classroom. It feels like a place where I can concentrate, focus and learn' or 'I use the resources in my classroom to help me with my learning. I know where to look if I need support.'

How do we capture the overall essence of rich learning that happens during the course of a theme?

One of the devices we use is a class floor book. Throughout the year, teachers and children experience learning in many different forms. It is important to capture this learning in a diverse range of ways, so the children understand that learning happens everywhere, not just when they are sitting in rows, facing forward and with a pen and book. In order to support and celebrate this understanding, each class creates a collective floor book (so named because they are large and ring-bound so are normally looked at on the floor). Teachers and children collect all the amazing learning that happens over the year; examples might include the wonderful visitor who came in to talk about birds of prey or the visit to a beehive to hear about the vital importance of bees in our ecosystem. The floor book might also capture debates and discussions held in class and include photos and sticky note comments about how well the children performed in concerts or poetry slams. The list is endless and only limited by the imagination of the teacher and class. In fact, the children love looking at the floor books so much that they are frequently sent up to the next class as a reminder of the incredible learning that has taken place during the previous year.

Through the eyes of the child: Our children should be shouting loud and proud about their learning: 'Come and see the amazing things we have learned about this year!' or 'Our floor book contains a collection of exciting things we have learned about, so we can look back and talk about them.'

How else do we communicate the quality of learning?

An interesting question. Audience, purpose and opportunity provide the answer; they are the starting points for our exhibitions. When talking to the children about memorable events and times when they were proud of their work and learning, there were commonalities. These were events or times when the children had an opportunity to work towards something purposeful, to refine and redraft their learning. They valued the times when they knew someone would read, see, admire and ask about their efforts. They appreciated the opportunity to show their efforts to parents and the wider community, to show progress to other teachers who had taught them in the past, and to explain their learning to other children from around the school and the trust.

p. 255

From this evolved our exhibitions. They happen twice a year across the trust and involve two year groups: either Years 3 and 4 or Years 5 and 6. They are held at one of our secondary schools in order to have enough space to display the work and accommodate visitors. The children write a list of questions that they think other children might ask about their work, which are collated and form a visitor pack. Visitors, including parents and carers, spend time at each school's stand, asking questions of the children whose work is exhibited. It is a privilege to see the pride on their faces when talking to visiting adults about their learning.

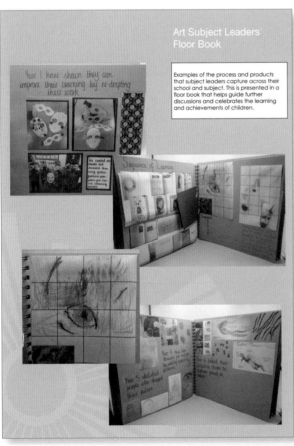

Art Subject Leaders' Floor Book

Examples of the process and products that subject leaders capture across their school and subject. This is presented in a floor book that helps guide further discussions and celebrates the learning and achievements of children.

There are two principles at play here. Firstly, children rise to the challenge when they know their work will be displayed and viewed. Secondly, an audience is a good driver for excellence. If, when you are working on and learning something, you know that your final piece of work will be put on display and shared across the trust, with you present to explain and answer questions, the purpose and audience become very real.

How else are families involved?

We use a trust-wide initiative called Curious Curriculum Unleashed, which aims to capture the essence of the Sustainable Development Goals while also supporting children to live life to the full – experiencing nature, cooking, making and being creative. Curious Curriculum Unleashed is more than some activities to do and tick off. It includes extracurricular challenges and experiences for children and their families, which aim to extend their cultural capital. We produce booklets that contain twenty challenges for the children to complete throughout each year of their primary school life (see Figure 1.7).

The children are encouraged to do some of the challenges at home and some will be experienced in school or perhaps set as home learning. When the children have completed the challenges they can share them on Seesaw (the trust's blended learning platform),[38] on controlled social media or with their class teacher. Part of this

38 See https://web.seesaw.me.

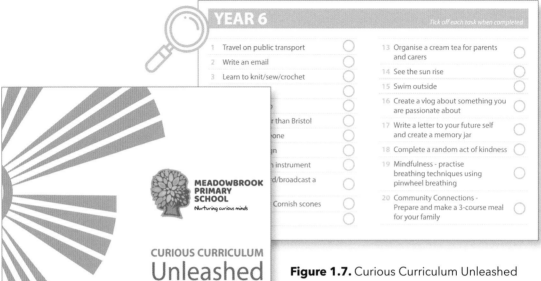

YEAR 6 — *Tick off each task when completed*

1   Travel on public transport
2   Write an email
3   Learn to knit/sew/crochet

r than Bristol
one
n
instrument
d/broadcast a

Cornish scones

13 Organise a cream tea for parents and carers
14 See the sun rise
15 Swim outside
16 Create a vlog about something you are passionate about
17 Write a letter to your future self and create a memory jar
18 Complete a random act of kindness
19 Mindfulness - practise breathing techniques using pinwheel breathing
20 Community Connections - Prepare and make a 3-course meal for your family

MEADOWBROOK PRIMARY SCHOOL
Nurturing curious minds

CURIOUS CURRICULUM
Unleashed

Figure 1.7. Curious Curriculum Unleashed

approach to support the Sustainable Development Goals leads back to our principles – in particular, the one that pledges to develop local, national and global knowledge and understanding in children by providing enriching experiences, developing global citizenship, celebrating diversity and creating cultural capital.

As a group of schools, we are always thinking about the responsibilities that come with being global citizens – for example, working hard to become an Eco-School[39] or gaining a Green Tree Schools Award.[40] The Curious Curriculum Unleashed challenges are no different. Many primary schools devise comparable challenges, which are similar to the National Trust's '50 things to do before you are 11¾'[41] or the Children's University Passport to Learning scheme.[42] However, we try to make sure that these challenges are not one-off

---

39 See https://www.eco-schools.org.uk.
40 See https://www.woodlandtrust.org.uk/support-us/act/your-school/green-tree-schools-award.
41 See https://www.nationaltrust.org.uk/50-things-to-do.
42 See https://www.childrensuniversity.co.uk.

random activities or experiences; they are linked not only to the Sustainable Development Goals but also to the learning that is taking place within the Curious Curriculum themes. They encourage and engage children, parents and families to venture into experiences that perhaps they would not do otherwise, and they are supported by the school curriculum in order to ensure that all children get an opportunity to experience them, regardless of home circumstances.

Olympus Schools' Exhibitions

Examples of the regular celebratory exhibitions that the Olympus Trust holds for children and parents.

Year 4

Year 5

What is the pledge?

When discussing and deciding on our pedagogic principles, we were agreed that every curriculum we had read about, seen or even taught did little to acknowledge the many other amazing things that happen within a primary school as an integral part of the curriculum. Some refer to the 'taught' and 'caught' curriculum. Some talk about the 'hidden' curriculum. Some talk of 'enrichment'. We knew these aspects were not add-ons, extras or frills. We thought of it more as a 'cultivated' curriculum – a curriculum that sits outside of what is planned and taught explicitly in subject disciplines. There were eight areas that we all felt passionately were the essence of what our primary schools were about. We wanted our children to leave our schools feeling confident in all of them. We wanted them to be performers, global citizens, adventurers, scholars, Olympians, activists, entrepreneurs and leaders.

In order to deliver on this ambition, we decided to pledge to parents and carers that we would be true to our principles and cultivate

Figure 1.8. Our pledge to you

Figure 1.9. Opportunities to thrive: knowledge in context

the whole child (see Figure 1.8). We understood that these eight elements were important to parents, and that in order for their child to develop and grow we would offer them opportunities outside of the national curriculum to improve in these areas.

In bringing learning alive and teaching it in context, we would be giving our children the chance to develop these skill areas and extend their knowledge, especially substantive and inter-disciplinary knowledge. These experiences would create openings for the children to take responsibility, organise and manage, to work in teams and to work towards a range of outcomes, successes and failures – real-world learning (see Figure 1.9).

p. 58

How do the Sustainable Development Goals fit in?

An important principle of our Curious Curriculum is the significance we place on the need for children to understand the shift between local, national and global interests and concerns. The curriculum needs to be grounded in the local area, which is easily recognisable to the children and has an immediate impact on their lives, but it is also essential that they develop into global citizens – adults who understand wider international issues.

The United Nations Climate Change Conference of the Parties (COP) summits emphasise the importance of education in global sustainability, so, as educators, we have a responsibility to teach our children about the world around them.[43] This links directly with Goal 13 on taking urgent action to address climate change. We have linked our Curious Curriculum enquiry themes with

---

43 See https://ukcop26.org. See also Department for Education, *Sustainability & Climate Change: A Draft Strategy for the Education & Children's Services Systems* (November 2021). Available at: https://assets.publishing.service.gov.uk/government/uploads/system/uploads/attachment_data/file/1031454/SCC_DRAFT_Strategy.pdf.

Figure 1.10. The United Nations Sustainable Development Goals

these global issues and encourage the children to explore the related big ideas, concepts and reality. We have also signed up to help deliver on the United Nations' seventeen Sustainable Development Goals.

The United Nations says of the goals: 'The Sustainable Development Goals are the blueprint to achieve a better and more sustainable future for all. They address the global challenges we face, including poverty, inequality, climate change, environmental degradation, peace and justice.'[44]

They are a call for action by all people and countries to promote prosperity while also protecting the planet.[45] To support us to do

---

44 See the United Nations Sustainable Development Goals website: https://www.un.org/sustainabledevelopment/. The content of this publication has not been approved by the United Nations and does not reflect the views of the United Nations or its officials or Member States.

45 If you would like to know more about this, you can do some research at www.un.org/sustainabledevelopment.

this, we have trained staff in each of our schools using Lyfta, an organisation that is partnered with the British Council. Lyfta is an interactive and immersive learning platform where teachers can construct lessons that bring learning to life. The content is ideal for teaching a range of subjects, including literacy, personal, social, health and economic (PSHE) education, relationships and sex education, geography, citizenship, science, and DT, as well as the Sustainable Development Goals.[46]

We integrate Lyfta into our themes to help provide learners with interactive, real-life scenarios of families, children and adults from around the world all telling their stories. We know that stories are an excellent way to learn about complex and geographically removed issues.

In essence, that is our Curious Curriculum. It is an agreed way of structuring learning for children to try to achieve high standards within and through the foundation subjects. It tries to economise on work for the teacher, while still providing opportunities for them to use their initiative and bring their own ideas to the children they teach. It provides detail without being burdensome. On its own, though, it can only go so far, which is why we also support our teachers in their work.

---

46 See https://www.lyfta.com.

CHAPTER 2

What structures does the Curious Curriculum offer to support the individual teacher?

Is there a central resource to help teachers?

The Olympus portal: it is the natural place to visit. Our portal supports staff with planning resources, and it enables teachers to plan directly using the planning tool and to see other colleagues' planning in schools across the trust (see Figure 2.1). It contains many examples of worked strategies and planning support, especially for English and mathematics. The portal also offers a platform for conversation with colleagues. It contains shared professional development resources, which allows staff to take responsibility for their own continuing professional development. We prefer to talk about 'economic work' rather than 'reducing workload': we want our teachers to be working on the right things and enjoying their productive work.

It is exciting to have one central repository where we store all our resources and planning. We have the same internal website for all our schools, which is administered by one IT web designer and by the central teaching and learning team. This means we are able to control and monitor centrally what is uploaded and stored for staff to access. The challenge is to make sure that the portal does not become like many shared drives – a dumping ground for things that might be useful. In order to create synergy with the printed resources, the landing page has the same styling as our staff handbooks. The titles and layout are also the same. This is not simply for the sake of appearance and image; it is to ensure consistency in many other ways.

The website is multifunctional. Firstly, it is a place where we share our principles and educational philosophy. Secondly, it holds an expanding bank of resources and examples to support high-quality planning and pedagogy, although we want our teachers to be discerning rather than simply harvesting resources. The third function of the website is as a dynamic and online planning portal.

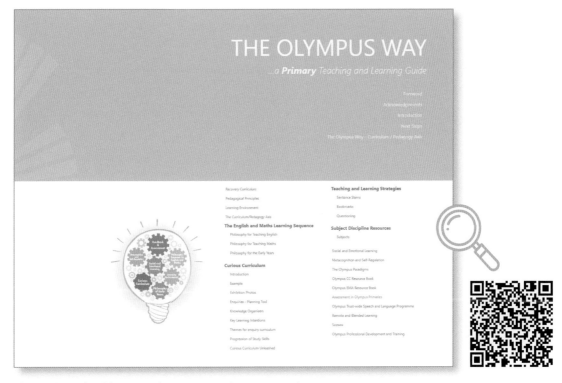

Figure 2.1. The Olympus planning portal

Why do we produce printed documentation?

It is one thing to provide staff with principles, expectations and resources, but it is another to build commitment. We have carefully considered the logistics of communication in our schools. We need to be able to share resources quickly and easily, yet we also want a place to share our educational philosophy and rationale.

We have settled on two formats: a digital portal and printed handbooks and resource books (see Figure 2.2). Initially, this meant that we wrote down and documented the thinking behind our curriculum, as well as recording the process and the journey we had been on as a group of schools. Ultimately, we produced a staff handbook to enable them to reflect on and refer back to as a record of our development.

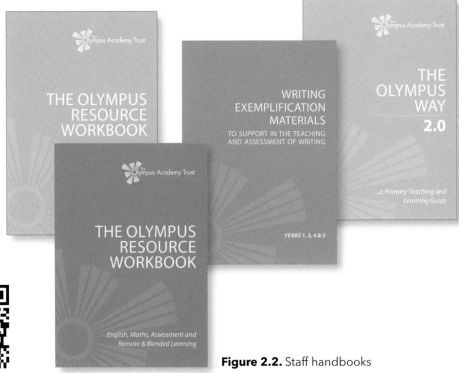

Figure 2.2. Staff handbooks

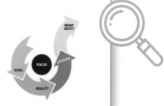

Professional GROWth
My next step to excellence
in the paradigms

My current professional growth focus is:

GOAL
What do I want next?   What do I need to achieve?   What outcome would be ideal?   Imagine being
really successful in this venture.   What would be different?   What are the benefits?

Figure 2.3. Professional GROWth document

How should staff take ownership of their own professional development?

Valuing and developing staff are hallmarks of good organisations and schools, and trusts are no different. As part of our support for staff, and alongside the portal and documentation, we have asked Chris Moyse, an educational consultant specialising in professional development and teacher performance,[1] to develop a self-reflection template that is included at the end of each section of our handbook, so that teachers can reflect and make notes on areas they feel are a strength or they might need to develop.

Both the Olympus Way handbook and online portal include GROWth pages. These appear at the end of each section and enable staff to use the coaching GROW (grow, reality, options, what next?) model to identify their areas for strength and development. The idea is that each teacher uses the model to have a conversation with a member of the senior leadership team and identify areas for their professional

---

1   See https://chrismoyse.wordpress.com/about.

development that year. The trust organises and runs professional development in any area that several people have identified.

Do teachers have to source all their own resources?

We want to take the strain out of resourcing for teachers who are planning the Curious Curriculum. Obviously, there is a fine balance between taking away teacher autonomy and providing everything on a theme or subject area and just leaving them to go it alone. Previously, our teachers were spending an inordinate amount of time using popular search engines to find worksheets and resources. Not only was this a ridiculous waste of their time, it was also unproductive because many of the resources were of poor quality and did not fit with our pedagogical approach. When we asked them what would be helpful, this is what they said – and is what we now provide:

What teachers requested	What we offer
An opportunity to plan with other teachers in the same year group.	We organised year-group planning sessions across the trust.
High-quality planning ideas and resources for each subject.	We subscribe to professional subject associations on behalf of our teachers. p. 332
An opportunity to try out new ideas and lesson structures within foundation subjects.	We organise conferences.
A place where you can see the planning for the previous year group and other planning for year groups across the trust.	We provide an online interactive planning tool on our portal where everyone plans and can see each other's planning across the trust.
Artefacts and resources to teach subject-specific things.	We spend time in INSET sessions checking the sequence of learning in each year group and in each theme, and then audit and purchase the resources necessary for teaching these subject disciplines and themes.
A place where good quality resources are stored and are easily accessible.	The online portal stores many quality-assured resources that teachers may wish to use.

Who does a teacher turn to for advice?

We were aware that some of the areas that teachers were teaching within the KLIs were unfamiliar or not within their areas of expertise. Due to the cross-phase nature of our trust, we are able to support teachers with continuing professional development (CPD) opportunities. Sometimes these are led by secondary subject specialists and sometimes by primary specialists and consultants. INSET sessions and conferences help to develop confidence in teachers, who can be supported by their school subject leader specialist or perhaps one from elsewhere in the trust.[2] Subject leaders supported by external specialists meet regularly to develop their own expertise and support each other with their role. This gives them the confidence, in turn, to support staff in teaching the range of foundation subjects.

What are the roles and expectations of a subject leader?

Subject leaders at Olympus have an important role to play in ensuring that teachers' planning for their class is age appropriate, pitched correctly, has detailed coverage and aligns with the subject discipline. How do we know whether, even if the teacher has planned for progression, it has been taught well and then learned? Enter, stage left, the subject leader.

> The power of the subject leader work has had a big impact on staff as valued professionals with expertise.
>
> *Nicola Bailey*

---

2   Some schools refer to INSETs, others to CPD, others to in-service training and others to the professional learning of teachers. We use the term INSET (in-service training day).

Meadowbrook Primary School - Knowledge Curriculum Overview - **YEAR 6**

YEAR 6	Term 1	Term 2	Term 3	Term 4	Term 5	Term 6 and 1
THEME Y6	Whole world in our hands	Exploration		Bravery		Identity
Class text	Non-fiction Discussion (for/against)	Non-fiction Non chron report	Non-fiction Biography	Non-fiction Police report	Non-fiction Newspaper report	Transition unit Explanations
Major focus Substantive Knowledge	GEOGRAPHY Place-North/South American region-PERU Understand geographical similarities & differences through the study of human & physical geography of a region of north or South America. Describe & understand key aspects of physical geography including: Climate zones, biomes & vegetation belts, rivers, mountains, volcanoes & earthquakes & the water cycle & Types of economic activity, including trade links, & the distribution of natural resources including energy, food, minerals & water.	SCIENCE Evolution and inheritance Recognise that living things have changed over time & that fossils provide information about living things that inhabited the earth millions of years ago. Recognise that living things produce offspring of the same kind, but normally offspring vary & are not identical to their parents. Identify how animals & plants are adapted to suit their environment in different ways & that adaptation may lead to evolution.		HISTORY Extended Chronological study- WWII and Geography KLI's Study of an aspect or theme in British history that extends pupils' chronological knowledge beyond 1066 (World War II)		GEOGRAPHY Local area (Bradley Stoke) Understand geographical similarities & differences through the study of human & physical geography of a region of the UK Types of settlement & land use
Disciplinary Knowledge (skills)	Locate at least two regions of North or South America. Understand how to use knowledge & understanding to suggest relevant geographical questions specific to particular, key environments. Compare key regions around the world using research to justify findings. Understand how to describe the location of key places at local, national & global scales. Study maps of the regions in North or South America to identify environmental features, Compare & contrast these regions. Locate the key physical & human characteristics. Relate these features to the locality e.g. population sizes near tourist landmarks/rivers, transport links to mountains. Understand how to select & use appropriate skills & ways of presenting information to help investigate places & environments. Know how & why it is important to present findings both graphically & in writing using appropriate geographical vocabulary. Understand geographical diversity by describing how physical & human processes can lead to similarities & differences in environments & in the lives of people who live there. To suggest ways in which humans can live sustainably in places near & far. Understand how to construct a geographical investigation & be able to explain why this is so important skill (locate, question data collection, data presentation, conclusions, evaluation). Know how to describe how locations around the world are changing & give reasons for this change. Understand ways in which some social issues can be improved in near & far places.	Investigation Pupils might work scientifically by observing and raising questions about local animals and how they are adapted to their environment comparing how some living things are adapted to survive in extreme conditions, for example, cactuses, penguins and camels. Skills focus Reason & present findings from enquiries, including conclusions, causal relationships & explanations of & degree of trust in results, in oral & written forms such as displays & other presentations. Identify scientific evidence that has been used to support or refute ideas.		Chronological understanding Place current study on timeline in relation to other studies. Use relevant dates & terms accurately in describing events. Sequence up to ten events on a timeline. Interpretations of history Start to link sources together to arrive at conclusions. Consider ways of checking accuracy of interpretations - how can they find out if interpretations are fact, fiction of opinion? Show an awareness of propaganda & how that might affect how the past is represented. Historical enquiry Recognise primary & secondary evidence. Use a range of sources to find out about an event. Use several sources to produce a fluent account. Select a wide range of evidence to help their questioning of the past & consider what is most useful. Identify periods of rapid change in history & compare them with times of relatively little change. Use literacy, numeracy & computing skills to an exceptional standard to communicate information about the past. Use original ways to present information & ideas. Geography KLI objectives Study photographs, aerial photographs and maps of local area - now & post war and present day. Make comparisons and reflect on the reasons for the differences. Study population numbers throughout the course of WWII and reflect on the reasons for changes. Study pictures of land use during these three periods.		Plan a full geographical enquiry e.g. survey the use of land in the immediate locality of the school e.g. local high street, making distance area, using the following classifications: • Residential: houses, flats, hotels, hostels. • Retail: food, clothing, footwear, sports, toys, furniture, etc. • Professional/Commercial: solicitors, banks, building societies, company offices etc. • Industrial & Storage: machine tools, engineering, factories, warehouses. • Entertainment/Leisure: theatres & cinemas, public houses, restaurants, cafes. • Public Authorities, local government offices, police, libraries, hospitals, churches, chapels, schools. • Other: vacant property, car parking, open space, development sites. Compare the land use to the area closest with old maps & photographs of the same area to examine how the land use has changed over time. Investigate why the land use has changed. Undertake a survey of buildings & materials. Investigate what jobs people do within & beyond the school in the local area. Sort them into categories & investigate where & how far people travel to work. Compare shops in the local area with the nearest city centre. Interview question people who use the shops about the services/ types of shop provided/ shopping habits. Study photographs, aerial photographs & maps of local area pre-war, post war & present day. (teach through history) Compare maps & aerial photographs. Make comparisons & reflect on the reasons for the differences. Study population numbers throughout the course of WWII & reflect on the reasons for changes. (teach through history) Study pictures of land use during these three periods. (Teach through history) Draw conclusions & develop informed reasons for the changes. Study one key building in the locality during the three periods (e.g. hospital) & reflect on the changes. Understand how to explain geographical interactions between humans & the environment & begin to discuss the consequences. Identify personal bias in primary observations & explain to what degree both primary & secondary evidence can be. Know how to explain how the UK's location influences the weather pattern across the country.

It is the role of the subject leader to ensure that all teachers use and secure the KLIs described in Chapter 1. Each school and subject leader homes in on the detail and adapts the trust's KLIs to meet the specific needs of their school. Alongside this, each subject leader is responsible for our three subject leader key words – seek, track and capture:

1. Seek learning. What opportunities do subject leads across the trust provide to support and facilitate creative engagement and aspiration, while having fidelity to the subject discipline?

2. Track learning. How is their subject tracked and assessed across schools and the trust to ensure that all children are making progress?

3. Capture learning. How will subject leads capture the learning for their particular subject discipline? By capture, we mean record and keep examples and then use them to seek improved outcomes in the future.

How this is documented, organised and collected in each subject area has been decided collectively by the subject leads in each school across the trust. The subject leads work collaboratively across the organisation, supporting each other and ensuring a trust-wide approach and expectations. This economy eases workload and ensures that new or less experienced leads can develop and grow.

In order to easily monitor and assess their subject discipline across the school, each subject lead is responsible for keeping two documents: a subject leader folder and a subject floor book. We use two documents because, when colleagues discussed the role of the subject leader, we realised that, while it was necessary to have a formal record of activities, it was more important to be able to capture and monitor the progression of what had actually been taught in their subject against what was planned. Explanations and examples of how the folders and floor books are used in schools are set out on the following pages.

What is a subject leader folder?

A subject leader's folder contains information that will help them to talk confidently to anyone (internally or externally) about what, how, when and why a subject sequence of learning (KLI) is taught in a particular way at a particular point across the school.

The folder contains:

1. Seek learning – knowing what we are looking for:

   a. Key learning intentions

   b. Curriculum sequence maps

Meadowbrook Primary School - Design and Technology Curriculum Overview - **YEAR 1**

YEAR 1	Term 1	Term 2	Term 3	Term 4	Term 5	Term 6 and 1
THEME Y1	*The world around us*	*I wonder*		*Machines*		*Wild things*
DT Substantive Knowledge	**Cooking** Assemble or cook ingredients. Identify where food comes from.			**Cardboard product** Investigate a product or theme. Record their ideas using words and drawing. Safely perform a range of cutting and shaping techniques (such as tearing, cutting, joining, rolling, folding, curling & finishing). Use a range of joining techniques (such as gluing, stitching, hinges or combining materials to strengthen). Explore existing products. Test their own products.		
Disciplinary Knowledge (skills)	Use the basic principles of a healthy and varied diet to prepare dishes. Wash their hands & make sure that surfaces are clean. Cut, peel or grate ingredients safely and hygienically. Explain what it means to be hygienic. Describe the texture of foods. Measure or weigh using measuring cups or electronic scales. Think of interesting ways of decorating food they have made; for example,x cakes.			Design purposeful, functional and appealing products for themselves & other users. Generate and use design criteria. Generate, develop, model and communicate their ideas. Develop their own ideas from initial starting points. Design parts of the process; for example, the decoration of a simple product. Select from and use a range of tools and equipment to perform practical tasks. Talk with others about how they want to construct their product. Create simple plans before making objects using pictures and words, e.g. drawings, arranging pieces of construction before hand. Describe how something works. Talk about their own work and things that other people have done. Explain what went well with their work. Explain what they would improve if they did it again. Explore objects and designs to identify likes and dislikes of the designs. Describe the materials using different words. Cut materials safely using tools provided (scissors).		

    c. Examples of planning

    d. Resources, including websites of subject associations and other professional communities of interest

2. Track learning – delving into quality:

    a. Achievement in your subject discipline: seeking greater depth where possible

    b. Subject evaluation: reflecting on quality and effectiveness for each discipline

    c. Triangulation: looking at learning from different viewpoints

3. Capture learning – recognising progress and achievement:

    a. Subject celebration walk

    b. Portfolio/book/learning scrutiny

    c. Photos of work (this may be in the floor book)

    d. Any other examples of capturing learning

As we have seen, it is the subject lead's responsibility to seek, track and capture the quality of the learning in their subject discipline across the school. Support is given in subject network groups, where subject leads from across the trust meet together with a senior leader from one of the schools to share best practice and discuss areas of strength and development in their subject area. On the basis of these discussions, we organise additional INSET, conference time or professional development.

Olympus Subject Leader Floor Books

Each subject leader captures examples of learning from across the school and presents them in a floor book.

History floor book examples

What is a subject floor book?

A floor book (or portfolio) is a way of recording the incredible learning that is happening across the school that is often difficult to document. It is one way for subject leads to help monitor the subject discipline progression across a school. A subject floor book also chronicles excellence and progression from year groups and key stages within the subject discipline. Floor books include examples of practical experiments, educational visits, performances, campaigns and school competitions. They also log work from subjects such as music, PSHE and PE that are practical in nature with little written learning. The variety of evidence captured is down to the subject leader, but it is a wonderful model for children to see what excellence looks like.

In order to promote the subject well, the subject leader will track both substantive and disciplinary knowledge connected to the specific subject discipline that is mapped out in the KLIs. They will monitor the spiralling knowledge across the year groups to ensure that learning progresses. For example, electricity in science is taught explicitly in Years 4 and 6 (Figure 2.5–2.9), and systematic progression in the use of and development of map work in geography is followed carefully through the year groups.

Figure 2.5.

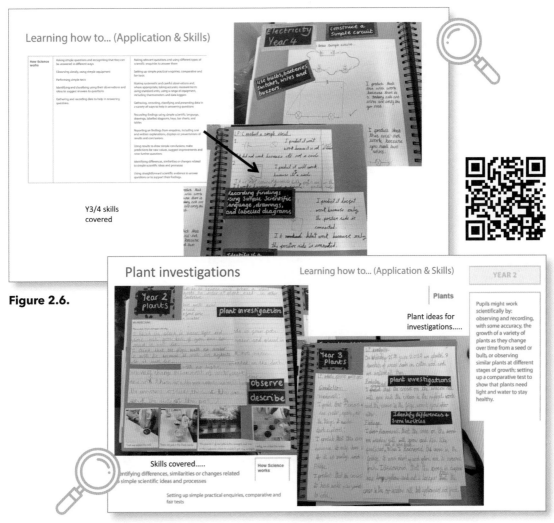

Figure 2.6.

Figure 2.7.

> The school-level curriculum maps are great. Subject leaders are able to track their subject across themes and ensure that there is not only purposeful repetition but the spiralling linking of knowledge.
>
> *Sharon Clark*

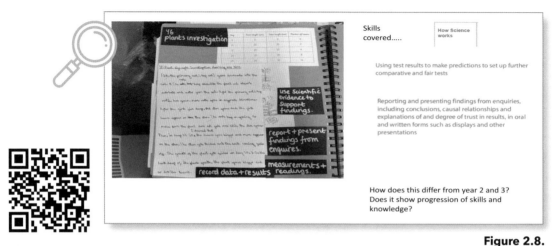

Figure 2.8.

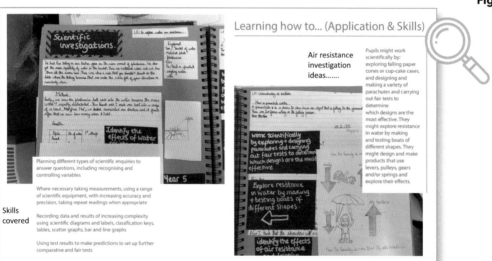

Figure 2.9.

> Subject leaders have produced floor books, which have been presented at school improvement committee meetings as evidence of the progression of skills, and we have been able to see excellent examples of the polished products that are the outcomes of a sequence of learning.
>
> *Kate Sheldon*

The subject lead tracks the captured learning in the floor book to monitor and support teachers through conversations about the progression of knowledge, skills and application.

How do we grow expertise in the subject disciplines?

As we have said, the importance of good subject leadership cannot be underestimated and is the foundation for curriculum development. So, how do we grow that expertise? Firstly, it is about good recruitment: thinking about gaps in subject expertise and where new appointments can be used to bring new skill sets to the organisation or school. But it is also about growing our own: talent-spotting, mentoring and nurturing potential talent. Within professional development conversations, head teachers talk to staff about their areas of expertise and areas they would like to develop. Training, courses and support are put in place and our networks provide a collective safety net where more experienced subject leaders can support and bring on new recruits.

 p. 173

The trust offers and organises external consultancy and support to help subject leads to be more effective, and the director of education and teaching and learning leads meet with and offer advice and encouragement to subject leaders. In one particular area, PE, schools have pooled their funding to employ secondary specialist expertise to work alongside teachers in a lesson study model,[3] so that not only does PE teaching improve but also the subject leadership of PE within the school. Any professional development needs to build on current practice, to keep nudging professionals to progress.

---

3   P. Dudley, The 'Lesson Study' Model of Classroom Enquiry, *Teaching Expertise* (n.d.). Available at: https://www.teachingexpertise.com/articles/the-lesson-study-model-of-classroom-enquiry.

We hope you have enjoyed reading (and perhaps rereading) this part of the book and using the resources on our website to build a picture of the Curious Curriculum. Different readers will delve deeply into different sections, but we hope that our overview has whet the appetite for what we do and that it has made you curious enough to want to read the story of how it unfolded. We are proud of our Curious Curriculum; in two years' time it will have developed even further. It is the process of its development that we believe will help school and trust leaders and teachers to address some of the challenges they may face in their own work. Part Two takes you through our story.

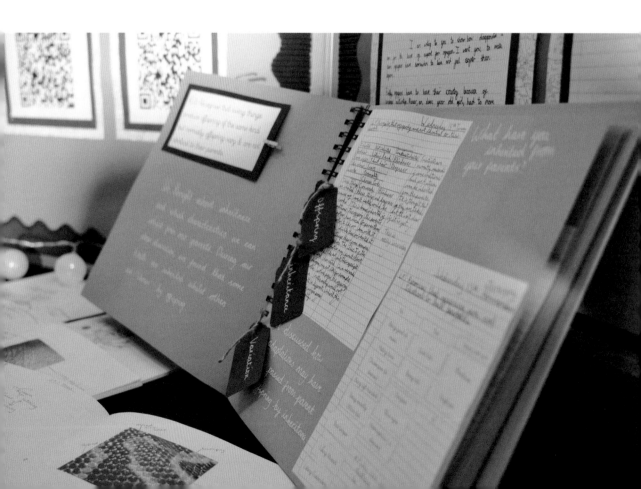

PART TWO

How we have made progress. Securing good practice, outcomes and quality. A story of communicating, convincing and problem-solving.

Between us, we have read many books on project management, leadership approaches and securing objectives. We have heard many lectures on change management theory. We have studied plenty of reference materials on curriculum design and teacher development. Nearly all of them have merit, but the one thing we know is there is no blueprint that applies to every context, and we don't offer one here.

When trying to help others think through and support their own challenge, it is natural to present a clear action plan: a model with an overall pattern or symmetry. Memorable key words or acronyms always help, and a diagram of the main stages or phases is a bonus. Everyone, including the people who develop these models, knows that it is extremely rare for everything to go to plan. Development is messy; it is affected by people, circumstances and events.

That is not to say that models and structures have no place. They can provide a theoretical framework or mirror to hold up to the thinking and progress being made. They can offer insights that ease the path of progress. The reality, however, is that it is the combination of theoretical perspectives linked with versatility in action that enables success. The progress we have made is due to applying those theoretical perspectives in context, and doing so with subtlety and sensitivity at what we thought was the right moment, while also being prepared to rethink, revisit and retread our steps when necessary.

We had a plan for development, but we knew from the outset that it would have to be modified and adapted. However, we were clear that we would not be deflected from our goals and nor would we allow the imperative to wane. We had agreed on our principles, and we would not change them for something more convenient. We knew that in schooling, as in many other spheres, it is common to set new goals or establish different and revised priorities without necessarily securing those that have been set previously. We were working with what Nigel McLennan refers to as 'awesome purpose',[1] and to achieve it we would require strategy and tactics, ideas to move practice forward, problem-solving to overcome setbacks, flexibility to adjust timescales without allowing the pace to drop, opportunism to take advantage of possibilities, tenacity to address shortcomings and difficulties – and a good dollop of luck.

We acknowledge that we haven't 'finished' our curriculum development and that it will continue to develop and improve, even though we have probably achieved more than most of those involved would have believed possible – in the sense that the curriculum work we imagined as a statement of intent is now being lived by children, with better outcomes than we could have envisaged. Not that we would say that too loudly; we want to encourage our current outlook of exploring possibilities and seeking further success. Everyone wanted success from the beginning but describing what it looked like would have been difficult.

We have used the usual techniques to try to encourage curriculum development:

- Communication through conferences, workshops and documentation.

- Consultation and involvement through meetings.

---

1 N. McLennan, *Awesome Purpose* (Aldershot: Gower Publishing Company, 1999).

- Creating opportunities for people to work together and see good practice.

- Clarifying agreements through research, theory and investigation.

- Checking for quality and excellence.

- Coordination at every level.

These could be our own six Cs of curriculum development, but there is nothing revolutionary or new here. Our work is not something that can be replicated step by step elsewhere. We couldn't go to another school and say, 'First, do this; second, do that …' and know that the required development would happen to get to the sixth step, when we could say, 'All done.' Therefore, the following account includes a description of the actions and steps we took, as well as the thinking and problem-solving that accompanied them.

As we reflect on our work on the Curious Curriculum, we realise that it was like a game of snakes and ladders: a lot of small steps, waiting for the roll of the dice that would provide the surge forward, occasionally meeting a ladder that would accelerate our climb, only to meet a snake which would send us slithering back down to a problem we thought we had overcome.[2]

---

2 The children's board game is thought to have originated in ancient India in the thirteenth century and represents part of children's moral education. Most significant developments in schools experience ups and downs: the challenge is not to give up.

Here, we tell our story and invite you to spot the ways in which what we describe fits with circumstances in your own setting, and to use our examples to inform your own work. We have tried to record our decisions and agreements as well as leaving you with some suggestions of things to consider. Sometimes, we explain what we did to make progress, occasionally with a big step forward. When we do so, we offer some illustrations of our pragmatic responses, actions and decisions. Here and there, we describe the ladders or snakes, which provide a summary of the possibilities, successes and difficulties we faced, and which we think many schools face: a sort of lived theoretical perspective, which gives you the chance to hover above your school and think about the issues.

This part of the book combines the pragmatic and the theoretical: it is an account of the actions and work we did, coupled with an analysis of the issues we faced. It is about the seizing of opportunities and the negotiating of challenges, both of which have helped us to get to the point that we now enjoy. We are still looking for the next ladder, while also watching out for the snakes.

CHAPTER 3

Our professional challenge

When books explain how to build a renewed curriculum and pedagogy, they often use the metaphorical self-assembly model. There are precise and detailed instructions and the assumption that the right tools will be used. However, we all know that each school is different, for many reasons, and so the blueprint is rarely applicable everywhere.

Too often, schools work hard to sort things out in order. They work on a vision, then the curriculum plan, then teaching, assessment and resourcing. There is a seeming logic and coherence to this process: spreadsheets, wall charts and documents record the decisions made and agreements reached. Too often, though, doing things in order doesn't work because, in reality, the various elements are interdependent and influence each other. Working life is complicated.

From the outset, we knew that our conversations needed to be about more than curriculum and more than developing a curriculum plan that could be aligned within and across the schools in the trust. There was going to be a focus on curriculum *and* pedagogy working in harmony in order to create the sort of learning opportunities and outcomes for all children that we believed was the purpose of the schools being joined together in the first place. Of course, if curriculum and pedagogy are going to work in harmony then, by implication, so do other aspects of schooling. Leadership, assessment, resourcing and external support all have to synchronise to enable the pedagogy to work in harmony with the curriculum that is going to secure the vision for learning.

For many teachers, and some in leadership positions, this was not easy to grasp. For many years, schools had been working back from the 'measurables' to define the approach to learning. Measuring implementation had become more significant than considering intentions in terms of effectiveness: teachers' and leaders' behaviours were often about checking that processes were taking place rather than checking whether those processes were effective. In short, if our schools were going to be successful in terms of curriculum and pedagogy, then success would hinge on all of the aspects of learning policy already mentioned, but fundamentally on one other too: professionalism.

The indicators of commitment were there to be seen. Early arrival at school, clerical planning in abundance and marking being up to date were the sorts of issues that seemed to matter to teachers. For leadership teams, lesson observations using common criteria driven by Ofsted to enable judgement was important, as was being able to determine the proportion of acceptable teaching as an indicator of professional effectiveness. These indicators contributed to the 'workload' issue, probably because all those involved were also aware of the burdens being created. Just as these indicators were habits of mind, so they were habits of activity. Classrooms were busy and industrious. Organisation was tight and time was used efficiently. Leaders checked that the signs of good lessons were evident in regular observations and scrutinised planning and children's work. In turn, these habits set the parameters for the children's experience.

Children experienced comfortable but relatively undemanding schooling. They spent their time with caring staff who they knew worked hard to support them. They appreciated the obvious effort being made to help them to learn and generally complied with the expectations upon them. In order to achieve success, teachers devised fail-safe learning experiences for the children – for example, writing frames to enable children to plan extended writing had become the finished product, with extensive writing rarely being required or expected. Because of the pressure of the sharply defined timetable, practical learning such as art, design or science was structured in such a way that the children's contribution would be only a minimal addition to the teacher's considerable planning and preparation. A class of children being creative in art would see thirty finished products, not identical, but each with just a 5 per cent difference from the template provided by the teacher.

The upshot was an outlook from staff which implied that, as long as the new parameters were clearly defined, people would commit to working within them and accept quality assurance to match. Any proposed new curriculum approach would receive their support. The message was, basically, 'Tell us what to do and we will do it.'

Ironically, the prospect of a school becoming an academy and joining a trust in order to secure autonomy risks creating an even more compliant community. Those in leadership positions can enact the decisions of the trust and use them as a reference point for controlling their staff. Instead of taking decisions together, the notion of trust can become one of deference to those with the ultimate responsibility.

From the beginning, we made it clear that the development of a shared curriculum, and the pedagogy to go with it, would be a shared enterprise. This would be the case in individual schools and across a group of schools. This was broadly accepted by all the schools involved, although the idea of what a 'shared enterprise' meant varied significantly, from those who waited for clear edicts, to those who thought that various options would be presented for consultation and agreement, to those who believed that a new

commercial product would be sourced for implementation on an agreed timescale. Expectations for the process of sharing were very different. Few anticipated that the onus for development would rest with them as part of an evolutionary process and a collaborative endeavour.

The process would rely on heightened and extended professional involvement at every level: leadership, teachers, teaching assistants and other staff. We wanted staff to embrace the view that decisions should be made closest to the point at which they matter. Over several years, decision-making for many in the profession had become something that was done elsewhere, in order that the effectiveness of implementation could be monitored.

We wanted teachers to make informed decisions about learning within a clearly understood set of principles that they could articulate and support. This was not the soft option of everyone doing their own thing. The trust needed to be ready for some serious conversations, for holding people to account for what they had agreed to do, for building the confidence to support and challenge each other, and for lifting expectations in the search for the attainment of the trust's vision.

A significant pivotal point was the clarification of the role of the curriculum leads – the individuals from each school who would work together to build the curriculum in a different image. Initially, not only were there different perceptions of the role in terms of their relationships with one another, but each individual had a different perception of their own role within their own school. For some, the head teacher had delegated responsibility for the curriculum entirely to them. For others, the post was a token role – they were simply the representative of the school at trust meetings. These were the coordinators, supporting their colleagues but with limited influence. Few had any authority to influence practice in the classrooms of others. Yet they were all called curriculum leaders.

When they came together as a collective, the curriculum leads would demonstrate their own and/or their school's perception of the task in hand; few saw a long-term task ahead. Most came to meetings to collect the next requirement for their school. There was little expectation that they would be asked to debate, consider, decide or agree on curriculum matters, and even less that they would be expected to share thinking in their own school or influence the quality of their colleagues' practice.

The early curriculum lead meetings were characterised by a sense of enjoying the debate for themselves, but always under a cloud of uncertainty when they remembered that they were expected to shape conversations in their own schools. They would imagine and then voice concerns about the probable reactions of certain individuals, as well as about their own vulnerability, which was prompted by being only one step further along the pathway of thinking than their colleagues. Some were concerned about the response of their head teacher, who might agree in principle with the big picture for change, but may have to amend various school approaches or policies. Just as the excitement and exhilaration of a conference can vanish like mist on a summer morning, so the splash of enthusiasm of a group of curriculum leads can dry up on the way back to school.

These individuals were professional in terms of their commitment and willingness to work hard. What they felt they needed to extend their reach was authority from their school leadership and implicit support from the togetherness of their group, which built over time. While this sounds obvious and fits with much leadership theory of the recent past, the reality of many schools was short-term, measurable actions to be implemented, ticked off and ready to show external agencies as necessary – and this differed from the broader expectations now required of them.

Ownership is a much-used term, but it became vital in the development of our curriculum and pedagogy. The curriculum leads had to own the drive towards a different set of expectations and, in turn, help their colleagues to own the efforts they were making too. Similarly, head teachers had to own their commitment to their trust, and to trust their commitment and their colleagues both within and beyond their school.

It was when the leadership of each school had come to terms with the need for a change in emphasis that the challenge really began. It can be difficult for classroom teachers to appreciate the need for a different approach, especially when they have been asked to follow certain practices for so many years on the basis that 'this is what inspectors are looking for' and when the school is deemed successful by its community. The challenge is even more pronounced in schools which find themselves under the cosh of inspection difficulties, where the notion of doing things harder, faster and stronger tends to beat doing things differently. The teachers had to believe that they were central to the process from the beginning and throughout, so from the teachers' point of view, change began with a conference.

Conferences as a vehicle for development

The value of conferences to build shared experience and commitment is well known. An initial half-day conference on curriculum for the trust at the start of the school year was a sensible place to begin. It would bring the whole trust together and provide a chance for people to feel part of a collective community of endeavour. And where else would we start other than with a consideration of what we should teach? However, the problem with conferences is that, on their own, their impact can be fleeting.

The first conference we staged put the children at the heart of the learning. Mick led a half-day session for all the staff on curriculum and learning. It included videos of children talking and classrooms where learning was taking place, as well as an analysis of what constitutes success and progress for children. Teachers and teaching assistants were asked to do 'at their level' some of the tasks that children in classrooms are asked to do and to draw from that some conclusions about how we might sometimes unwittingly distort our aims. The session was fast-paced with short talks and guided group discussions. There were references to research and images of the reality for teachers, whether it matched research or not. There were flashes of intense concentration on sharp details. There was also much laughter, often followed by a moment of uncomfortable silence when it dawned on people what they were laughing about. While schools are often funny places, their impact on children is profound and serious. There were many murmurs of approval.

As they left the conference to get ready for the reality of the new term, the staff were buoyant, positive and invigorated about the impact they could have through a purposeful curriculum. Staff would be returning to their real world of the new school year having had a reminder of their core purpose and a glimpse of what they knew was within themselves. They could subscribe to the principles they had heard during the conference and could commit to trying to bring them to life. At the same time, they had a new term to navigate, new children to work with and all the old inhibitors were still there.

Teachers have become accustomed to attending conferences in anticipation of being reminded why they came into teaching, while at the same time being conscious that they will then have to return to the world they have come to know: a conference as a sort of respite, like a journey in a G4 van on the way to and from court offering a glimpse of a life of freedom to sustain the next period of incarceration; a Brigadoon moment. For that reason, it was important to follow up, reinforce and put in place structures to build a long-term conversation with and between all those involved. Our first conference was not something to tick off as 'done'. It was like a searchlight illuminating the terrain and showing the lie of the land,

but not enough to make out the detail. It secured enthusiasm and gave some pointers and ideas, but the investment would make little difference overall without consolidated and sustained development.

Until we started to discuss teaching, learning and the curriculum in a serious and professional way, the role of the child in their own learning was lower down the agenda. That is not to say that the children were ignored or neglected. Indeed, we were making considerable effort to provide appropriately for each child, with teachers planning tasks that would cover the curriculum and the children set fair for the rigours of testing, the results of which would demonstrate progress and teaching effectiveness. The new driving force had to be something that would resonate with the core purpose of all staff: the learning experience of the children for whom they cared.

In truth, while the teachers and teaching assistants enjoyed the first conference and we whetted their appetites for the prospect of new learning ambitions, the head teachers were aware that we were opening up a wholesale review of the work of their schools where it mattered most: the impact on the children's learning.

Our initial conference was important and set the tone for what was to come, but we needed to follow things up swiftly – and we have been doing so ever since.

A few words about conference effectiveness

Staff conferences can be a big investment in terms of the cost of venues and speakers, of course, but also in the outlay on staff time. For a single-form entry primary school to hold a conference for their teachers and teaching assistants, the investment can be many thousands of pounds in terms of salary costs. As a matter of policy we never use conference venues. Instead, we exploit the flexibility that our secondary school buildings provide and the opportunities that primary schools offer for looking at classrooms while in each other's setting. Any external speakers are selected because their expertise is compatible with the development point of our work, and they are carefully briefed in terms of expectations.

At Olympus, our conferences need to fit with our other efforts to develop longitudinally. As a one-off event they can have an impact but it is rarely significant or lasting. We have an annual conference in October to take stock and point to next steps – a sort of signpost. They are focused on learning and teaching, and we resist allowing organisational matters into the agenda. Our other professional development time is spaced carefully throughout the year to make sure we keep the momentum and, once again, the agenda is carefully and tightly managed.

In planning any conference, it might be worth thinking through:

- Exactly what can be achieved by a short conference.
- Who is going to follow up with staff to keep up the momentum?
- Where the conference will point people's thinking and anticipation.
- How the 'eyes of the child' provide a productive way to look at practice.

We will return to conferences, workshops and meetings at other times during our story, as they have been essential parts of our communication. They are important steps on our pathway of progress, but on their own they would achieve very little.

CHAPTER 4

Towards an agreed common purpose for a school's curriculum

Agreeing our intentions: setting in place a shared objective

In simple terms, when working as a head teacher, you have one curriculum, one philosophy, one set of principles and, hopefully, one shared culture. Most theories on leadership single out establishing a shared vision as the starting point for a successful organisation. Obviously, when working with a group of schools, the starting point is multiplied by the number of schools in the trust.

The first and obvious question to ask ourselves when embarking on the quest of trying to establish common objectives and vision is, why? Why is it important to us within a school or a trust to have an aligned, shared philosophy of education? If the answer is that it isn't important, then there is absolutely no point in putting yourself through the pain of trying to design a curriculum at scale across a school or group of schools. The point of a curriculum is to develop the agreed course through which the children will travel. The decision to align the curriculum must be driven by the shared values and principles of all the schools involved.

However, if our values promise equitable provision, opportunity and high quality, and we have a belief that we are one entity that is stronger together and we wish to use our collective power to support children's learning, enhance professional development and reduce pressure on staff in terms of workload, then there are many reasons why we may undertake such a journey.

At Olympus, our values are stated as collaboration, excellence and opportunity, which emerged out of the process of defining our *raison d'être* when the trust was established. When we embarked on our curriculum journey, it was for several straight-forward reasons. We had identified our three values because they suited our aspirations, but we knew that we would have to work hard to achieve them. Each school that had joined the trust brought strengths; and, at the same time, one of the reasons they joined the trust was to develop further.

We also recognised that we were discomforted by our own aspirations. Each head teacher accepted that the quality of the teaching of subjects other than English and mathematics was not at a high enough standard across our schools and was often variable within schools. This meant that our quest for excellence was already falling short in terms of our values. Due to the high-stakes accountability measures and the focus in the 2016 Ofsted framework on end of Key Stage 2 results, our foundation subjects did not have sufficiently high importance or status within our curriculum, and where foundation subjects were taught the approach gave us cause for concern.

Leaders paid less attention to foundation subjects, and so did most teachers, who tried to provide 'interesting' things for the children to do rather than identify important learning experiences. Planning was haphazard, and educational visits and school trips were regarded as opportunities for social and recreational benefit rather than as structured opportunities to deepen learning.

We acknowledged that much of the teaching in subjects other than English and mathematics was focused on 'What do I want the children to *do*?' instead of 'What do I want the children to *learn*?' Within most classes across the trust, there was an overuse of planning lifted from the internet and downloaded printed worksheets rather than a clear, well-constructed sequence of learning that systematically built on previously acquired knowledge, skills and understanding. Teachers were mainly focusing on substantive knowledge. For example, the children might know a few facts about Henry VIII's wives but little on the importance of Henry VIII's break from the Catholic Church and how this impacted on the future of England.

Most significantly, we recognised that the schools did not have a shared understanding of what we were trying to achieve and what we believed was the appropriate and ethically correct way to achieve it. There was little discourse about learning or approaches to teaching; in contrast, there was a lot of discourse about how to lift results in English and mathematics. Our group of primary schools needed what is commonly called a unique selling point: what did we stand for? What did we believe in? How was this demonstrated through our curriculum design and implementation?

It is worth mentioning governance here. While most of the work has taken place within our schools, driven by head teachers and staff and supported by colleagues from the wider trust, our trustees and school governors have played a central role. From the outset, they have been involved and engaged. They helped to formulate thinking about our curriculum purpose. They challenged practice – and continue to challenge us to seek new horizons for children. They have signed off our plans and then backed them with resources. They have been present to support conferences and taken every opportunity to be seen to support our work in the eyes of parents.

We do not discuss governance in detail in this book, as we know that schools across the country have various approaches to governance. Multi-academy trusts have developed different models of trustee and local governing board arrangements. Local authority schools differ

again. However, in terms of curriculum and pedagogy, it is worth working with governors to:

- Ensure a shared commitment to curriculum purpose.

- Develop an ongoing articulation of pedagogic decisions.

- Clarify the distinction between strategic and operational engagement and ensure that the governance appreciates that its role is the former.

- Bring decisions back to the shared purpose.

- Demonstrate to governance the success or otherwise of curriculum and pedagogic practice in terms of the shared purpose.

- Welcome challenge and invite support.

For our head teachers, the first step was a group visit to schools elsewhere. Notably, we went to academies in the Inspire Partnership where we engaged in discussion with colleagues who were generous with their time and, more importantly, their professional thinking. This was an excellent opportunity for our head teachers to begin to build close professional relationships. The visit also set the tone for the sort of learning we wanted to see. As is often the case, though, agreeing with an approach and recognising the sorts of practice and standards to which we aspired is very different from knowing how to get there.

For our schools, therefore, the real starting point was to identify and articulate a baseline. What was the practice like in each of our schools and in each year group? We started with a curriculum review in each school.

CHAPTER 5

Looking at learning and working out where to start

Our curriculum reviews

Leadership theory usually advises that, once the vision and objectives are clear, the place to start is with a baseline. Sometimes the baseline is established in comparative terms against the envisaged end point or goal. If we can agree what constitutes success, then the baseline would signal gaps in performance. Most head teachers know this; they have completed the various national professional qualifications.[1] Our head teacher colleagues knew this too.

The challenge is to find the right source of evidence that will prompt the right sort of response, because the risk of being thrown off course by the baseline itself is very real. If you use data to analyse the baseline then chasing the data might become the strategy. If you survey inspection reports then the task becomes beating the inspectors. If you use staff or parent opinions then the possibility of being swayed by majorities and prejudice increases.

---

1   The national professional qualification programme began in the 1990s with the National Professional Qualification for Headship (NPQH) and now extends to a suite of voluntary qualifications designed to provide training and support for teachers and school leaders at all levels.

We decided that the way to begin was looking at the children's experiences. What was their current day-by-day encounter with learning like, and was that what we wanted it to be?

Getting people talking about variable and disparate practice

The first step was to acquire a snapshot of current practice that would form the basis for our discussion of the curriculum and teaching and learning. Head teachers had their most recent Ofsted inspection reports, but these contained little commentary on the curriculum or on teaching and learning beyond English and mathematics. While there were recommendations, it was often the case that head teachers admitted to not fully understanding what to do about them.

The head teachers agreed that a good starting point would be a visit to each school for half a day by Claire and Mick, with an open review of common issues to follow. They were keen to get an external view of their school from trusted colleagues. We set up a schedule for all the schools to be visited for their half a day over the course of four weeks to look at and talk about classrooms: curriculum and teaching and learning. We emphasised that this would be low key rather than high stakes – we were not going to produce a summative report on the schools. No preparation was needed on the part of leadership – there were no documents to assemble and no data were required – but this did not lessen the importance. The visits would be a vital step on the path towards enabling teachers and ensuring that children across all the schools experienced the very best of learning.

The pattern of each visit was similar. For the morning visits, we would arrive together about half an hour before the school day began. We would talk with the head teacher and whomever else they had invited to be part of the session as a curriculum lead. We would then spend time in classrooms (as we describe below), which was followed, from around 11.30am, by a conversation between us lasting about 45 minutes. The format was the same for afternoon visits, although with the shorter afternoons in school, the conversation did not begin until after the end of the school day.

The introductory conversation would be very informal, exploring how the curriculum worked in the school, how decisions about content were made and who made them, how planning took place and their impression of the quality, success and effectiveness of the themes. These short exchanges told us much about the variability between the schools.

We heard about examples from some schools with a plan. Each year was divided into half-terms, each of which contained a theme so that, through the primary years, each child would have a balanced and coherent experience across the subjects on the list by progressing through the sequenced logic of the planner. Where curriculum plans existed, we explored them briefly, and found that some had emanated from staff discussion, some from curriculum lead negotiation and some from leadership decisions.

We also heard examples from schools with no plan. These were schools where the teachers were invited to teach what they thought would be appropriate. There were only a couple of these.

The third example was schools that had agreed a title for a half-termly theme, which would range across the whole school, and the teachers would decide on the interpretation for their year group.

While we were talking with the head teachers in their rooms, we were already gaining an insight into the type of school we were visiting. In some, a table was set up in a business-like room with documentation for us to look at or to be talked through, while tea and coffee were provided. In others, a mug of tea was thrust into our hands as we found a seat to perch on while finding out about the school. In others, we were shown the tea and coffee and invited to help ourselves.

None of this mattered to us – years of visiting schools teaches you adaptability and ease – but it is always worth wondering how the unexpected parent is treated.

Similarly, in those minutes before the school day began, we gained an impression of the leadership of the school. In some schools, the head teacher was able to talk without outside interruption, while in others there were issues to deal with momentarily. In one school, the deputy head interrupted three times to ask the head teacher, 'Was it okay to …?' – always over small matters and always with consent.

In some of our schools, the head teachers wanted to tell us about their own journey – their time at the school, the problems they had faced and the successes they had experienced so far. Some told us openly of their development problems: awkward members of staff, parental expectations, recruitment challenges, the home background of children and the building – all of which were very real to them. All but one volunteered to us where their school stood in terms of Ofsted judgements, as though that gave an instant indicator as to the quality of the school. These impressions then had to be qualified based on how long ago the inspection took place, what framework had applied and whether they thought the inspection team was correct. This analysis of the Ofsted judgement was usually followed by an assessment of what the inspectors might think if they came now – depending on whether the team was any good!

In each school, towards the end of the initial conversation, we asked, 'What are you grappling with now in terms of curriculum and teaching and learning?' The answers varied: from seeking consistency to seeking quality, and from ensuring staff complied with agreements, policies and plans to wanting staff to feel they could express themselves. In some instances we got 'Ofsted-ready' answers; at the time, Ofsted was rumoured to be focusing on feedback and marking, so these were mentioned as though they were part of the school's agenda.

We then set off to visit the classrooms, Mick with the head teacher and Claire with the curriculum lead, one pair starting with the classes of younger children and one at the older end of the school. We would change partners and starting points at breaktime after our twenty-minute catch-up.

Visits to classrooms were simple in their complexity. We were simply looking at teaching and learning – and that is complex. We had no clipboard, no pro forma and no checklist of issues to observe. We were not judging against preordained criteria. We were not grading or passing judgement. The pairs would enter a classroom as unobtrusively as possible, watch what was happening between teacher and children, children and children, and consider our impressions.

After perhaps ten minutes, which can seem a very long time when you are not writing notes, we could move on to the next room. In some parallel classes, the same session was in train, either duplicated on the other side of the wall or running in the same sequence ahead or behind their identical twin next door. In some cases, the same lesson title had been plucked from the plan to be interpreted in totally different ways by the two teachers.

After a further ten minutes or so, another move to another room with barely a few seconds for discussion in-between – perhaps time to write an odd memory-jogging phrase on the back of an envelope to slip into the back pocket for later. Around twenty-five minutes after setting off, on leaving, say, the third classroom, we might double back to the first room to see where the lesson had reached, what had unfolded from that introduction and how the children were responding. From there, it might be back to the third room to see where the task that was just beginning when we were there was developing and what the children were producing.

And then it was on to another new room and another, before going back to the second room where they would be well into the task that had been set and reaching a point where the teacher would be responding and reacting. How had those drawings turned out? What had happened to that group work? Had the children had the sorts of ideas we expected? Did that distribution of lots of printed sheets ensure that all the children understood? How did the children's ideas get used? What was the quality of the work the children had produced? Between each room, there was chance for the swiftest of snatched conversations.

When the four of us reconvened at breaktime, the school hosts were invariably waiting for feedback, sometimes with notepad and pen at the ready. However informal, there was still the question, spoken directly or implied, 'What did you think?' It wasn't a game but our response – 'What do you think we were thinking?' – was vital in setting the tone, not just for the conversation but for all of our future work together. We were not simply giving feedback; we were engaging with each other in extensive and active dialogue. The kaleidoscope of images we had gathered over an hour in a range of classrooms would be enough to sustain conversation for double the time available.

We wanted to encourage and develop a relationship built on openness and exploration of the possible, though linked to reality. We needed to get away from the compliance-led, managerially efficient model that most were expecting. In that breaktime conversation, we would begin to explore some of the stark realities of learning in the school. We were not playing 'three stars and wish' or 'even better if'. We were talking as professionals about what we had seen of the children's experience of learning over the course of a couple of hours.

Usually, the focus was on overarching issues – the degree of challenge, the pace of the sessions, the level of the children's engagement – and it was these areas that started to shape the second phase of time in the classrooms between breaktime and the end of the session. With Claire and Mick starting again at opposite ends of the age groups, and perhaps but not always changing partners, they threaded their way between classrooms, watching, moving on, doubling back and building the bigger picture. The conversations continued in corridors between the classrooms, but not for too long as there was always another room to visit. Of course, in the afternoon session there was usually no break, so the interval chats were not as practicable, which definitely affected the final discussion.

The final review conversations were electric. They were sparked by the head teacher and curriculum lead wondering aloud, at times pleased and at times disappointed, about what we had seen, but using detail within the context of big picture ideas about learning in their school. Our task was to keep the dialogue focused on the impact of small moments and the repercussions of such moments repeated over time, and not allow them to be about judging teacher against teacher.

As visitors we had just a snapshot of learning within the school. Although this was the starting point for our discussions, it also put an onus on the school-based people. How typical was what we had seen? Was this a 'normal' day in classrooms? If so, how good was normal? What would they usually do about some of the practice we had seen, good or bad? We kept drawing the school folk to consider what we had observed in the light of what they had told us at the beginning of the session about their approach to themes and what they were trying to achieve.

Every one of the head teachers and curriculum leads said that the approach we had used was helpful to them in better understanding their school. Until that time, they had been observing learning rather than carrying out lesson observations. They had been trying to gauge the effectiveness of learning rather than grading a teacher's lesson. They had been reviewing their thinking rather than completing an analysis of teaching quality.

Some noted that they now realised that the standard lesson observation failed to open their eyes to learning because what they were watching was a teacher who knew what was on their pro forma making sure they had enough examples to tick. Some also commented on how unfulfilling the 'standard' lesson was, both for teacher and children. Our head teachers were probably little different from most primary head teachers across the country at the time. They were busy doing what was expected of them and had little time to lift their eyes to what was really happening in the foundation subjects.

Some of the practices being done, just so they were done, often did little to enhance the learning. Starters, learning objectives and plenaries, for example, all have value but only when used effectively. Many of the lessons we observed were busy without being productive, active without being rigorous and exciting without making progress or consolidating progress. Some were embarrassingly confusing, some disorganised and a few both.

Head teachers were particularly aware of missed opportunities in the way teaching was being managed, of the poor understanding of certain teachers and of some of the bizarre links made by teachers, which almost encouraged the children to build incorrect knowledge or concepts (Viking longships in the Caribbean was one – don't ask!). The slow approach to learning became very apparent to head teachers and curriculum leads in a way that it had not done before; not in the sense that teachers needed to work faster but that they needed help to do the right things better.

Early years was often a worry because of under-stimulation and over-direction by adults or, conversely, because of the apparent aimlessness of children left too long by adults busy over-stimulating other children. Year 6 was often a concern because the quality of the children's products was not very high and remarkably uniform. What came through in all year groups was the low expectation of children in terms of their capacity to drive their own learning, think for themselves and manage their work. Too much of the learning experience was organised from the starting point of the teacher delivering the lesson rather than decisions about what it was we wanted the children to learn.

We saw an example of a class of children trying to engage in choral speaking. However, they were unable to read the words on the screen and only gained energy when the poem reached the refrain in the chorus which they recognised. We saw a teacher take some children to a 'bug hotel' in the school grounds to study mini-beasts and then, when no bugs emerged, pass around a photograph of some insects. We saw children being asked to describe and experience an avocado in the form of a 2D picture on an interactive whiteboard rather than as a real fruit in front of them. We met a teacher who had produced a class set of illustrated books for the children to colour in rather than asking them to make their own books.

How do we refocus teachers' commitment, so we support them in planning to enable the children to take more responsibility for their own learning? How do we know whether teachers recognise this problem? And, if we raise it with them, will it be seen as criticism (which it is – but of the problem, not the teacher) that will dishearten and devalue their professional effort? This is why conversations are better than feedback. It is why summative judgements and records of the observation will always take second place to formative considerations and conversations, which can be broached over time and 'forgotten' when the time is right and issues pass.

Such shortcomings are not the end of the world. The teachers have not committed a professional sin. But, we do have to work out how to help them see other possibilities and recognise for themselves that they could use their undoubted professional energy to greater effect and even greater satisfaction.

One teacher wanted to talk about a passing question about bugs that Mick had asked of a group of children: 'How big do you think that creature will be if you see one? Show me on your hand.' She wanted to discuss why she hadn't realised that the children wouldn't necessarily know what they were looking for and why she hadn't thought about it before they left the classroom.

In our conversations with head teachers, we might have dodged around certain issues, not been as effusive as would be expected, asked questions or made comments that left thoughts hanging in the air. We might have picked up teachers' conversations and pushed them further, subtly letting them take the lead.

To return to the teacher who had produced the class set of colouring books, we knew that the reason they had done so was because the children did not possess the skills to do it themselves. The prerequisites were not in place. The teacher knew it too, which is why she had done the work for them. Just setting them the task would lead to far less satisfaction on the part of the teacher and the children if they produced a mess of pottage, and so, defeated by her own intention, the teacher would resort to printed sheets. Our challenge was to work out how to assist such committed teachers in the long term.

It is important to recognise professionalism and effort, however misplaced they may be. Use what teachers are currently doing as the starting point for a discussion about how it compares with what they intend. Appreciative inquiry is a good way into a conversation.[2] Asking people what they think we are thinking is better than telling them what we are actually thinking. It helps to work out where they stand and gives them a chance to see what they are doing from another viewpoint. Of course, challenge is important, but it should be mixed judiciously with appreciative inquiry in a balance of about one to four.

Consistency of message matters too, as does the willingness to articulate some of the common misunderstandings about practice that emerge from generalisations. Trying to figure out with teachers what would be a good step forward, so they feel they are taking the step rather than being told what's next, is vital in terms of maintaining enthusiasm. When the time is right, we need to introduce teachers to others who are grappling with the same challenge or have a slightly

---

2   Appreciative inquiry has resurfaced in the last few years as a legitimate leadership approach. See D. L. Cooperrider and D. Whitney, Appreciative Inquiry: A Positive Revolution in Change. In P. Holman and T. Devane (eds), *The Change Handbook: Group Methods for Shaping the Future* (San Francisco, CA: Berrett-Koehler, 1999), pp. 275-289.

different perspective. A problem shared is a problem not necessarily halved but is at least on its way to being solved.

For anyone observing teaching

It is important to look at learning rather than lessons and to watch what is going on over time as opposed to making a summative judgement on the quality of a lesson. If we do the latter, the chances are that we end up grading the management of the learning and the teacher's performance rather than really getting underneath the quality of the child's experience.

It is always better to raise questions rather than to make judgements. 'What did the children learn?' is always a good starter for consideration, followed by, 'Did all of them learn this?' Wondering how the session could have hit the target better, brought about higher quality products, sustained attention for longer or responded more appropriately to the children's interests might be more effective than simply determining whether certain aspects were good enough or not.

Finding magic or not-so-magic moments to dwell on can also open up key conversations. The moment when the whole class 'got it' or the children seemed to suddenly switch on. The occasion when a child asked a pertinent question that was seized on or allowed to pass. The question a girl asked, or why a boy got stuck or gave up. These are all starting points for a dialogue about the fascination of learning. It is always worth visiting classrooms several times during a session. It is less intrusive without a clipboard and notes being taken. The observation of the learning is more important than the record of the observation.

It is important to watch what is holding children back when teachers have planned a good learning experience. Too often, teachers get dispirited when the children don't possess the requisite skills and the product is inferior to what they had envisaged. Their instinct can be to do it for the children next time, when what is really required is a focus on teaching the necessary skills. By tackling the missing prerequisites, we can support teachers and children by addressing the core concerns.

Leadership's role in sharing the insights and issues

For a head teacher in a school, the issues raised and insights gained from the observation need to be shared with the team at some point. If we seek a collective approach to our curriculum, we need to work as a collective. This is a very different approach from trying to 'improve' each teacher separately in the hope of seeing an overall improvement. This is not to say that each individual should not be helped to be the best they can be starting from where they are, but the group needs to appreciate the broader issues that matter and that are being addressed.

For us, it was a case of talking with head teachers from all the schools together in one room. We gathered, and we showed them our collated thoughts about the curriculum in their group of schools. After just half a day in each school, this was no more than a set of snapshots, food for thought, a spur to further consideration. The caveats were spelled out: the limited time we had spent in the schools, the danger of snapshots, that the time might not be typical, that our thoughts could be accurate or distorted. Only they would know whether what we had portrayed matched their own image of the daily experience of a child in their school.

The head teachers were offered a series of eight very basic PowerPoint slides with some impressions of the learning offer in their schools. After each couple of slides, we slipped into group response and discussion. The atmosphere was quietly dynamic. The head teachers were engaged, thoughtful and intrigued. They questioned virtually nothing but wanted to go deeper into why the images were as they were.

While each individual was being asked to look at the slides as a collective impression of the six schools, it was clear that each individual was focused on their own school. As a community of leaders, they were positive about a situation which was largely lacking in compliments about the quality of the learning on offer.

> The initial observations of our own school proved to be challenging conversation moments. These were really important in setting an agenda for improvement.
>
> *Jen Wathan*

The list that follows is a summary of the snapshot visits to the schools. It is what we showed to head teachers over two slides. Each item is deliberately brief because the conversation, explanation and examples were more important. You might like to read them through and relate them to the circumstances in your own school. What would your snapshots look like over the last few terms (disrupted, as we know, by the pandemic)? This is what was replayed to head teachers about their own schools:

1. Considerable effort put into planning but lack of clarity about rationale.

2. Teachers putting an emphasis on the beginning session/introduction to a new topic.

3. 'Wow' beginnings and teachers sometimes putting effort into endings, often with 'celebrations' being held.

4. Many visits and visitors being included.

5. Some of the visits and visitors not exploited to full advantage.

6. A lot of the more imaginative work is done as homework.

7. There is comparatively more clerical work and less practical work.

8. Morning rigor; afternoon muddle.

9. Little science and few experiments.

10. Variable learning environments.

11. Little real geography or history.

12. Kite marks, awards and 'weeks' evident.

13. Art, dance and PE given over to specialists/artists in residence.

14. Considerable use of web-based video.

15. A lot of mindset posters and a multitude of acronyms and mnemonics.

16. A lot of writing about not much, but not much writing by each child.

17. Little children's work on display in many schools, and little example of the use of children's work on display.

It was quite amazing that not much of this came as a surprise to the head teachers. Nevertheless, it provided a reasonable and agreed baseline from which to start planning and designing a curriculum and approach to teaching and learning that would do the job we thought we wanted to do.

Probably, for the first time in a long while, these professionals were debating quality without being given a summative judgement from which to start. Terms like 'outstanding', 'good' and 'requiring improvement' did not feature. The head teachers were offered depictions of their schools that spoke of 'a lot of', 'rarely' and 'frequently'. Pictures were painted, and they were asked whether they seemed realistic and whether they were the sorts of pictures they wanted to see.

There were two main anchors or criteria for their level of satisfaction, or otherwise, with the portrayal of their school. The first, which was significantly driving their discussion, was their in-built professional purpose as a teacher. When they were considering the learning offer in their schools, they were doing so as the professional teacher they wanted to be. The second criteria, to which we kept alluding, was the series of school visions from across the group. Even the straplines that appeared on letter headings, websites and school signs provided a sufficient nudge of discomfort.

The head teachers made some key decisions. They agreed that the pictures painted were realistic, and also that they were not content with them. Learning had to be a better experience than this, and we had to get on with it. Importantly, they agreed that they would take a lead on this agenda and also properly delegate to their designated curriculum leads, so that decisions could be taken and they could be empowered to drive action in their schools.

They also agreed that, while curriculum was the drive for their initial consideration, the real agenda that had been discussed was the diet of learning the children consumed. The head teachers had nodded previously when we said that the curriculum never stands alone and always stands with pedagogy. Now, they recognised that talking about curriculum meant also talking about teaching and learning, and they were starting to realise that talking about curriculum also meant talking about leadership. The curriculum is the reason we have schools, and therefore it affects, and is affected by, pretty well every other aspect of schooling.

The head teachers were invited to stay for the next meeting, which was a repeat of the first with the curriculum leads from each school.

Only one head teacher elected to stay. The others felt compelled to get back into school to continue to be indispensable and deal with important crises of the immediate kind rather than the ticking time bomb that was the learning life of their school.

We recognised later on that this was a symptom of the underlying challenge for schools. Over the years, the distance between leadership and teachers, between leadership and children, and between leadership and learning had been allowed to grow. It had widened to such an extent that, for many head teachers, the chasm is enormous. As a result, working together on a collaborative professional endeavour can feel threatening, as much to the head teachers as to their colleagues. How sad that discourse about teaching, learning, curriculum and the children themselves has been reduced to a perfunctory management transaction rather than the joy of professional consideration and problem-solving that opens understanding for all involved to the benefit of the children.

On their way back to school, a third criteria for head teachers' level of satisfaction or otherwise with the picture of their own school's offer to children would start to cloud the others and they would remember why they had allowed things to become as we had described. The true anchor for their decisions and practice – the one they had almost forgotten for the previous two hours – was the spectre of an Ofsted inspection. This wolf at the door was their rationale for much of the practice they had just criticised so heartily. Worse still, Ofsted was also a justification to their teachers and other staff for much of the classroom practice they had just acknowledged to be counterproductive. Like Saul on the road to Damascus, they had seen the light and knew they had to change, but the shadows behind them were enormous.

For this reason, the chances of immediate change and development would reduce. Indeed, an acceptance of the need for improvement, the heartfelt wish 'to do better than this' and the stated urgency 'to get on with it' would all come to seem like out-of-body experiences once back in the learning routine of their school of which they had been so critical. It is sometimes simpler to live with a leaking roof than to set about the task of replacing the tiles.

At this early stage, one of our first steps – observing the learning offer in classrooms – might now be seen as a final step. We were considering whether what the schools were offering, providing and achieving was what they said they were doing. We were looking at the impact of their work on the children's learning in the widest sense – their accomplishments, their accumulation of knowledge and skills, their experiences, their image of themselves as learners and their potential to build on their learning in the next phase of their lives. We had looked together and we were less than impressed with what we saw.

Ofsted has always looked at impact. It has been one of their watchwords for quality; one of their determinants for judgements. 'If we say teaching is good but learning outcomes are not strong, then teaching has not had the expected impact and cannot be judged as good.' 'If teaching is not seen as good overall, then the impact of leadership upon teaching falls short and leadership cannot be judged as good.' There is something seductive about this logic. The problem is that it leads to algorithms whereby inspectors, in the search for consistency, start unwittingly to define the acceptable levels for their judgements and schools try to work out the algorithm in order to demonstrate the success being sought. Ironically, the impact that emerges as the criteria for the judgement becomes the intended outcome and limits the ambition. Tails do wag dogs.

A couple of years later, in 2019, schools in England were reflecting on their practice in the light of the new inspection framework. Ofsted's pilot work began to influence schools to focus on their intent, so many were reconsidering what they were trying to achieve. The idea that schools didn't know previously what they were trying to do is a worrying prospect, yet the reality was that many didn't know because they had become fixated on meeting Ofsted's previous demands rather than being secure on first principles. Since inspection itself has focused on English and mathematics for so long, schools had naturally done the same, thereby neglecting a wider curriculum focus.

The three steps of the inspection framework – intent, implementation and impact – are reasonable and realistic. The piece that is missing, perhaps, is an emphasis on the cyclical nature of the process. The impact is what the children really experience and, equally, it can be the starting point for consideration. While the nationwide consideration by schools of what their intent should be and the urgency to devise a clear statement of intent has been beneficial to some degree, a look at the impact of learning in terms of the intent already in place (often called something like a 'vision') may well have saved time and achieved more. Having reached step one of three, schools and inspectors have two more steps to address – and the final step is the vital one, but it doesn't always need to come last.

Starting with impact is possible. Building urgency and clarity is important. Asking a trusted, experienced educator to spend time in the school and paint a picture of the curriculum offer as it appears to them is productive. Comparing those impressions with the pictures you have already painted on your website and school literature can be salutary. How close is the match between the daily learning of children and the posed photographs for school websites?

Asking probing questions is crucial. How accurate is the picture of the learning experience for all children, including those with special needs, those that few notice, those that seem to have a limited experience at home, those who keep having to miss what everybody else is doing so they can go off into a room to do something different to close a gap? How big is the gap between what you want to offer the children and what you currently do offer them? If it is a big gap, you will probably need stepping stones; in leadership speak, it is called a plan.

CHAPTER 6

Making a start

Where do we begin with planning?

Of course, we begin our planning with our vision and purpose. As we explained in Chapter 1, we had agreed the seven statements of educational belief that would bind us and the eight pedagogic principles would help us to achieve those beliefs. Reaching such agreements creates a sense of togetherness and joint commitment.

p. 27

Going forward, we faced several challenges if we were going to make those beliefs and principles a reality in terms of learning and outcomes for children. The first challenge was related to decisions about what we meant by curriculum and what would be included. When we reached our agreement on beliefs and principles, individuals made certain assumptions about what other people meant by the terms that were used or else they presumed that everyone else meant the same thing. If we didn't agree on what the curriculum was, how could we shape it and make it work? Should we include the national curriculum? Should it be followed, flogged or forgotten?

What follows is an example of one of our considerations – our starting point explained and articulated. It is quite extensive and aims to encourage the reader to ask themselves whether this is what they believe. It takes account of the brief history described in the introduction and looks at what the curriculum might offer today for our children's futures. As you read it, consider your own articulation of the curriculum to your own community, and whether you have a consensus about what the curriculum is and what it is trying to achieve.

Defining the school curriculum

It has always been the case that the curriculum of a school is bigger than the national curriculum – the expectations that are an entitlement for all the children in our country. The best schools ensure that they offer a vibrant, challenging and well-structured learning experience, and somewhere within that are the expectations of the national curriculum. However, this clarity of focus is far from universal. Many schools continue to grapple with the false idols of the very early days of the national curriculum: coverage and delivery. These are imperatives that became more deeply embedded as a result of the early wave of inspections thirty years ago. The planning blight which set in as a consequence has had an impact on the learning of a generation of young people.

The national statutory expectations have always formed a short document. There are no time allocations for subjects, and nor are there any expectations that a subject should be taught weekly, termly or even yearly. Some say there should be enforced requirements … and then they say that the government should not dictate to schools. Indeed, they want a more precise national curriculum and at the same time they want to free schools from it.

Academies are not bound by the national curriculum; in fact, release from it was one of the incentives offered to attract schools to convert to academy status. At the same time as the government was offering schools the opportunity to reject one of the foundations of schools' success, it was, ironically, constructing a new national curriculum. In practice, most academies use the national curriculum as a basis for their learning offer. The fact that inspection looks at schools through a national curriculum lens has and will continue to influence the prominence of the national curriculum.

The curriculum is the entire planned learning experience that happens in schools. It happens in lessons, events, routines and that range of activities around and beyond the school day. Good primary schools design learning for their children and then cross-check it against national expectations to make sure they have done right by their children in terms of the agreed, precious entitlement for all the nation's children. The attainment targets provide a touchstone for the expected standards, and that is it.

Good schools get on and do things: dance, drama, music, art, using the outdoors, speaking in other languages, finding out about the past, growing things, cooking, going places, using computers and paint brushes, making things, experimenting, learning about their own bodies, working out how to get on with others in the real world. And, using all of those as vehicles, they do amazing English and mathematics to support the structured English and mathematics programmes, and at the same time bring purpose to learning for children. The curriculum is not a difficult concept; it never was. In fact, without all this nit-picking from people who rarely read it, the national curriculum is a good attempt to bring a sense of consistency and entitlement for all children.

Some confuse the curriculum with a scheme of learning (or scheme of work) or long-term plan. Secondary teachers of subject disciplines leading to exams use the specifications to guide their planning, ensuring they touch every point in the expected syllabus and gradually focus on the 'banker' questions for the exam. Too often, a syllabus-style approach to study means that children end up with no time to apply the learning because they are hurtling through the

Leaders

Little Leaders
EXCEPTIONAL MEN
IN
BLACK HISTORY

Little Leaders
BOLD WOMEN
IN
BLACK HISTORY

VASHTI HARRISON

lessons. The need for results puts so much pressure on some schools that their children become simply a currency for accountability.[1]

The learning diet becomes more limited as we move away from rounded learning into the production of fragmented crumbs. This style of learning will neither excite a passion for a subject as a discipline of understanding, and nor will it help young people to develop insights into the way the world has been shaped for good or ill. Our society wants the best for young people and the best for the future of our society. Good schools are committed to a set of values that underpin good learning, and the curriculum enables that. Often, schools state their values as a starting point for the curriculum and, in terms of responding to schools being urged to think about and articulate their intent, many schools begin from their values or vision statements.

People know that the future offers today's young people opportunity and challenge like never before. They see the importance of preparing children for their futures, while at the same time recognising that the most precious gift we can give them is the present of a good childhood, where all children experience some childhood 'must dos'. People recognise that employers and businesses will need skilled employees in the future, while also realising that, without being able to read and write and manage numbers, most will not thrive. They acknowledge that the world has moved on from the more passive childhood era of post-war Britain, and that the learning experience has to matter to the child.

There is always talk of a slimmed-down national curriculum; the teaching profession has argued for it for years. But a slim national curriculum simply focuses on less content, so then the argument is about what detail should be included. There is talk of a focus on

---

1   See Ofsted and A. Spielman, Amanda Spielman's Speech at the Wellington Festival of Education (22 June 2018). Available at: https://www.gov.uk/government/speeches/amanda-spielmans-speech-at-the-wellington-festival-of-education.

essentials; but the danger then is that we fill the time with the bare necessities. There is talk of kings and queens; well, they are important so let's do them – and then do emperors, tsars and pharaohs too. There is talk of chalk-and-talk pedagogy as an essential (presumably that is now whiteboard and mouse); well, that's fine and important for some of the time, so let's get on with it and then build the range of learning approaches that will help the children to move on. There is talk of back to basics; well, some of us have been back to basics so many times we are on elastic.

In twenty years' time, today's children will not recall their learning about synthetic phonics, fronted adverbials or apostrophes, important as they are. They will recall the impact that reading made on them, the skills they learned, the knowledge they gained, the insights they had and the moments that took their breath away.

Many children are natural physical performers – they dance, do gymnastics, sing, speak out. They strive to improve, to have impact and to reach a peak of performance. We need them to build the same enthusiasm for quality in writing, mathematics and every subject discipline. They have to understand the concepts of hard work, endeavour, polish, depth and finish, and to work with panache to show what they can achieve.

Subjects matter, for their knowledge base as well as for their discipline. Among other aspects, mathematics is about proof, art about observation and appreciation, science about hypothesis and testing, history about evidence, and design and technology about fitness for purpose. The true historian shares their excitement at the discovery of Roman mosaics in a farmer's field in Rutland. The true scientist delights in the *Perseverance* spacecraft on Mars or the deployment of the James Webb Space Telescope. The true geographer is excited by the impact of a container ship blocking the Suez Canal. The true design technologist kindles interest by reflecting on the death of Richard Rogers and his impact on the urban landscape. The true technologist is intrigued by the drone display during the Queen's Platinum Jubilee celebrations. We can also exploit the Olympic and Paralympic Games as a way into debates about fitness, lifestyle and big horizons in spite of adversity. People who are true subject enthusiasts know that their subject is a living thing to be enjoyed and explored as it unfolds in the modern and future worlds.

What needs to remain constant is our commitment to helping young people understand the value of their education, to see it as never-ending, door-opening and threshold-crossing. When the national curriculum was introduced in 1980s, it seemed to be packed with almost everything our young people needed to learn – or, at least, everything needed to pass A level. There was too much. After a very short time, we adapted it and tried to hang on to the best while changing the rest. In the end, it comes down to some very simple values: do we want our children to grow up and become responsible adults, secure in themselves and their futures and successful in learning? If we do, the curriculum has to be wide-ranging, relevant, challenging, knowledge-seeking and skill-finding.

While what comes from government matters, the real and living curriculum is the one that children in schools meet day in, day out. As a profession, we owe it to our children to offer them learning that will give them the skills to manage their own lives, leave them with a desire to continue learning, and allow them to look back years later and reflect that it was worth it. Let's just get on with it – but get on with it well!

Our curriculum experience

Across our own school community, there was general agreement with the curriculum thinking described above. The problem was that this was not the reality of the school experience for the children. Our schools were agreed on what they would like to do and achieve, but they were living a different reality in the classroom. Our visits to schools had shown this beyond doubt. Our head teachers both agreed and were determined that it was the schools that needed to change rather than the curriculum ambition. We would need to shift to meet our own aspirations.

We decided to:

- Root our school curriculum in the national curriculum.

- Ensure we met the expectations of the national curriculum.

- Supplement national curriculum expectations with local imperatives, while also meeting our statements of educational belief and pedagogic principles.

- Change aspects of pedagogy in order to meet our aims.

- Ensure depth and quality in the children's learning.

For those schools deciding on their starting point for curriculum content, it might be worth considering:

- Whether to use the national curriculum as a basis for curriculum provision. We decided early on that we would in our Curious Curriculum. In a democracy, why would we not wish to use what the government had provided? In any case, when the children reached Year 11, they would take compulsory exams based on the national curriculum.
- To what extent you wish to supplement and expand on the national curriculum and, supplemented by other resources, focus on how it meets the needs of your children. Our approach was to enable the national curriculum to do its job well by taking teachers, and the children they taught, deeply into the possibilities for learning that it offered. We also believed that the scope of the national curriculum was limited to the essentials, and therefore that we wanted to look at broader issues with the children in order to fulfil our guiding principles.
- That the success of the curriculum relies on a well-structured learning sequence. For a curriculum to work throughout the age ranges, there needs to be a structure to the learning experience, which is what we began to articulate in Part One.
- That teaching deeply and taking children to depth is central to curriculum effectiveness. The work of our Curious Curriculum is as much about effective pedagogy as it is about curriculum content.

p. 48

What about the early years? Should it be included in a primary curriculum plan?

The early years foundation stage should be exactly that: a stage that establishes strong foundations for lifelong learning for *all* children in the early years of their life.

This belief was a large part of the remit that we agreed on when Alistair Bryce-Clegg was invited to work with our trust as an external support for early years provision and learning. The outlook we agreed was described by Alistair in this way:

Whilst undoubtedly, an element of the foundations will be based on knowledge, a much more important and significant aspect of what makes a child a happy, accomplished and successful learner is how they perceive themselves in that context, and the range of dispositions for learning that they possess.

How we as adults feel about the people we are with and the spaces we are in can deeply affect our mood, enjoyment and engagement in any situation. This is no different from children in the primary phase. In fact, it is more amplified for younger children as they do not have years of varied life experience to help make sense of, and rationalise, what and how they are feeling.

Even though early child development research and theory is grounded in the knowledge that effective play provision is the most developmentally appropriate way for children of this age to learn, the early years foundation stage is very much outcome based. This can shift the ultimate aim to achieving the early learning goals which, in turn, can result in a narrow, adult-focused approach to teaching and learning.

It is paramount as education leaders and practitioners that we have a strong understanding of the most appropriate journey for children to take, based on current child development and scientific research, rather than just the most familiar route to the required destination: 'not everything that can be counted counts, and not everything that counts can be counted'.[2]

Alistair told the following story to illustrate the point:

I was once working with a reception teacher who was delivering an Easter-themed maths session to her whole class. The planned objective of the session was for the children to count and then

---

2   C. Middleton, J. Gubbay and C. Ballard (eds), *The Student's Companion to Sociology* (St Malden, MA: Blackwell, 1997), p. 92, col. 2.

add one more in their head. The chosen counting apparatus were some Easter chick toys. A little way into the activity a child put up his hand and, rather than predict the next number in the sequence as the adult expected, he asked: 'Do chickens have belly buttons?'

The adult responded with 'I don't know, what do you all think?' What resulted from this question was a really interesting and animated discussion that led to all sorts of questions, theories and routes of enquiry. A really curious exploration of the question that was supported, but not led, by the adult.

Afterwards, I discussed with the teacher the benefits of moving away from the planned maths focus and taking the lead from the child. She responded. 'I know, it was great. Mind you, I wouldn't have done it if Ofsted were in.'

Many of the dominant discourses that are currently shaping our early years practice also stifle the exploration of other possibilities. An understanding of child development and what underpins successful, engaged learning is paramount if we want our children to be curious lifelong learners.

We should not be aiming to track national curriculum or 'subject specific' activities using a curious curriculum in the early years. Instead, we should look for delighted children who can demonstrate high levels of well-being, engagement, resilience and curiosity. Children are offered environments that reflect current child development research with opportunities for knowledge and skill development through a range of experiences that are the beginnings of everything they will encounter, not just in the national curriculum but in life.

The Curious Curriculum is one that sets out, through its content and pedagogy, to develop the disposition for curiosity in both adults and children. It is not one that provides outcome-driven activities created by adults for children to hopefully be curious about!

We decided that:

- Our primary stage curriculum and early years curriculum experiences were separate entities, but they would have the same ethos for learning.

- Early years would have its own integrity and would enable future learning without being a slave to it.

- Our early years teams and our Key Stage 1 teams would liaise to effect learning transition.

CHAPTER 7

Curriculum complexity

Setting priorities for teaching and learning and why organising curriculum content is difficult

Our schools were already teaching a curriculum and some had spent a lot of time trying to get it right. However, as our observational visits and discussions had shown, there was as much frustration as there was success. For most schools, organising what goes into the curriculum - what we often call curriculum mapping - is one of those snakes. We put in so much effort and think we have sorted things out, only to meet much exasperation. This chapter stands back from the challenge and attempts to unpick what it is that causes difficulties. As you read it, try to think about experiences you have had in different schools and to what degree this describes your own perceptions.

Assuming that we are designing and pursuing a curriculum that is based on the national curriculum and supplemented by a range of other imperatives, it is reasonable to think this can be articulated in some sort of document. The next question that arises is: what sort of document? Does a document alone do the job? If not, what else is needed to support it? As our school observations had shown, and head teachers had agreed, what was going on in our classrooms was not securing the sort of learning we sought. All of the schools had plenty of policies, but they were hidden away in electronic filing cabinets ready to show external visitors who asked to see them. The policies were not being lived in the daily life of the schools, which was where they would or would not have impact.

The two of us spent much time considering how to support schools by producing documentation, and, if we did, whether it would be effective. What was wrong with what we had already produced? In this chapter, we include our musings on why schools have so many false starts over curriculum and why it becomes so complicated. What follows here is not about our schools in particular, but about schools more generally – and reading it might resonate and provide some clues about how to sort out curriculum expectations.

The problem of explaining the curriculum for teachers: what is in the curriculum diet?

Schooling is a serious business but it also makes us smile. We need to enjoy the odd, the bizarre, the strange and the sometimes daft world of schools, so this section includes a bit of humour. One of the common problems in moving learning forward is that teachers are keen to do it but don't know where to start. In fact, they are offered so much help that they don't know what to do. Read what follows and see whether it rings true for you.

One problem with the curriculum is that there is just too much of it. Leaders often have the view that they mustn't leave anything out, so they add every element. This means that, if challenged, they are seen to be on message, up with the latest thinking, doing what they have to and, most importantly, giving the children the best possible opportunities.

This leads to the temptation for leadership to produce documentation about curriculum structure, where the amount of policy and guidance increases and, along with it, the complexity. The relationship between curriculum and pedagogy is complex, but as leadership strives to wrestle the complexity into a coherent explanation, there is a risk that the teachers, who have to make it real where it meets the child, become bemused.

A salient question for leadership teams to ask is: does a Year 1, Year 3 or Year 5 teacher know what they have to do? Do they have a picture of what this will look like in the classroom when they are doing it? Are they clear what they will do to improve learning, as opposed to going through a bureaucratic process of planning in PPA time and not focusing enough on preparation or assessment? Too often, clerical imperative rather than consideration of effective teaching becomes the planning that arises from documentation – and with that goes much of the excitement.

We often talk of the children's 'learning diet', so let's have look at the leadership problem of producing a curriculum overview in terms of the analogy of providing a buffet for a group of guests.

The learning buffet

We know we have to include certain staples (the national curriculum, phonics, and spelling, punctuation and grammar (SPAG). We know there is widespread concern about the importance of diet in sustaining well-being, such as five a day, so we add our four Rs (the learning values).[1] We want some drinks to wash it down, so we add some drivers that will carry our curriculum along – some bold statements about creativity, opportunity or imagination.

We pick things up at courses and conferences or in books and add them to our buffet too. Aspects of teaching, such as questioning or models and 'what a good one looks like' (WAGOLLs), are included because

---

1   Guy Claxton's four Rs are resilience, resourcefulness, reciprocity and reflectiveness.

everyone else seems to be having them with their meals. These are the 'party packs' we can buy, containing some new trendy bites, such as knowledge organisers.

p. 62

> Once we got teachers to share examples of knowledge organisers that were purposely written for children and not just teachers, we saw them making an impact.
>
> **Ian Oake**

Our children need some treats so we add those as well: novelties they have never tried or visits and special events. We also need sauces and custards to pour on, dip into and help to blend things together, so we have jugs of positive relationships with families and local community links.

We need to make sure we have everything in place should the health and safety inspectors appear, so we have serviettes and clean cutlery – that is, safeguarding.

Believing the feast is now prepared, we stand back and look at the learning menu for our buffet – the overview.

Finally, we invite our teachers to construct their meal from the buffet to feed the children in their class. The trouble is that the teachers don't always choose sensibly: they pick what they think is best or they 'help themselves'. Some select a balanced diet but don't have time to try everything before the end of the learning meal. Some opt for only what they like and leave out the things that would do them good – all treats and nothing healthy. Some eat all the sweet things and nothing enriching. The Twiglets are always left at the end, hardly touched. Some people didn't select anything at all from what we had prepared, choosing instead to eat from their own Tupperware box of special delights that they always enjoy.

Because everyone chooses differently from the buffet, and many don't regulate the diet for their children, we must make sure that we manage it better next time.

Next time

The same overview buffet is available, but now different items are on different tables and we make sure teachers know the rules for selection. First (in the morning), they must have fruit and veg (English and maths) and later (afternoon), they can opt for a balance from different small tables of meaty and fishy things (subjects such as history, science and geography … and there would be alternatives for vegans and vegetarians) and of sweet things (subjects such as art, drama, music and PE). Then they can collect their treats, sauces, drinks and cutlery (special events, days and weeks).

This time, we have encouraged the teachers to select a balanced meal for the children, but again, their choices mean that they have left some dishes untouched. They have had lots of peas (calculation), beans (time) and carrots (shape) from the vegetable (maths) table, but the cabbage (measuring), purple sprouting broccoli (capacity) and spinach (estimation) have been ignored. The same with the fruit (English) table: they took the easy peelers (phonics) and the easy-to-swallow strawberries (fronted adverbials) but the hard-to-get-into pineapples (extended novels of Stevenson) were left as people devoured the readily consumed grapes (Roald Dahl and Harry Potter). From the dessert tables they took the pastries – the strawberry pies (history) and apple tarts (geography) – where the fruit filling meant that history provided a chance to do writing about the past and geography to write about somewhere else, but they rejected the pastry itself (the geographic and historic knowledge and skills).

Lots of drinks were taken (opportunities and creativity) but they were mixed with treats, such as visits and special events. In the end, nobody tasted much and they had little to chew on.

Third time lucky

The leaders organise the buffet even more and have even more rules. The teachers can only eat from designated tables and food is apportioned appropriately. With this assigned menu (long-term plan), the leaders can be sure the children will get a varied diet.

All the tables have some easy peelers (phonics) and lots of peas (calculation), and different tables have different vegetables and fruit to ensure coverage. One table has turnips, another has onions and one even has pak choi. The melons, kiwis and mangos are spread out so the teachers have to make sure the children experience the whole range. On other tables, the teachers find that some science, art, PE and music decisions have been made for them.

The trouble is that, now, even though they take the balanced foods from their assigned tables, they can't work out how to get the children to eat it. The children turn their noses up at pak choi (geometry), so the teachers let them eat peas (calculation) instead and they just nibble at the pak choi. The teachers aren't sure what to do with the kiwi (ocean currents), so they just leave that and get stuck into the easy peelers (water cycle). The mango (church reformation) is much too hard. As for the pastries, they still tend to scrape out the jam and do the literacy, but leave the chewy dough of geography and history on the side.

Science is the worst: nobody has even nibbled yet at the salad drawer of science. Therefore, the leaders decide that the salad drawer should be on one special table and every teacher has to visit it weekly. They also tell the teachers which elements of the salad they have to select.

We can't keep this analogy going, but we have been told that it is a useful way to describe the dilemma we all face. And we hope you get the drift about the challenge for leadership in getting teachers to address properly the curriculum we construct. In the end, we verify whether the buffet has been successful. Have the children put on weight? Are they fit? Are they healthy? Are they addicted to bad things to the extent that they have illnesses linked to poor diet? Can they feed themselves? Do they enjoy a varied intake?

The government checks mainly that the children have grown physically. Yet, we know they need far more than that, which is what Ofsted has woken up to recently, although they have caused many of the disorders they think they are now uncovering.

It seems that the majority of schools have similar documentation to most other schools and much of it is the same and some of it better. For most schools, the overview is a scattering (or buffet) of terminology that they try to organise into something coherent, which makes sense as long as teachers understand it. That is what the documentation of our Curious Curriculum represents: the logical organisation of our thinking as an aid to collective understanding and support.

The problem is that these overviews are often two-dimensional – we work across and down a page – whereas, organising learning for a school or classroom is multidimensional. Think of a Rubik's cube with six faces each with nine squares: each twist has an impact on the other faces. Some teachers don't like working on certain faces and some schools struggle with particular faces more than others. And because they do struggle, the other faces get out of sequence too.

The more we insist on one face of the cube looking right, with a more perfect pattern, the less the other faces are likely to be in the right configuration. Teachers tend to stick with the face they like the most, or is the easiest, or seems to be the most important.

So, do values matter more than drivers, more than subjects and more than visits, or is teaching and learning essential – or progression or questioning? While a school might be fixated on covering content for the national curriculum or developing better science teaching, individual teachers might be gripped by making creative art or by questioning, because they believe that to be the answer. Another might just like organising visits. All of this goes some way to explaining why continuous dialogue is so important. It is through dialogue that teachers can ask questions, voice their concerns, articulate what they don't understand, share their misgivings, offer their ideas, help each other and prompt improvement.

Documents need to be discursive and illustrative, helping teachers to see the thinking behind the policy, to understand the way decisions have evolved, to offer examples and to remind them of the agreements reached. This was the case with our own documentation. Transplanting the solution wholesale is not advisable, if you seek success for your children as opposed to a document to show observers.

The curriculum buffet in our schools

Our schools had the buffet problem in abundance. The amount of waste planning filling the bins at the end of the week or year could have been recycled into several schools. One of the frustrating issues for head teachers was that they knew provision in the schools was variable, but they found it hard to put their finger on why. Most teachers were teaching from the menu prescribed by their school, but there was so much on offer at the buffet and the range of curriculum diet in classrooms was so great, that it was hard to know where to start to secure consistency.

With documentation describing the curriculum in the way it did, teachers were invited to attempt what they could and, as a consequence, the overall curriculum was becoming distorted. p. 152 There was no explanation of what a teacher had to teach and what we intended every child to learn.

We decided to:

- Ensure that our curriculum is not a separate entity and fits with our pedagogy. Our documentation needs to reflect that.

- Define curriculum expectations clearly.

- Ensure the expectations are manageable.

- Specify what we call the key learning intentions. ◀ p. 37

- Monitor the curriculum in terms of our expectations.

- Seek quality and depth.

- Provide sustained support for staff to develop effective curriculum and pedagogy.

In terms of a curriculum policy outlook, it might be worth considering:

- Spending time discussing what principles the curriculum is trying to address and then making sure people know how the various elements of content included fit with those principles.
- Holding detailed and extended discussions with staff about the places where the curriculum might run away with itself or whether there may be bare patches.
- Using the buffet analogy to help staff see the problems the school may face (it will be fun!).
- Talking with staff about the potential distortion of the curriculum, which will help them to see it as a shared problem rather than as a criticism.
- Asking staff what type of support they need.

CHAPTER 8

How to avoid good intent going wrong

A key decision: curriculum is not a separate entity and our work and documentation need to reflect that

We decided very early on that the curriculum could not be treated on its own without reference to the aspects of schooling that affect it. Our head teachers' disappointment in the variability of practice in their schools was compounded by the fact that they had produced the documentation. We spent time considering why documentation alone is not sufficient to secure the goal of effective learning.

Usually, schools construct a curriculum with a sound rationale. Usually, the curriculum is intellectually coherent and thorough, and clearly articulates the purpose, approach and expectations. Usually, the content builds on the intent and is set out in a formal document. On the whole, schools are pleased with the results – the intention is good. But having a curriculum plan is only the start of the process.

Our buffet analogy in the reality of our time: what can go wrong even with the best of intentions

The logic behind the purpose of the curriculum is typically well argued. It will include a collection of elements that address the philosophical challenge of responding to what we know about the world that the children will inhabit as adults. It will add a smattering of government buzzwords, some issues that Ofsted inspectors seem to be emphasising and some of the educational must-haves of the day.

Given all this justification, the customary conclusion is that the way to organise curriculum content is through subject disciplines. The national curriculum is arranged into subjects, as are many exams at 16, so should this be a guiding principle or even a hinge point where aims meet reality – a given? Alternatively, might it be possible to organise the content in line with the United Nations Convention on the Rights of the Child?[1] Could the Sustainable Development Goals, for example, be integrated into the curriculum, or could they be add-ons, invitations or expectations? Is the school aiming to achieve all the goals? Is each child supposed to respond to them constructively, or are we just being cognisant of them? How do we progress children's understanding and action across all of the seventeen goals as they mature? Similarly, British values feature in the curriculum of most schools, but what their status is beyond 'important' or even 'fundamental' is often unclear.[2]

While the curriculum includes the entire planned learning experience, English and mathematics are often described and treated

---

1   UNICEF, *The United Nations Convention on the Rights of the Child* (1989). Available at: https://downloads.unicef.org.uk/wp-content/uploads/2010/05/UNCRC_united_nations_convention_on_the_rights_of_the_child.pdf.

2   Department for Education and Lord Nash, Guidance on Promoting British Values in Schools Published [press release] (27 November 2014). Available at: https://www.gov.uk/government/news/guidance-on-promoting-british-values-in-schools-published.

separately from the rest of the content. In effect, therefore, what is commonly developed is a 'morning curriculum' and an 'afternoon curriculum'.

As the implications spread outward, teachers need to understand the curriculum in a linear way to enable the pedagogy to develop alongside it. The danger then is that each teacher simply focuses on what they have to teach and loses sight of the big picture – and progression suffers for the children.

This is how it was in our schools. We had all of the ingredients mentioned above, so the key issue in moving forward was to help head teachers and teachers see why it was happening. The way the curriculum can so easily become distorted was one of our snakes. We describe below how we explained and encouraged discussion. This was not done in a critical way but in order to improve our understanding of the situation. This is what *we* see – do *you* see it too?

Following a curriculum map and some of the challenges that arise

The step towards influencing practice in classrooms over time is a big one. Teachers tend to enjoy presentations and explanations of what is required of them by new approaches, and they appreciate being involved in organising subject discipline content. It is the range of ways in which the planned curriculum is interpreted that leads to variability in practice.

Any curriculum model is built on connections between big ideas, sometimes by taking a thematic approach and sometimes in discrete subject disciplines. It then plots a route through those connections. So, how do we stop lessons from becoming fragmented and disembodied, and retain the coherence of our intentions?

> A pivotal moment for me was the introduction of the 'intellectual concept'. This moved my understanding on how to ensure a theme was linked but not in a topic with tenuous links.
>
> *Sharon Clark*

Understanding the essence of civilisations is the reason why we opt to study the Greeks, Romans, Egyptians, Ming Dynasty or Aztecs. Geography ought to lead naturally back to the Sustainable Development Goals. The trouble with any content map is that it implies that coverage and the production of evidence denote success. Do teachers understand how to draw together the big ideas and make connections in learning, as opposed to covering or delivering content? 'Delivery' implies that teachers are akin to the people who leave parcels on our doorsteps or bring fast food. For professional teachers, curriculum is the outline and their task is to use that architecture to make the learning take shape and build learning that will last.

◄ p. 77

As the *planned curriculum* moves on from documentation it becomes the *taught curriculum*, and the risk of distortion occurs. Firstly, teachers select from that curriculum buffet. They then tend to teach those aspects of the curriculum that are inspected or tested, that they know about, that they think the children will enjoy learning and that they like to teach. Unless they are required to teach everything, they will omit things. For example, speaking and listening have always been part of the English curriculum, but they are rarely given the same attention as reading and writing, which are tested and inspected more thoroughly. Experimental science is taught in a limited way: teachers teach staple concepts each year because 'they always do'. This is where inspection will highlight any gaps between intent and implementation.

As the taught curriculum moves towards the children it becomes the *experienced curriculum*, and distorts again as teachers are influenced by what they see as the expectations on them: timetable, resources, limited time, separation or integration of subjects, the perceived potential of some children to disrupt and the requirement for evidence of learning. All of this can lead to the curriculum experienced by the children in practice to be very different from the one that looks so good in the original document.

Often, teachers are invited to tweak the content. If they are allowed to pick and choose from the menu or buffet of learning, distortion

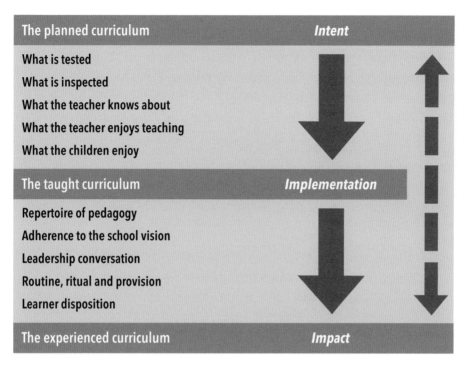

The planned curriculum	Intent
What is tested	
What is inspected	
What the teacher knows about	
What the teacher enjoys teaching	
What the children enjoy	
The taught curriculum	Implementation
Repertoire of pedagogy	
Adherence to the school vision	
Leadership conversation	
Routine, ritual and provision	
Learner disposition	
The experienced curriculum	Impact

Figure 8.1. From curriculum vision to practice – coherence or distortion?

is guaranteed, so what is acceptable? Are there any minimum expectations? Is the curriculum a guide to get the teacher started and then expand, is it a minimum expectation or is it a pick-and-mix offer? Are there clear guidelines on the learning diet of a child for every week, month or year? Is the model of a fair subject division per week through the timetable imposed or agreed with the teacher? What degree of agility and flexibility over curriculum content and pedagogic approach is permissible?

The challenge for leaders, therefore, is to ensure that the practice in the classroom corresponds with what is envisaged in the curriculum document. That means being awake to the potential for the distortion summarised in Figure 8.1, recognising that it is likely to happen, noting when it does and being prepared to do something about it.

We had all of these concerns but they were spread across each of the schools. While one teacher was distorting the curriculum because 'I always teach the *Titanic* because the children enjoy it', another was distorting because he 'avoids anything to do with biology' and yet another because 'I only do art if I have to'. Several schools were completely distorted by feeling under the cosh of inspection and had an almost total diet of literacy and numeracy.

We agreed and decided that:

- Reducing distortion was the job of leadership at every level.

- This could be achieved by building teachers' skills, competence and confidence.

- Teachers needed clarity about what constitutes quality in children's learning.

- Teachers needed help with pedagogy to make the curriculum come alive.

In terms of planning for curriculum development, it might be worth considering:

- The immediate challenge is to link curriculum with pedagogy and to consider and be clear about the extent of the job to be done. What is the gap between what is envisaged and what is happening now in school?
- A curriculum development plan will bring clarity about where culture change is needed. The expectations and pace of change will be important, as will be the sorts of support that will be offered. Some people get nervous about doing things wrong and then don't do them at all. How can we help them to take early productive steps?

- Most teachers looking at a proposed new curriculum model will approve and be impressed. Equally, many will believe they are doing it already, give or take a bit of adjustment to the content. Are they right?
- A good thing to do might be to write down what the new curriculum might mean for, say, five teachers (you don't have to name them). With that summary, it should be possible to think about the type of support people will need with planning, organisation, teaching and so on.
- Some of the issues are macro pedagogy – that is, school-wide influences on success that an individual teacher cannot control or is not expected to do: timetable, room allocations, resources and the provision of exercise books.
- Micro pedagogy might be seen as the teacher's organisational repertoire – what they can control: the range of teaching methods they use, their versatility and agility.
- More than anything else, what teachers will need is an extensive conversation about pedagogy and curriculum. As a teacher, is there an expectation about the hours I will spend per subject per week/term/year? Will I have a timetable? Will I use separate books to record learning in different subjects? Is homework included? Can I do my staple favourites? The answer to each of these questions carries a message about your expectations for the curriculum, and playing the answers back to the aims of the curriculum might clarify your challenges as linked to the leadership of learning and schools.
- It is often salutary to think: what will this mean for the teacher of Year 3 or Year 5? Articulating to staff the specific implications of what the proposed curriculum will mean to them is key to implementing it in the way you intend.

- If the aim is to teach the new curriculum in, say, 200 hours per year,[3] can the envisaged content be fitted into the available time or will it be chock-a-block? How will you help teachers to decide what falls off the edge? Does the intention of linking subject content together in themes resonate with the big concepts in your aims? Is the teacher a deliverer of content or the architect of a learning experience, the performer on the classroom stage or the oiler of a machine of learning?
- Some aspects of learning take a long while to teach in a discrete block, others build incrementally and some need to drip often, with teachers being really tuned into exploiting every moment and opportunity. Languages (including English) and mathematics are a case in point. Children's versatility grows when teachers draw attention to language features at just the right moment to reinforce the learning. Language vocabulary is hard to learn en masse: we manoeuvre around terminology without aiming for a terminus and we draw attention to the French, Germanic and Latin roots with our children (as in the sentence you are reading now). There is the playful inclusion of some little linguistic examples in this text if you want to look for them. Good teachers live learning all of the time, not just for an hour or so per week timetabled by subject.
- If the leadership team has produced a lot of planning, why not provide the next layer of planning and structure each term or half-term? (We might know the answer to this question, but are we clear about our reasons to others?) Some schools and trusts provide scripted lessons; we wouldn't suggest that you should, but you might like to talk about why you wouldn't.

---

3 This figure comes from thirty-nine weeks in a school year with two-hour afternoons for three days a week (less some for events such as sports days or similar).

- Do teachers understand that we want them to teach subject disciplines rather than cover subjects? It is the discipline that enables the children to mature into geographers, linguists, scientists and so on; they will have to behave as experimenters, researchers, scholars, designers, performers and so on. This is one way to avoid the issue mentioned earlier of history being literacy about the past or geography being writing about somewhere else.
- Is there any indication of the sorts of pupil products that might result from the curriculum?
- Is it anticipated that children will make models, carry out experiments, make presentations, use artefacts and so on? What prerequisite skills will they need in order to do well in the curriculum experience? Do teachers know how to teach them?

We have been addressing all of these considerations over the time we have been developing our Curious Curriculum. They were not dealt with all at once and some are still being addressed. The answers we found, the solutions we came up with and the tactics we used are all set out in this book, but reading about them here as we explore some of the challenges of getting from page to classroom will, we hope, set you fair for the task ahead.

An important question to consider is, how is the group driving the curriculum going to support pedagogy? Is it acceptable for teachers to take the new content and simply transfer it to their old teaching model? This is a challenge in most schools. It was one of the most significant problems we faced when transferring the Curious Curriculum from the page to the classroom. In the following pages, we have explained how we tried to encourage improvements. As you read on, you will have a foot on the rung of one of our ladders and the chance to make progress.

Moving on from intent

The articulation of curriculum intent can be a striking achievement. It is base camp achieved and a staff invigorated. Too often, though, schools seem to turn back at this point, too exhausted by the climb and the unexpected to revisit their curriculum planning. Planning a curriculum is relatively simple and usually enjoyable since we are imagining perfection. But some of our schools had seen so many false dawns with their curriculum that some teachers were almost resigned to the process of the rethinking being repeated every couple of years.

The steps required to make the curriculum achieve what we intend are hard, but we have to leave base camp behind and strike for a summit – and take our teachers with us. This goal was central to all our work from a very early stage. We know this can seem obvious; there will be few in school leadership who do not believe they should build their own team's competence and confidence. Our concern was that this would rely less on managerial approaches and more on being close to teachers and influencing their thinking, practice and belief in their own ability and professionalism.

While monitoring and in-school accountability would be important, we wanted to ensure that support structures were in place to gradually increase teachers' skills, effectiveness and growth. Documentation would matter but as a support rather than as an instruction, as a reminder of ground covered as well as a set of demands for what was ahead.

We knew from our work so far that the teachers were fascinated by how to teach better, how to bring the curriculum alive for the children and how to inspire greater achievement. We knew that job satisfaction in doing so would be a greater motivator than any performance management process.

CHAPTER 9

Reframing our model for implementation

Supporting teachers to improve children's learning: how to go about it

If we agree that the focus for development and improvement is on teachers and their classrooms, what do we do and how do we go about it? We had six central efforts:

1. Working directly with teachers themselves and finding ways to help them work with each other.

2. Working with school leadership to make sure that the effort to help teachers gained as much traction as possible and made the impact we agreed. We needed to support head teachers to organise themselves and get their eyes to focus as much within the school as with satisfying onlookers. We also needed curriculum leads and teaching and learning leads to exercise their responsibilities well.

3. Working with curriculum subject coordinators to develop their confidence and skill, and to help them see their role in influencing the quality of practice and learning outcomes across their schools.

4. Finding ways to encourage these three groups of people and to build collective effort and commitment. None of the

methods we used will surprise you: conferences, workshops, documentation, meetings and so on. The key issue was that we would aim for coherence and try to create a continuing story, and that any contribution to development would carry the expectation that it would be used effectively.

5. Working on the curriculum not as something static or inanimate but as a friend to learners, which had to be brought alive through the best teaching. If the curriculum represented what we intended for the children and the Curious Curriculum was part of that, how would we implement it successfully? Our view was that we should consider teaching and learning alongside the curriculum throughout and never let one or the other sleep.

6. Avoiding the possibility of losing momentum or grinding to a halt and all our efforts petering out. So often in schools, well-intentioned planning stumbles or stalls due to events elsewhere that distract. We were keen to address potential influences that would restrict development and not allow them to have undue impact.

It is these six aspects of our work effort that we explain as we go forward from here and this provides the backdrop to what we do now. Essentially, we have been engaged with the schools in an extended problem-solving programme. Solving problems is complex and occasionally frustrating. New steps are often faltering or misplaced and need to be re-trodden. At the same time, solving problems is also exhilarating when things go well. If only we could guarantee the latter! It was synchronising our efforts in each of these areas that kept us pointing in the right direction. Sometimes we were knocked off-track, but we had to regroup, rethink and return to the difficulties and challenges identified initially and keep improving the offer for the children.

Of course, while a timeline and schedule are useful in outline, events don't always go according to the plans set out in so many 'how to' books. This is why we think our experience was more like a game of snakes and ladders: our six priority efforts were the counters that we would try to move in sequence, but occasionally one would slide back down a snake and we had to recover. Occasionally, after a long slog of problem-solving we would a surge up a ladder – only to find that another development had slid down a snake. Leadership is too easily seen as a formulaic programme of actions, when, in reality, few developments turn out as imagined or intended. Learning to cope with complexity is fundamental.

We adopted an approach that relies on what Kotter et al. termed 'agile principles': seeing leadership as 'fast and nimble' and working in several dimensions beyond the 'reliable and efficient' hierarchically structured management processes, which are less prone to adaption when things take an unexpected turn.[1] We were doing what Kotter refers to as moulding the culture to be 'less of an anchor holding back change and more of a force that fosters speed and adaptability',[2] by activating 'want to' rather than relying on the 'have to' outlook of a 'management centric' approach.[3]

Supporting teachers' understanding of the curriculum structure

Our musings on the snakes of curriculum mapping and the distortion of intent were what led us to determine on a shared approach across our schools. It was the need for clarity that encouraged us to specify our themes and determine our KLIs.

---

1   J. P. Kotter, V. Akhtar and G. Gupta, *Change: How Organizations Achieve Hard to Imagine Results in Uncertain and Volatile Times* (Chichester: John Wiley, 2021), p. 149.

2   Kotter et al., *Change*, p. 101.

3   Kotter et al., *Change*, p. 58.

If we could agree these, then our support for pedagogy could follow, linked to a common provision with the aim of ensuring quality and depth.

◀ p.46

As a result, we have a set of themes that provide a focus for learning in year groups. This helps with continuity, progression and coherence. It also provides a common agenda for teachers to work on together, particularly in year group teams. A new teacher arriving in a school now is presented with the expected themes; they are non-negotiable. To explain the background, they have the Curious Curriculum document as well as colleagues who understand it and leaders who want to help them make it work. Our themes were co-constructed by the curriculum and teaching and learning leads together discussing how they could work collaboratively on agreed content across the trust, yet still retain teacher ownership and autonomy. Each of the leads talked to staff in a school staff meeting and shared some examples and ideas, discussed what they thought would be an interesting and engaging theme title and considered how the theme fitted with the already decided curriculum. The results were extraordinary. The big ideas were current, open and engaging. The teachers loved the thought of having an overarching theme from which they could shape the direction of their enquiry and from this

◀ p. 48

interpret the big idea or intellectual concept.

These ideas were then brought back to the curriculum planning group and a list was collated. This list was then returned to staff to consider what they thought would and wouldn't work. Over time, the list of themes has changed and evolved. Through review and feedback from teachers and leads, it became apparent that some themes were not working as well as others. Schools with split year groups have been imaginative in the way they have chosen their themes for the year. In reality, they are a conduit to enable teachers to see broader connections than a traditional topic would typically allow. The content of a theme can be wide, and in effect, it is the school curriculum plan, which is derived from the KLI, that dictates the direction and knowledge to be taught.

We have had conversations about the impact on staff workload. Initially, teachers were concerned about too much churn, as they would not be able to use the basic structure of the previous year's planning if the themes changed too much. By keeping them consistent, the staff could become familiar with the content of the curriculum and develop confidence in delivering through the agreed themes.

The reason for all year groups having the same theme was for classes to be able to take the big idea or intellectual concept in different directions, and then come back and share their thinking and learning. Thinking practically about where a theme such as 'exploration' could be taken within the Year 6 curriculum excited the teachers. They saw many hundreds of possible connections with the central element of the theme. This enabled them to explore specific aspects in detail, while other year groups across the trust explored different aspects. When the teachers came together, they focused on the same theme but from various angles and with alternative interpretations on how it could unfold in the classroom without becoming distorted.

> The reduction in workload for our teaching staff, due to being able to share planning, provide more collaborative opportunities and have a clear, consistent curriculum plan in one place, has helped with the work-life balance.
>
> *Sarah Williams*

However comprehensive the themes, there was always content that didn't fit or belong. When designing the curriculum, we were really clear that discrete subject lessons were to be expected, and actively encouraged, where subjects didn't fit into a theme. For example, the schools decided to pool their PE and sport premium funding to employ two PE specialists to support the delivery of high-quality PE across the trust. They work alongside teachers to further their development and build confidence in teaching PE.

Other subjects are taught discretely too. Music, RE and PSHE all have a bespoke curriculum that does not lend itself well to being incorporated into a theme. These subjects flourish when taught independently but with cognisance of the subjects that relate to them. The professional subject associations help subject leaders and teachers to make the necessary connections (see the Appendix for a list of associations). Obviously, where things fit naturally within a theme, those links are developed, but they are not forced.

Clarifying and extending the teacher's role in the planning process

Once our teachers had agreed and knew what theme fitted where in their school calendar, where the themes sat within the foundation curriculum generally and how they tuned in with English and mathematics, the real work began. What we seek is rigour and depth rather than coverage and delivery. We want teachers to help the children learn what is intended rather than plan a series of activities with a tenuous link to the title of the theme. We want teachers to focus on what the children are intended to learn and how their teaching supports that aim.

For this reason, the design of each theme is one of the fundamentals of our Curious Curriculum. It is why the learning intentions of a theme are set out in a diagrammatic way with the intellectual concept at the core. Images are important; there is a two-way link between the intellectual concept and each of the drivers for quality. It is why none of the boxes are at the top of a list and instead surround the big idea.

p. 48

The structure of the themes is a key element in our Curious Curriculum, so it is worth revisiting the explanations in Figure 1.5. As a result of the emphasis on facts and knowledge that Michael Gove was advocating for political purposes during the review of the national curriculum, schools were lurching towards factual accumulation for children. The debate about knowledge has settled since, but at the time we needed a more nuanced approach to the issue. In fact, Ofsted are now acknowledging that children need genuine understanding rather than disconnected facts,[4] which is something we were encouraging in the structure of our themes.

---

4   This has taken the form of a series of curriculum research reviews – see https://www. gov.uk/government/collections/curriculum-research-reviews. See also J. J. Schwab, The Concept of the Structure of a Discipline, *Educational Record*, 43 (1962), 197–205.

Taking stock

Our intention in this section has been to describe the complex process of bringing teachers together around curriculum purpose and mapping, both in theory and in practice, as a step on the way to quality and depth. This is all about supporting teachers to do the job they want to do well. It is widely known that effective planning is a precursor to effective teaching, so a teacher starting in one of our schools today would get the Curious Curriculum background document and other supportive materials. They would also be

◀ p.82

working with colleagues who could support them in a school environment where they would see expectations all around them. We didn't have this when we first introduced the theme design expectations. We had beaten the buffet problem by not providing a mountain of things for teachers to select from, and instead asked them to bring ingredients to create the menu for an appetising and nourishing (but not outfacing) theme.

But, of course, it didn't work straight away. Even for teachers who were enthusiastic and convinced that this was the right way forward, it was much more difficult than simply choosing from a buffet – a development that had deskilled them to some extent. It also revealed the degree of deskilling that had crept up on them over recent years. They wanted to teach well but, over time, the narrow, incessant and changing demands had squeezed out many of the skills they now required. We needed to support our teachers, and to do that we had to develop the skills of the curriculum subject discipline coordinators. These people would be one of our ladders because they would help us to make progress more swiftly. If we were going to use them well, then they, their head teachers and all the staff would need to appreciate their role.

Coordinating the subject disciplines

We knew that our subject discipline coordinators would be instrumental to our success, so wanted to use them to maximum effect. We had all the problems of variability that will be familiar to any school. From the beginning, we recognised that we would have to work with the coordinators and see them as key drivers of success in supporting teachers to make progress in their schools.

Most primary schools have some sort of system for subject coordination, usually related to staff responsibility and according to a logic of school leadership based on the size of the school, available resources, staff expertise and experience, school strengths and weaknesses. The effectiveness of the role of the coordinator is a key influence on curriculum success; just as important is the coordination of the coordinators themselves.

Leaders must be clear about the level of responsibility that is being delegated to coordinators, as this affects their self-belief, confidence and readiness to act. The list below is often used to illustrate the range of delegated levels of responsibility.

Nine levels of delegation:

1. Look into this problem. Give me all the facts. I will decide what to do.

2. Let me know the alternatives available and the pros and cons of each option. I will decide what to select.

3. Let me know the criteria for your recommendation, which alternatives you have identified and which ones appear best to you, with any risks identified. I will make the decision.

4. Recommend a course of action for my approval.

5. Let me know what you intend to do. Delay action until I approve.

6. Let me know what you intend to do. Do it unless I say not to.

7. Take action. Let me know what you did and how it turns out.

8. Take action. Communicate with me only if your action is unsuccessful.

9. Take action. No further communication with me is necessary.[1]

Asking people to coordinate aspects of leadership in primary schools linked to these nine levels of delegation is fraught with challenge. Too many head teachers imply a level 9 position through job descriptions or their attitude to the work expected, resulting in colleagues feeling under-led. Other head teachers operate at level 1, often without realising it, and in doing so, over-manage and frustrate individuals' ambitions. Occasionally there is a contradiction, with the pronouncement of level 9 and the actions of level 1.

So, what is the most effective level for supporting, for example, the curriculum coordinator or the teaching and learning lead? The truth is that there is no hard-and-fast rule. For the experienced and successful coordinator, most of their work might be towards the level 9 end. For the inexperienced and perhaps hesitant new coordinator, it might be towards the level 1 end. For new developments, innovations or areas

---

1   T. Brighouse and M. Waters, *About Our Schools: Improving on Previous Best* (Carmarthen: Crown House Publishing, 2022), p. 525.

of concern, the expectation of 'checking in' is likely to be different than for more routine or straightforward aspects of their work. The chances are that the coordinating team will comprise a blend of self-awareness and readiness, so the challenge is to be clear about which aspects of the role fit where and how one coordinator's role integrates with the others. In effect, the head teacher is the school's coordinator of coordinators, orchestrating their work in search of the essence of leadership – continuous improvement.

What does the subject discipline coordinator's job involve and how do we help them to be effective? In terms of Ofsted's recent outlook, it is to lead in respect of the three I's of intention, implementation and impact, which, when meshed with all the other efforts at coordination, will ensure the school achieves its overall vision and intent.

For our own schools, these considerations were important. Over time, people had been appointed to certain roles, worked hard and tried to do either what was expected of them or the role they gradually shaped for themselves. However, some were given little responsibility and others were virtually free-range. Our challenge was to determine how to motivate these individuals to have real impact across their schools, which was why the challenges we faced needed to be aired with head teachers as well as the coordinators themselves.

Too often, the role of a curriculum or teaching and learning lead or a subject discipline coordinator goes little beyond a managerial function. Supporting colleagues by producing school-level documentation, organising resources and compiling records are all important tasks, but they are only part of the story. During an era that has emphasised literacy and numeracy and focused on the teacher's 'performance' in a relatively stylised lesson format, many teachers have become deskilled in their approach to the wider curriculum. For example, they have had not been through the same assessment regimes as for English and maths, including a lack of opportunity to benchmark or moderate standards.

The limitations of present practice were inhibiting our development, which involved issues such as the repertoire of pedagogy, the range of pupil products and perceptions of excellence. We have said it before but, sadly, for many schools, teaching history meant literacy lessons set in the past, geography was literacy set in specific locations and science was literacy about famous discoveries or natural phenomena. In too many cases, art or music had become opportunities to experience learning using different parameters or different media; more open activities but often with perfunctory or limited outcomes and products. To move from this to learning about and through subject disciplines – building a knowledge base and interpreting that by beginning to understand the behaviours and practices of historians, geographers, scientists and artists – presented a shift in mindset and practice for teachers.

Overcoming such challenges demands more than documentation and observation. It demands changing perceptions through shared language, shared understandings, shared interpretation and shared endeavour. The coordinator needs to see their role as coordinating the school's efforts around the study of history, art or mathematics rather than coordinating the subject itself. It would be clumsy, but a better job title might be 'coordinator of the school's work in the arts' (or PE or computing, for example).

This is why our conferences became important vehicles for enabling the sharing and communicating of expectation in the widest sense – showing different horizons, challenging accepted practices in a positive way by presenting alternative aspirations and encouraging people to have new ambitions for children's learning. A new intent that put meaning into the fine words of the school vision and brought the curriculum off the page with renewed purpose at a school and national level.

> There is precious little preparation for the role of subject leader.
> We knew we had to help them.
>
> *Sharon Clark*

It is vital for the coordinator to see the role in the round. Many of our staff appreciate the coordinator's wheel (Figure 10.1), which outlines briefly what the role entails. It applies to those who lead on the effectiveness of a subject discipline as well as those who have designated leadership of teaching and learning or the curriculum – or even the learning effectiveness of the school. Leadership is often seen as tasks such as managing a budget or the performance management of staff when, in fact, these are examples of how the functions of the role are fulfilled, not of the role itself.

Figure 10.1. The coordinator's wheel: leading learning effectiveness

The coordinator's wheel was shared first with head teachers, so we could debate the scale of change that was needed. We discussed the extent to which the roles assumed by school coordinators were circling the wheel and whether they were taking their roles forward in a rounded way. There were muted chuckles when we talked about the danger of the role of head teachers being limited to the 'holy trinity' of policies, observing and checking, and quality assurance. Leadership teams poring over data and seeking to make improvements by producing policy changes, then checking that the policy is being followed, only to revisit the data a few weeks later to find that no change has taken place, is the story of schooling on so many levels, from government through to classroom teacher. What head teachers realised from their discussion about the coordinator's wheel was that they needed to expect and support all aspects of the role, and that they had the overall job of coordinating learning.

The purpose and function of the ten key roles on the wheel are self-explanatory. The challenge for the coordinator is to make sure that their work encompasses the entire wheel in an organised and coherent way. Each spoke is informed by the ones before and informs the ones beyond. This means that the policies we develop fit with the vision for the subject discipline and with the overall vision for the school. It also means that the resources we purchase align with the school's principles and policies; equipment, books or visits that are used as a learning resource should help to realise the vision. If we have a policy about children being practical scientists and researchers, we buy equipment that enables them to carry out experiments and ensure that it is organised effectively for them. We don't buy science resources that take children through printed sheets, however attractive they might appear to be.

In terms of the design and plan for the subject discipline, the coordinator would make sure that there is clarity about the subjects being pursued under the themed approach. If our vision is to make science matter by showing how it links to wider constructs, then we might reasonably try to incorporate science with history, geography and other subjects within a theme. However, if this means that science is being shoehorned into a theme where it doesn't really fit, we are at risk of denying our principles. In which case, we will adopt a separate and more appropriate subject discipline approach.

Modelling and influencing good practice are a vital part of the coordinator's role. Some coordinators have expertise in the subject discipline and some have greatness thrust upon them because a job needs to be done and they are willing to do it. Some coordinators in small schools collect music to go with science and DT and then cheerfully add modern languages too. Whatever the position, the coordinator must try to find and show examples of good pedagogy and demonstrate how the curriculum should meet the children. Part of the role is about demonstrating to colleagues the good practice that already exists among them and that meets the vision and principles of the school. Nothing builds enthusiasm like having good work recognised and valued.

Of course, the curriculum or teaching and learning lead for the school will be in the position of being better versed in some subject disciplines than others (and sometimes feel weaker in a few). The challenge is to develop any areas of personal weakness as well as drive the strengths. The role of the lead is to coordinate the effort across a range of disciplines, which means paying equal attention to all and supporting all staff, some of whom will have a better understanding. If each coordinator develops good principles and policies that are agreed and understood by everyone, those principles and policies become a watchword for practice across the school rather than something to shove in a filing cabinet in case the inspectors ask to see them. Policies need to be working documents; what makes them work effectively is the coordinator and the staff.

Within our schools, we have always accepted that our documentation is a working resource rather than the finished product. Each version of the Curious Curriculum is almost a draft for the next one because our thinking, practice and examples are always evolving. Once this mentality builds in the teachers and teaching assistants, they are not simply delivering a curriculum but helping to shape it through ongoing experience and growing knowledge and practice.

The spoke of the wheel that coordinators find the most difficult is the expectation that they will help to improve practice. Having provided a vision and policy, helped with planning and design, organised resources and led some staff workshops, surely the results will flow? Perhaps they will, but our experience has taught us that people tend to need more support in order to imagine what success might look like. (Doesn't some of this sound like leading learning with children?)

A teacher with three years of experience can feel very awkward when trying to support a teacher with twenty years in the classroom, although most teachers are very self-effacing and open to new learning. The point is that we are all attempting to help each other improve our practice. We are not looking for faults, but we are questioning whether what we are doing really achieves the principles we seek.

Some coordinators worry about carrying out observations. However, in schools where the professional climate is good, teachers and teaching assistants are used to spending time in each other's rooms, supported by leadership teams who make it happen as a sort of entitlement, which sets the right tone for making the experience productive. The worst approach is to mirror formal observation processes. Informative time spent with colleagues in classrooms is often informal (the clue is in the stem of the word).

The challenge is to know what to look for and how to see it. The place to clarify this is vision and policy statements and materials that have been developed through CPD (the whole job is on the wheel somewhere). Regular incidental conversations in classrooms can be far more productive than the once-a-term session of observation and form-filling. A few minutes of well-practised appreciative inquiry will drive progress more succinctly than official feedback, especially with the usual ducking and diving that is likely to ensue.

As the school community gets used to observing on another and talking naturally about what they see, progress is discernible. Leaders have the challenge of setting a culture that is both instinctively challenging and ultimately supportive – and always with the best interests of children in focus. This is why vision statements have to be more than just words on a page. It is another example of how the interconnected roles on the coordinator wheel rely on each other for effectiveness.

The need for data and evidence often drives coordinators because it can be a means of quality assurance, the proof that a subject discipline is being taught effectively. For the coordinator who is seeing their subject discipline genuinely develop, this can be one of the really joyous aspects of the role. Evidence is what we assemble to show that standards have been achieved, progress made, ground covered, high points reached and problems resolved.

One difficulty is that, over time, the use of data has grown exponentially. Some schools have become so reliant on spreadsheets that they believe this is the only valid form of evidence of learning. But evidence comes in many forms, not just numerical data. Evidence is not simply data stored to show someone else but a resource for extending development. For example, annotated examples of children's products that record the way they are working at greater depth than previously or demonstrating progress in understanding, knowledge and skills acquisition is a vital part of ongoing quality assurance.

Whether evidence is collected in the form of data showing achievement in spreadsheet form or a collection of teacher planning documents or observations, what matters is the use to which it is put. Good coordinators use evidence in a nuanced way to further the dialogue about continuous development and review areas for focused and concentrated effort – for example, particular groups of children or specific learning objectives that could be jumping off points for new developments.

Interacting with others is central to the role of the coordinator. The role is about communication rather than managerial or clerical tasks. It is also an influential position, as well as a persuasive one, in that it can shift practice in school for the better. Leaders need to enable dialogue within the school, across the school and beyond the school. One of the powerful elements in developments within our schools has been the way in which people from different schools have been able to share their experiences and insights: subject discipline coordinators talking with each other, phase leaders talking with each other, curriculum leads and teaching and learning leads working together, year groups of teachers working together with coordinators. Over time, the interaction of multiple communities of interest has helped to create a dynamic and positive emphasis on long-term development.

Coordinators, whatever their subject discipline, are more likely to be successful if they know about the discipline. It is impossible to overstate the benefit to be gained by reading around the subject and building a secure knowledge base. This is about more than reading for ideas on learning activities to do with the children. This is about reading at an adult level: understanding principles, key developments and momentous events, finding out about influential people, and exploring big ideas and intellectual concepts for their fascination and intrigue. Once that secure base has been established, helping colleagues to think through their work becomes much more rewarding and sharing delight in the subject discipline comes naturally.

Of course, it is harder when greatness has been thrust upon us or when we have walked reluctantly into the limelight. Sometimes needs must and we are asked to coordinate an area for which we have no natural warmth. However, the same principle applies: the more we know and understand, the more enjoyable it becomes. A good place to turn is always the subject associations; every subject has one. Most have a fund of resources and supportive guidance, as well as pointing the way to a literature base and the latest developments or research. There are also associations which bring together fields of interest in areas such as the early years, the environment or pedagogic approaches. It is a pity that the profession engages with itself so lightly through its membership of such bodies and relies

 p. 332

instead on guidance gleaned from interpreting inspection reports on individual schools. A strong profession drives thinking and practice, so schools would do well to invest in the membership of associations for their subject discipline coordinators.

In our schools, we have invested in the membership of subject associations for teachers as a way of gaining access to high-quality and up-to-date insights in every subject discipline. The investment is comparatively small and has paid dividends by linking our teachers to communities of interest across the country and abroad.

Subject discipline coordinators are vital cogs in the wheel of progress for curriculum and pedagogy. Over time, they have made a huge impact on the developments described in this book, once leaders had worked out how to use them effectively and productively. Careful and concerted investment in your coordinators will reap enormous benefits.

> Belonging to subject associations has seen an absolute transformation in the quality of subject leaders' knowledge.
>
> *Jen Wathan*

In terms of subject discipline coordinators, we agreed to:

- Ensure that the level of delegation was commensurate with their experience of leadership.

- Ensure that their role encompassed the coordinator's wheel.

- Expect coordinators to influence other teachers and classrooms.

- Provide opportunities to engage fully with their subject discipline, including membership of a relevant association.

- Encourage the collaborative and collective work of coordinators between schools.

> In terms of subject coordination, it might be worth considering:
>
> - How to ensure that subject discipline leaders have responsibility that is clearly delegated and dependent on their experience, expertise and confidence. The nine levels of delegation apply to different aspects of their work, so they should each know where they stand. If we want them to exert more influence, the degree of delegation should grow over time as they become more capable and experienced.
> - The importance of ensuring that the role is about improving practice rather than passively coordinating. Their role is to influence positively, not just be a watching brief.
> - How working together under a shared development programme, coordinators can build understanding and confidence.
> - How we keep the focus on depth and rigour in the subject disciplines.
> - How to measure the effectiveness of subject discipline coordination by more than the quality of documentation, and instead empower coordinators to influence widely.

p. 179

How might we help teachers with planning beyond structuring the content of a theme?

Our teachers all knew the words but they didn't know the tune. Breaking away from providing activity-focused lessons designed to generate evidence was proving to be a challenge. Too many teachers had developed the routine of downloading generic stand-alone lesson plans without realising the pitfalls. Their thinking was about their own performance and what they would do in the lesson rather than developing a long-term view of the children's learning.

We needed to find ways to encourage teachers to consider the child's role in the learning process. They had a natural affinity with the premise of an engaging curriculum and children being active in their learning processes. They enjoyed examples of how this was being done in other schools, they were positive about seeing children as instrumental in their own learning, and terms such as 'agency', 'exercising responsibility', 'organising' and 'making decisions' came easily to them. However, getting teachers to take the step of making these sorts of approaches to learning a daily reality proved difficult.

> Visiting other schools has been really valuable. But it had to be the right school at the right time, and we took advice on that.
>
> *Sharon Clark*

We set about this issue from different angles. We didn't necessarily have a master plan, but as one thing slid down a snake, we positioned a ladder to send it back up again. What was going up was the progress we were making on planning. However, it was failing to get through the classroom door in any significant way, so it kept coming down again.

We began by revisiting our curriculum content planning. We found that the teachers were struggling to get away from taking something from the national curriculum and building a 'standard' lesson around it in transmission and task mode. We set about trying to get them to see curriculum expectations from a different perspective – one that would inform their teaching. We were trying to avoid a snake while at the same time offering a ladder.

CHAPTER 11

Setting the expectations

Getting teachers to come to terms with what we are trying to teach and how to go about it

In this chapter, we will briefly explore the key components of any curriculum and the discussions we had with our coordinators to help them get to grips with their own subject and to support their colleagues to 'imagine' learning in the classroom. It is framed in the same way that we discussed these issues with our own teaching community, and we hope it will encourage you to think about your own understanding of your school.

Every curriculum contains the same three elements. Whether we are looking at a national curriculum from anywhere in the world, an off-the-shelf curriculum product, the curriculum of a school or even a scheme of work produced for a group of classes or year group, the three core elements are the same. Teasing out and exploring the balance between them is a good way to understand content and expectations.

So, what are the three elements in every curriculum everywhere?

Every curriculum contains a blend of things that children need to learn *about* in the subject discipline, to learn *how to do* within the subject discipline and to learn *through* the subject discipline.

Take three different coloured highlighter pens, one for each element, and go through the text of any curriculum: green for *about*, red for *how to* and blue for *through*. By the end of the highlighting process, there will be no blank paper in terms of curriculum learning expectations.

Of course, the three elements are those stalwarts of any primary classroom: knowledge (*about*), skills (*how to*) and themed learning (*through*). At present, the national curriculum in England is often described as 'knowledge driven' or 'knowledge rich'. However, while knowledge is emphasised, it is mostly not specified and more often refers to children learning about, for example, a range of artists or musicians and their accomplishments.

Knowledge expectations get very detailed (some would say prescriptive) in the GCSE exam specifications,[1] whereas in the primary sector expectations are more balanced and generalised. It is not essential for teachers to know the detailed balance of these elements, but simply producing a few pages of national or school curriculum documentation will give them an insight that few will have had previously.

The next step is another eye-opener for a lot of teachers: taking some individual examples of expected learning from the curriculum, using a few each of *about*, *how to* and *through*, and encouraging teachers to think about the best way of approaching them to make them stick with the children.

Some things are best learned using a drip approach, little and often – repetition, revisiting, incidental mentioning and reinforcing – and doing it so frequently that it becomes a habit. If we are practising scales in music, the best way is little and often. If we sat down to practise until we could do it, we would be a long time sitting.

p. 246

---

1 Different awarding bodies set different courses of study to satisfy the specifications set by Ofqual for each subject at GCSE.

Speaking a foreign language is enabled by regular reminders and induction. Similarly, becoming familiar with number bonds needs to be done in frequent bursts, whenever there is a chance to encourage confidence and ease, which means the teacher seeing the chance to draw attention to a fascinating feature of number or seizing a moment to practise and revisit until proficiency is secure. If we want to learn to draw, we can be taught the skills in formal sessions, but it is the regular, often brief, sessions of practice that will build confidence and skill.

Teachers instinctively warm to this insight. They know it to be true, they can grasp it and it appeals to their image of the teacher. However, cognitive dissonance takes hold when they set about planning their teaching with its one-hour sessions and formulaic approaches. Hence, we get a learning objective, which will be something like: 'We are learning to become proficient at number bonds to 10' or 'We are learning to use speech marks.'[2] While it is possible to plan and teach a one-hour lesson towards such objectives, they will not be embedded and the children will not be proficient in such a short period of time.

Mastery – that term which was so prevalent just a couple of years ago and remains relevant – is achieved through strong and clear understanding and confidence, such that whatever we have learned becomes second nature. It might come about through a well-led teaching session, but it will need additional application as well as constant reinforcement and familiarity. This occurs in snippets over time. It has to be part of the teacher's routine practice and must be allowed for in scoping-out plans.

If the drip, drip, drip of teaching is one vital approach, another way of addressing the content that needs to be taught is to create a module

---

2   In the 1990s, Shirley Clarke invented two characters, Walt (we are learning to) and Wilf (what I'm looking for), as a way of personalising learning objectives. Years later, she announced that it was time they left the scene – but they just won't go.

and teach it in a block. We might elect to teach about electricity over four consecutive Thursday afternoons or perhaps spend a whole day on the Caribbean. Typically, although not exclusively, the things we teach in blocks are those things we need to learn *about:* twelve afternoons on the Tudors (spread over a term) or eight lessons on explorers. The challenge is to take what is learned and refer to it, use it and apply it.

Other examples of blocked learning are 'specials', like Eco Week or World Book Day, where time is set aside in a block for a specific purpose. Nevertheless, the learning will only have lasting impact if it is used later and often. One day a year spent delighting in literature will capture few habitual readers. One week of environmentalism will not lead to global sustainability in a year of waste.

It is the timetable that inhibits the teacher who wants to block learning in any other form than one-hour weekly dollops. Timetables reassure leadership teams that content is managerially secure and can be quantified for inspection. They also reassure those who worry that learning will go off the boil if it is not turned up on a routine basis. If children spend four afternoons (or even mornings) in a row learning a block of science, what might happen to history? It might rot or calcify. Meanwhile, geography might get lost or eroded, never to be rediscovered.

If some content is ideally taught in a block and some by dripping, other things are best learned in the context of other things – that is, linked. Primary teachers readily associate with this idea. Themes and topics have long been a staple in primary schooling: seeing and exploiting natural connections between the content of different subject disciplines and teaching it in tandem under a thematic heading. Typically, aspects of art and design are taught alongside history or geography, or mathematics is combined with geography or science. We might draw maps of explorers' expeditions, linking geography and history, or use exercise in PE as a way of measuring heart rate for science. Linking learning in this way is usually appropriate for content that we think the children should learn *through* another subject discipline.

This often brings relevance to learning across subject disciplines and allows content to ride on the shoulders of another subject. Too often, though, teaching is once again inhibited by a timetabled outlook on the part of teachers who have been prompted into offering learning in one-hour chunks to comply with evidence production in a range of differently coloured exercise books to help with inspection scrutiny. While longer term planning envisages themed learning overall, content within the themes is often re-blocked into one-hour sessions and re-separated into subject lessons in the seeming hope that the children themselves will make the links.

The main reason that theme and topic-based approaches to content are undermined is that when two pieces of learning are linked, neither are taught properly. If a child spends all afternoon painting a picture of a Roman soldier, but is no more proficient at painting and knows nothing new about Roman soldiers by the end of the day, we have a wounded bird and a redundant stone. Teachers must be really clear about the status of an activity for the children, so that when two subject disciplines are learned together, they know which is major and which is minor. That is, which one are we really trying to make inroads into, cover new ground, address new concepts or build new knowledge? That is the major one. The other one is being used as a vehicle. It is minor in the sense that the child can already do it and, therefore, is using this experience to practise or become more proficient. Returning to the Roman soldier, if a child is able to paint well, then that is a given and can carry the major learning, which might be encouraging them to observe closely the uniforms of Roman soldiers of various ranks (e.g. tunic, weaponry, insignia), with different children painting different ranks and discussing with a well-informed teacher the uniform features that are linked to status.

So, in looking at elements of content and how best to teach them, we can see two dimensions: learning *about*, *how to* and *through* on the vertical dimension and *drip*, *block* and *link* on the horizontal. To illustrate this, we have included some examples below (see Tables 11.1–11.4). In our work, these were dynamic talking points for staff who saw the logic and potential influence on their planning.

Using these grids will provoke conversation about that crucial link between curriculum and pedagogy. Some teachers think of the grid as a planning tool, a new method of producing long-term planning (teachers tend to love completing grids; it must be the pleasant feeling of completion). However, the purpose is intellectual rather than organisational. Getting teachers to build a mindset which begins by thinking about the best way to achieve learning is a step towards better outcomes. It moves the conversation from how to record evidence for someone else to how best to help learning stick for children.

Teachers know that one approach to teaching spelling is a list of, say, twenty words in a family of sounds to learn each week. They also know the vocabulary can be there for the test on a Friday and gone by the following Wednesday, unless we grab every opportunity to dwell on common word beginnings or endings. It is the same with word meanings. 'Word of the week' is fine but, at thirty-nine words a year, it will be a long while before we meet the 170,000 words in our language.

The switched-on teacher helps children to accumulate words as well as gather them, construct a strong vocabulary as well as build one, and seek, search and retrieve the best, most appropriate, apposite or apt word for the context or situation in which it will be used or utilised. Good teachers of word meanings are walking homonym and synonym spotters, supporting children with the etymology and morphology of the new vocabulary they come across. We spark, ignite or light children's enthusiasm for language by using it with them endlessly and showing them its versatility by using, employing, utilising, grabbing, maximising and taking opportunities to do so.

This doesn't mean that we don't teach aspects of vocabulary, spelling or punctuation in a formal way, but it does raise the question of whether formal teaching is the best approach when it continues for an hour at a time. Alex Quigley's work on vocabulary became one of those waves passing through just a few years ago; his book is full of examples of ways in which we can close the vocabulary gap.[3] Yet, many teachers were unable to keep the momentum going because of their inhibiting slavery to the four starts a day of the timetable. We needed to help our teachers build the confidence not to reach for the easy lists of twenty words per week, but to consider why vocabulary matters in the first place and to make it work for our children.

Sorting out content: English			
	Drip	Block	Link
How to	Spell	Make a book	Write up an experiment
About	Meanings of words	Author techniques	Recipes/ instructions
Through	Speech marks	Historical novels	Newspapers/ICT

Table 11.1. English

Helping children to understand the techniques of different authors might be taught discretely in a block (see Table 11.1). Over several set lessons, the teacher could introduce the concept of novelists' techniques with a focus on, say, a Dickens novel. Examples might be Dickens' use of intense description and setting to place the reader

---

3   Quigley, *Closing the Vocabulary Gap*. Routledge, p. 136.

as the equivalent of an audience at a play, or the way he takes the reader inside the mind of individuals to 'explain' the plot or events. Of course, most of Dickens' novels are episodic, having been written as accumulated weekly publications in the style of today's soap operas. If a Year 6 class studied *David Copperfield* in this way, the children could be given six other novels to read with a further four sessions in the next half-term devoted to five groups of children exploring the techniques in the context of their own novel and sharing the findings between groups. In this way, the children read in depth, which in the next term can transfer into a study of other authors, with different children studying different texts and novelists: Stevenson, Carroll,

YEAR 4			
Our Blue Planet	Civilisations	Flora and Fauna	Natural Phenomena
Ocean Meets Sky by The Fan Brothers	The Wizards of Once by Cressida Cowell	The Lost Words by Robert Macfarlane (Picture book)	The Miraculous Journey of Edward Tulane by Kate DiCamillo
This Morning I Met a Whale by Michael Morpurgo	Tales from the Inner City by Shaun Tan	Tom's Midnight Garden by Philippa Pearce	The Abominables by Eva Ibbotson (Picture book)
Brightstorm by Vashti Hardy	Escape from Pompeii by Christina Balit	Krindlekrax by Philip Ridley	The Brockenspectre by Linda Newbery
The Storm Keeper's Island by Catherine Doyle	Jeremy Button by Alix Barzelay	The Great Kapok Tree by Lynne Cherry	Ice Palace by Robert Swindells (Picture book)
Town is by the Sea by Joanne Schwartz	The Story of Tutankhamun by Patricia Cleveland-Peck	Fly, Eagle, Fly! by Christopher Gregorowski (Picture book)	Escape from Pompeii by Christina Balit
Where the Forest Meets the Sea by Jeannie Baker	Diary of An Edo Princess by Fidelia Nimmons	The Little Gardener by Emily Hughes	Flood by Alvaro F. Villa
My Wounded Island by Jacques Pasquet	The Thieves of Ostia by Caroline Lawrence	The Chocolate Tree by Richard Keep and Linda Lowry	Hurricane by David Wiesner
The Proudest Blue by Ibtihaj Muhammad and S. K. A Ali	My Story: Roman Invasion by Jim Eldridge	Jemmy Button by Alix Barzelay	Each Kindness by Jaqueline Woodson
Circle by Jeannie Baker	Beowolf by Rob Lloyd Jones	Kaya's Heart Song by Diwa Tharan Sanders	
Island by Mark Janssen	Revolt Against the Romans by Tony Bradman	The Secret Sky Garden by Linda Sarah	
	Mystery of the Egyptian Scroll by Scott Peters	The Land of Neverbelieve by Norman Messenger	
	Rain Player by David Wisniewski	The Wonder Garden by Jenny Broom	
	Secrets of a Sun King by Emma Caroll		
	The 1000 Year Old Boy by Ross Welford		

Wilson, Raúf, Walliams, Pearce, Zephaniah, Rowling, Dahl, Blackman, Nesbit, Alcott and others. In this block of learning spread over the course of a year, a class would know about many authors, develop an awareness of the techniques of several and each child would have a working understanding of a few – as well as a growing appreciation of literature.

If we wanted the children to learn about recipes, it would make sense to teach that linked to practical work in cooking; learning about writing up experiments would be best linked to doing experiments; and learning about newspapers would link with many points in history.

Table 11.2 on art and design similarly explores the *drip*, *block*, *link* arrangement of aspects of *about*, *how to* and *through*. Again, the purpose is to get staff thinking about the appropriate organisation of their approach rather than planning the timetable. If children are going to truly understand colour mixing, then a lesson on primary, secondary and tertiary colours, along with the colour wheel, will help with the concept. To become good at mixing and using colour, they will need exercise and practise over time. Photography can be linked to many elements of learning in history, geography, mathematics and so on, to be followed, perhaps, by a short block on the history of photography and the *how to* of some techniques.

p. 212

Sorting out content: **Art and design**			
	Drip	**Block**	**Link**
How to	Draw and paint	Sculpt	Photography
About	Colour mixing	Art movements	Art Deco
Through	L. S. Lowry	Protest art	Newspapers/ICT

Table 11.2. Art and design

In mathematics (see Table 11.3), the pattern continues with facility with money or telling and manipulating time, growing as the children get used to it on a drip, drip, drip basis to supplement the lesson guided by the teacher. Counting actual money (or even plastic) will lead to competence and confidence much more quickly and securely than colouring in printed sheets of coins for evidence of having done so in a one-hour lesson.

Learning about data is supported by the astute teacher consistently referring to examples of graphs, charts and tables in a range of media to show how data is accumulated and displayed. In all subjects, the drip of learning is about seizing the moment to make explicit some of the KLIs that are being addressed in a structured, blocked or linked way.

How to use a protractor and a pair of compasses (once the initial instruction is complete) is best linked with real situations in DT or art and design to apply the learning in authentic situations. Ratio and proportion come alive when linked to science, geography or art, where they become a vehicle for the exposition of data.

Sorting out content: Mathematics			
	Drip	Block	Link
How to	Count money	Use pairs of compasses	Use a protractor and compass
About	Data	Geometric shapes	Ratio and proportion
Through	Graphs	Timelines	Mass, volume and capacity

Table 11.3. Mathematics

In history (Table 11.4), the novels of Dickens might cast light on Victorian life or *Goodnight Mister Tom* provide insights into the Second World War. The proficient teacher reads the novel over a couple of weeks and, in doing so, dwells on the historical aspects as appropriate, teaching them through the vehicle of the novel. If we want to educate children on how to investigate a historical site it is best done in context, so a visit to a cathedral, synagogue, mosque or temple as part of an RE theme is the linked opportunity. Similarly, teaching the geography of former empires – whether Roman, Greek or British – teaches history through a link with geography. Learning how to use artefacts, a fundamental of historical learning, is best done on a drip basis as children's understanding of events over time will grow best through continuous attention. A lesson where the children play a game of putting events in order with arrows on a printed sheet will be enjoyable, but the learning won't necessarily last. Understanding about time grows gradually, building through references to timelines that drip into their consciousness.

Sorting out content: History			
	Drip	**Block**	**Link**
How to	Use artefacts	Research from documents, records and objects	Investigate a site such as a cathedral (within RE)
About	Timelines as records of development	Period of history	Famous inventors (within science)
Through	Dates and events	Novels	Former empires (within geography)

Table 11.4. History

> The focus on dripping, blocking and linking teaching of knowledge of skills opened up all sorts of conversations. I knew it was working when children were saying things like 'I know this because when we learned about Romans in Year 3, we …' and linking it to the Year 5 themed work.
>
> *Sharon Clark*

Understanding and recognising the way these elements of content can be utilised to help the children – whether dripped, blocked or linked – is fundamental to the planning process. It was an important turning point for our teachers, and also for school leadership, in

doing what is sadly often called 'giving permission' to rethink aspects of pedagogy and particularly planning.

All of this was challenging – and still is; mastery is tough for teachers too. For our teachers, the change to their use of time was tough initially, but now we see them thinking carefully about how long the children need to be working on tasks and what time span is appropriate for developing skills or knowledge as a matter of routine. Most have mastered it, but it was difficult at first for them to break away from the metronome of routine for fear of getting it wrong: worries about what outsiders would say, worries about questions from parents who had become used to old routines, worries about whether it would work (not that the previous model did!). For some, ingrained practice was hard to shift. New teachers in our schools are unsettled when they are asked to consider their use of time, and often need support from head teachers and coordinators to take important steps in their own practice.

Some of these practices, when discussed openly, cause the scales to fall from teachers' eyes and they adapt quickly. We no longer see perfunctory or futile learning objectives, and we have worked hard to encourage teachers to better appreciate the purpose of learning.

> Why would you teach electricity on a worksheet instead of with circuits and containers?
>
> *Will Ferris*

To begin to address the effective use of learning time within pedagogy, we agreed to:

- Encourage teachers to think and be discerning rather than impose artificial time expectations.

- Hold conversations in classrooms about appropriate time use.

- Demonstrate the impact of practice on accuracy or speed by working in short periods over time.

- Discourage seeing drip, block and link as a new planning pro forma.

- Keep teachers talking about teaching and learning over time, as opposed to one-hour spasms.

In trying to help teachers think through curriculum content and the best way for it to meet the needs of the children, it might be worth thinking about:

- Using thinking about the notions of learning *about*, *how to* and *through*, along with *drip*, *block* and *link*, as a way of making sense of the content demand.
- The trick, though, is to avoid teachers making it into a clerical activity. They are attracted to this way of working, but they need to turn their thinking into action.
- Encouraging teachers to think differently about the way they use their time and breaking the metronomic approach that many have developed.
- How leadership will think about issues of timetabling which can constrain teaching terribly.

As well as returning to planning, our next ladder would need to take us up a level in our consideration of pedagogy. This was another ladder that could take us forwards, and unless we addressed it properly, it would be a snake that would take us backwards.

Again, first with head teachers and then with all the staff, we talked about the issues along with endless examples. Staff need to see the bigger picture, to consider what role they have become used to playing within the learning agenda and to ask whether this is as effective as they would wish. What follows is an explanation of the issues we presented to our various groups as food for thought. We offer it to you here in the same spirit.

CHAPTER 12

Looking closely at pedagogy

How it enables curriculum success

Teachers clearly understand that curriculum and pedagogy are entwined. However, in recent times, events have conspired to constrain teachers' thinking as they look over their shoulders at the ever-present accountability system. Like travellers in the Middle Ages wary of highwaymen, rumours about the threat of inspection inhibit the likelihood of teachers going off course or down rabbit holes as they mimic what they have heard the inspectors are seeking. Given the ongoing narrative of a knowledge-focused curriculum and the impression that inspectors wish to see 'standard' lessons, there is little wonder that curriculum and pedagogy have found themselves in a straitjacket.

For over twenty years, teachers have become used to 'performing'. The introduction of performance management around the turn of the century linked performance to pay. As Ofsted focused on teacher effectiveness and school self-evaluation (the self-evaluation form, or SEF), leaders were increasingly encouraged to observe teachers.[1] As this observation process developed, so regression to the mean led to

---

1   Ofsted, Education Inspection Framework (14 May 2019; updated 23 July 2021). Available at: https://www.gov.uk/government/publications/education-inspection-framework/education-inspection-framework.

a standard, almost formulaic approach to lessons on the part of the teacher, which would tick all the boxes.

In our schools, most teachers recognised the formulaic nature of their lessons, which affected their planning and the very nature of their working lives. Since they are so often observed, the teacher almost becomes the performer on the stage. The lesson begins as the curtain goes up and the teacher enters with an attention-grabber – the equivalent of executing a flicflac or dressing in a tutu. Having gained their attention, a starter follows to settle the children into the lesson after breaktime or their arrival from another lesson elsewhere, such as the hall. Next comes the learning objective, the WALT or the WOLF,[2] where children write down what they are expected to learn in the lesson, regardless of whether they can understand it, read it or whether it will be referenced again. The aim is to link the objective with the main point of the lesson, which has become the gathering of 'evidence' to match the objective by the end of the lesson in order to show impact. If children often write down their WALT without knowing what it means, it is much the same for some teachers.[3]

The next phase of the lesson drives towards the part that will occur about ten minutes or so later, when children will have to write or complete a pro forma printed sheet to generate evidence of learning in the lesson. Following the learning objective, the teacher will lead a short instruction or explanation (mostly using the whiteboard) around a concept or principle, perhaps exploring knowledge. Usually, this is a veiled attempt at showing the children what they will have to do for the evidence production. Next comes a class effort at some examples, so the children grasp the idea prior to doing it themselves

---

2   'What Ofsted's looking for'. It is a joke, but one of the reasons many teachers write objectives is that they believe it will keep Ofsted happy. It won't, but good teaching will.

3   It might seem that we are mentioning WALT a lot. Many children meet WALT at least 500 times a year for six years and still don't know what it means.

and producing the evidence. Sometimes the teacher will organise an activity with apparatus or equipment to reinforce concepts through concrete activity, but this is rare as there is enormous pressure on teachers to leave sufficient time to generate evidence.

After allocating some time for evidence production, the teacher might organise a plenary. These were common a few years ago when Ofsted inspectors commented on them, but nowadays they don't appear to be expected, so are often omitted if the evidence gathering requires more time.

With all the boxes ticked, all that remains is for the teacher to bring the lesson to a close as the curtain falls, preferably with something memorable to set the scene for next time. There is then the chance of a short break, maybe with a cup of tea, before the whole process begins again.

Okay, while tongue is in cheek, it is not that far in cheek. We recognise that the formulaic, one-hour lesson does have its merits when done well. It is the relentlessness and perfunctoriness of its use that means so many things are poorly taught in the pursuit of the few things that are well taught.

The standard lesson has its roots in the national strategies of twenty years ago, with their literacy and numeracy hours.[4] This was the first time that central government had intervened in pedagogy and the programmes had significant impact. The idea was that a model one-hour lesson would form the backbone of the teaching of concepts in numeracy and English. Teachers were encouraged to use a range of approaches during the hour, as opposed to the single dimension that many lessons had traditionally.

The hour was divided into the segments as indicated in the first dial in Figure 12.1. Teachers of a certain vintage may smile at

---

4   Department for Education, *The National Strategies 1997–2011*.

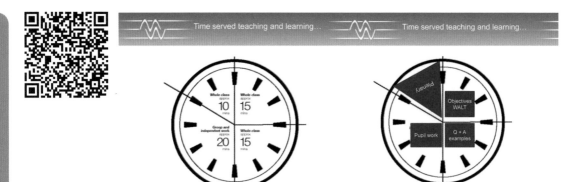

Figure 12.1. Time served teaching and learning from the national strategies to 2022

the memory of needing to stick to the schedule (some even set kitchen timers to tell them when to move on!). Our current standard lessons have carried this model forward, as indicated in the second dial.

However, there is one important distinction today. The segment allocated to group work – using apparatus and equipment to exemplify the concept – has largely disappeared for all sorts of reasons, the main one being the need to allocate enough time to gather written evidence.

There is another issue at play too. Teachers have an uncanny ability to suck new pedagogic developments into an old story. For example, when interactive whiteboards were first introduced, classrooms came alive with teachers and children using the boards interactively. Children would add to or amend diagrams on screen and teachers would make adjustments based on children's responses and suggestions. Now, even though the technology has moved on and been replaced by touchscreens, in many classrooms the whiteboard is just that; it is not interactive. In many cases, it is a dust-free, electronic version of the blackboard that preceded it.

This phenomenon also makes other developments hard to embed. For example, our pattern of gaining agreement from head teachers and then working with curriculum and teaching and learning leads was fine in theory, but the ease with which good intentions can slip between cup and lip was still apparent. Nobody would deliberately scupper or stunt a new development, but achieving progress requires more than optimism and a couple of meetings. Hence, the conferences and other approaches we reference elsewhere in this book. What was important for teachers was the notion of working together to move practice forward, and for that, the support of the curriculum leads and head teachers needed to be tangible and consolidated.

This is complicated yet simple stuff. Getting away from an over-reliance on formulaic, staccato lessons meant providing alternatives and then ensuring they were allowed to work in schools, with an expectation of tentative beginnings. Firstly, there is the issue of big-picture planning for pedagogy – that is, the macro pedagogy that is decided for teachers. Secondly, there is the micro pedagogy – the fine detail of teachers' pedagogy and what goes on between teacher and children. Figure 12.2 proved p. 36 useful in explaining the issues around pedagogy. It is not that the standard one-hour lesson is wrong; it is simply that it implies a one-size-fits-all approach, regardless of what is being taught, and that is wrong.

> Teaching that uses the curriculum/pedagogy axis has put teaching and learning quality at the heart of our work.
>
> *Will Ferris*

The figure outlines some of the range of techniques that teachers need to use in order to enable learning, looking at pedagogy in

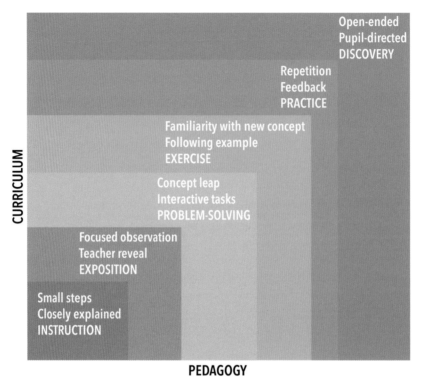

Figure 12.2. Curriculum and pedagogy

tandem with curriculum. These are the techniques that form part of lessons where teachers ask themselves, 'How can I get this to stick?'[5]

Let's look at the techniques in Figure 12.2 more closely.

If we want children to take a small step in being able to do something, they need careful and close *instruction*. Examples would be the use of tools in DT and the skills of sketching or creating

---

5   In the last three years, there has been much reference to Fiorella and Mayer's work on what they call generative learning (*Learning as a Generative Activity*) and Sweller's work on cognitive load (J. Sweller, Cognitive Load During Problem Solving: Effects on Learning, *Cognitive Science*, 12(2) (1988), 257–285. doi:10.1207/s15516709cog1202_4). This chapter illustrates both of these concepts in practical terms.

perspective in art, as well as the myriad of cross-curricular skills that children need to generate good learning products. (Note: Instruction is a specific pedagogical approach. However, there is some confusion because the term *instruction* has also been 'borrowed' from the United States where it is used as a generic term for teaching).

Exposition is the tool to use to encourage children to observe carefully and pay attention as the teacher gradually reveals information. This is the essence of many PowerPoint presentations. It is also used in processes such as studying an artefact, when features are revealed one at a time.

If we want children to engage with *problem-solving*, which involves making a concept leap, interactive tasks (if carefully employed) can prompt them to ask questions of the teacher and other children, encouraging them to explore possibilities deeply. Asking questions of the teacher is important. In most instructional theories, the teacher asks the children questions, which is pertinent in many contexts (indeed, it is regularly commented on in teaching observations). However, teacher questions might sometimes have consequences we do not seek – for example, incorrect answers being heard by everyone – and remembered by some.

Too often, questions are used as a means of keeping the lesson flowing, avoiding the teacher talking too much (another point that observers frequently note) or keeping the children involved. Sprayed around for these reasons, though, questions can elicit answers that are wrong and, worse, broadcast misconceptions to the rest of the class. A few of these in a row and the problem being solved has become even more complicated. Are classrooms the only place in society where the person who knows the answers asks questions of those who do not? Often, especially when grasping a new concept, the children asking the teacher questions leads to more coherent and clear comprehension on their part. 'Why do you say …?' 'How does that work?' 'I don't understand the bit about … please can you explain again?' might reasonably be asked by the children as a way of making a breakthrough in their understanding.

When a concept has been grasped, becoming more familiar with it through further examples in different contexts builds confidence and embeds it, helping it to become understood fully. This is *exercise*. Exercise is where the learner comes to terms with a new process or concept. If they can read a four-digit map reference, getting used to a six-digit grid reference can help them to understand the principle with greater accuracy and then become proficient. The same applies to threading a needle, playing notes on a glockenspiel or drawing with charcoal.

Once acquired, all these processes need to be honed: this is *practice*. Familiarity with concepts and processes makes practice possible, with the aim of increasing speed or accuracy through repetition. The teacher's role is to provide feedback to enable improved performance. Examples would be coaching a child in instrumental practice in music, where playing a piece of music might elicit feedback about the need for more pressure on the keys or more controlled breathing in the search for accuracy. Alternatively, the practice of forty calculations might be achieved correctly in one minute today; reaching the same goal in forty seconds would be a valid reason for practice tomorrow.

Sometimes, the teacher might set children an open-ended challenge with clear criteria for success, allocating time and resources and setting limitations. After that, it is up to the children to make decisions and present their efforts to compare with others. In doing so, if well managed and supported, they engage in *discovery*. Often, the teacher can make such activities competitive – for example, in a 'great model boat race' or 'paper aeroplane competition', where planes are judged on time in the air, accuracy, quality of landing or distance travelled, as well as style and decoration. Of course, the level of discovery links to and depends on the children's prior knowledge. A paper aeroplane activity will be more fulfilling if the children understand some principles of aerodynamics, as well as possess paper-folding or measuring skills. Otherwise, it risks being just messing about and throwing paper around, with the occasional good effort accompanied by cheers. This is why younger children's learning needs to include elements that encourage them to be self-sustaining as learners, able to organise themselves, manage equipment and work in teams. These qualities need to be taught and practised as prerequisites.

 p. 245

This list of approaches to pedagogy is by no means exhaustive – there is no mention of role play, simulation or rote learning, for example – but it does start to paint the picture of a repertoire of pedagogy with appropriate aspects woven into practice for the right purpose. The problem was that this repertoire was being underexploited in our schools. Because of the standardised, formulaic 'performed' lesson, the techniques were often not considered and lessons were becoming PowerPoint driven.

If this was the detail of the sort of micro pedagogy we wanted our teachers to become proficient in, we also needed to encourage them to see teaching as more than a 'one lesson at a time' experience.

We agreed to:

- Provide illustrations of different aspects of the pedagogic repertoire at our conferences and within INSET sessions.

- Encourage planning of specific approaches to teaching within our scoping of learning experiences over time.

- Positively reinforce teachers who were extending their pedagogic repertoire.

- Encourage subject discipline coordinators to support the extension of pedagogic approaches.

- Discourage formulaic lessons as a habit while recognising they have a value in certain contexts.

> In order to widen the pedagogic repertoire of teachers, it might be worth considering:
>
> - A careful analysis of the right approach for the learning envisaged as part of staff discussion over time.

- Spending time considering the issues raised in the discussion of Figure 12.2.
- Challenging the effectiveness of the formulaic lesson within all learning contexts.
- Setting up different working groups to explore and master different aspects of the pedagogic repertoire.

A narrative for teaching and learning

 p. 63

One of the issues that was evident in our initial observations and considerations was that of hand-to-mouth teaching. We were trying to address the issue of teachers conducting one-off lessons as fragments of learning rather than seeing a theme as a coherent exploration of big ideas over several weeks. Teachers described themselves as being on a treadmill of 'plan and deliver' – and the treadmill was going quicker and quicker, leading to the tendency of thinking of things to teach rather than planning for what we wanted the children to learn. With the treadmill came the temptation to resort to downloaded lessons and printed sheets, with an early start at the photocopier getting us through the next day.

We began to encourage teachers to look beyond tomorrow, this week or even next week, and to imagine the learning experience of their theme over time. We urged them to see it as a story that would unfold in front of the children. If they could envisage, say, six weeks of learning, they could plan the general pedagogic direction and add in the detail later. We wanted teachers to feel in charge rather than administrating learning through a planning compliance approach.

We began to talk about these as 'narratives': the unfolding of a theme over time as a coherent learning experience for the children rather than a series of learning tablets to swallow every hour. Constructing a narrative means building a mental image of the way a theme will evolve in the classroom: visualising how it will work to achieve the teaching ambitions we have set ourselves and imagining ways in which the teacher will organise drips, blocks and links to make it work.

> I remember when Mick riffed freestyle and modelled how he would plan a narrative for an insects theme. It opened our eyes to how a theme should evolve.
>
> *Ian Oake*

> Our children have the same curriculum entitlement, regardless of which setting they are in, and are enthusiastic about a holistic approach which develops them as a whole person.
>
> *Parent*

If we seek children who engage with disciplines as researchers, makers, performers, activists, inventors and scholars, how will we manage the time to provide opportunities for them to take on these roles and address them seriously? These are the roles that real historians, geographers, scientists, artists, linguists and mathematicians adopt through the exercise of their discipline.

From here it is a case of thinking about logistics, first in outline and then in more detail. What is going to be the essence of our theme? Is it finding out, organising, explaining and sharing what has been learned, so we accumulate and assimilate lots of knowledge? Is it going to be understanding some big ideas through the observation of phenomena over time? Is it going to be a starting point with lots of investigations radiating out from it? Is it all of these and more? If so, how are we going to fit them together? This is an important question. It is different from saying: 'We have got six weeks of two half-days per week, so that will be twenty-four lessons. Let's look for twenty-four things to teach!' It starts from the question, what do we want the children to learn? Start big and then drop down into the detail.

We must include the KLIs in our planning – everything from the big ideas to knowledge, skills and experiences – with a clarity about what all the children need to do and what some will do to achieve those intentions. That is, differentiation. This is when we will think about the novels or poetry we will use, the visits to support the theme, the visitors who might come into school to inject a different perspective, the great works of art – a bank of content from which we can make our withdrawals. All these resources or learning opportunities support our learning agenda; our challenge is to make it work effectively.

 p. 50

Much of this is about logistics. We could study ten works of art or carry out six different experiments in the time available. Our classroom turns from a series of productions with the teacher on the stage to a machine generating learning, with everyone in the room playing their part. This is how Robert Fisher sees the classroom – a 'community of enquiry' which stimulates thinking and deals with big ideas,[6] and what Marcelo Staricoff explores as lifelong learning dispositions, with seven dispositions that can be extended through experience and practice.[7]

So, if we want the children to be researchers, makers, presenters and organisers, who will start doing what and when? What sorts of culminations will there be – presentations, mini-exhibitions, low-stakes quizzes,[8] assemblies? How do we sequence these through the course of the theme?

---

6   R. Fisher, *Teaching Thinking*, 2nd edn (London and New York: Bloomsbury Academic, 2003).

7   M. Staricoff, *The Joy of Not Knowing: A Philosophy of Education Transforming Teaching, Thinking, Learning and Leadership in Schools* (Abingdon and New York: Routledge, 2021).

8   See Fiorella and Mayer, *Learning as a Generative Activity*, p. 97. See also B. Rosenshine, Principles of Instruction: Research-Based Strategies That All Teachers Should Know, *American Educator* (Spring 2012), 12–19, 39. Available at: https://www.aft.org/sites/default/files/periodicals/Rosenshine.pdf.

What emerges is the role of the teacher as the orchestrator of the classroom, the person who oils the machine of learning and makes sure that individual children get their moment in the limelight of presentation, that different groups get access to resources at the right time, that an experiment is seen close up by everyone and that they all have a role as an experimenter.

> We have been able to see the systematic and progressive approach to each subject in the key learning intentions and detailed planning by subject leaders.
>
> *Kate Sheldon*

A narrative is not another piece of planning for submission. It is the teacher's working image of their classroom activity – who will do what and when, how to synchronise activity to bring pots to the boil at the right time.

Teachers taking stock and buying into the enjoyment – we were on a ladder

Teachers were 'getting it' and warming to their task. They were intrigued, they appreciated the arguments being made and they were willing to try different approaches. The main problem was the old one: time. How could teachers fit all this new thinking into their day-to-day reality when they were already working flat out? Of course, the answer was an old one too: they would have to stop some of their current practices and substitute the improved ones.

As ever in teaching, people worried about getting things wrong and needed constant reinforcement to take the important steps. We found that an effective way of encouraging teachers was to talk about the children's outlook on learning and what mattered in terms of learner agency. Most people subscribed to the images of the sorts of learners we wanted to see, so by working with curriculum leads and head teachers, it was fairly simple to reach agreement on eight pedagogical principles that would set the children well in terms of their futures. Teachers were also excited about considering the sorts of experiences all children should have in the breadth of our curriculum offer. They could see the value of learning approaches in the activities to which all the teachers were committed to some degree. However, securing them represented a challenge.

◀ p. 27

This had the effect of illustrating the mass of activities in which schools engage and which tend to get taken for granted. It also achieved another shift that we needed to make. If we believe children become more entrepreneurial through this experience, or more adventurous through that experience, or more scholarly through another experience, how much stronger would their learning be if we could infuse classroom-based learning into the process with this set of experiences and incorporate these types of experiences into themes? We were trying to avoid teachers seeing this aspect of their work as supplementary or as an extra curriculum; we had already agreed that the curriculum was the entire planned learning experience.

> We wanted to do more for our children. We wanted to develop their interests. We wanted to give them opportunities to grow. We wanted to give them the foundations to be lifelong learners.
> **Sarah Williams**

We came up with idea of calling these aspects of learning 'our pledge' to the children. We produced this, like everything else, in a high-quality way to show how much it mattered. Producing the pledge on a postcard to send home was another good idea (see

Figure 12.3), which both excited families about the learning offer and committed teachers to an outlook and practice.

Teachers were also asked to contribute to a list of the sorts of experiences children might have beyond school as part of a rich childhood, which they loved doing. It offers a sort of escapism, giving them the chance to relive happy memories as well as simply enjoying the promise of childhood in a perfect world. Many schools produce something similar – they are sometimes called 'learning passports', 'cultural journeys' or 'magic moments'. The purpose is to try to engage families in developing their own children's experiences, widening their horizons and providing connections with the real world that will open their eyes and build vocabulary. The accumulation of what has become known as 'cultural capital' is vital for many schools, including ours, where a significant proportion of children have not had the same experiences as those fortunate enough to have families with the means to take them on visits and expose them to cultural knowledge and experiences.[9] We called our version 'Curious Curriculum Unleashed'. There was a subtle message in this about the benefits of bringing learning alive, especially when teachers saw most parents' delight in the suggested activities.

We had talked with teachers about some aspects of the curriculum being *taught*, some *caught* and some *cultivated*. Our unleashed curriculum would have to be caught by the children, and we wanted them to cultivate the skills necessary to be leaders, activists or performers. We would cultivate these opportunities by providing contexts where they would be taught how to develop the skills to become proficient.

---

9   A. Reid, Cultural Capital, Critical Theory and Curriculum. In C. Sealy and T. Bennett (eds), *The researchED Guide to the Curriculum: An Evidence-Informed Guide for Teachers* (Woodbridge: John Catt Educational, 2020), pp. 41–48.

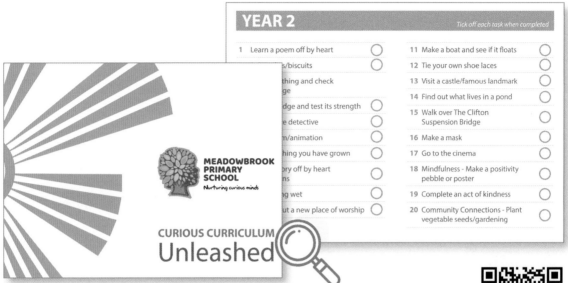

YEAR 2			*Tick off each task when completed*	
1	Learn a poem off by heart	○	11 Make a boat and see if it floats	○
	s/biscuits	○	12 Tie your own shoe laces	○
	thing and check		13 Visit a castle/famous landmark	○
	ge		14 Find out what lives in a pond	○
	dge and test its strength	○	15 Walk over The Clifton Suspension Bridge	○
	e detective	○	16 Make a mask	○
	m/animation	○	17 Go to the cinema	○
	hing you have grown	○	18 Mindfulness - Make a positivity pebble or poster	○
	ry off by heart ns	○	19 Complete an act of kindness	○
	ng wet	○	20 Community Connections - Plant vegetable seeds/gardening	○
	ut a new place of worship	○		

Figure 12.3. Example of Curious Curriculum Unleashed postcard

As our curriculum and pedagogic approach became more developed, they also became more complex, so we wanted to avoid the problem of the curriculum buffet. In our regular workshops with coordinators, in our less frequent but vital conferences with teachers and in all the meetings between teacher groups, we had to keep the conversation going and keep it focused on our pedagogic principles. We needed to keep explaining, keep revisiting and keep finding other ways of helping teachers to exploit the curriculum through effective pedagogy. However, we were still struggling to get most teachers to see their weekly timetable in anything but one-hour chunks. We weren't necessarily meeting snakes but we definitely needed ladders.

◀ p. 152

What follows in the next chapter is a summary of how we tried to get teachers to see themes in a longitudinal way as opposed to in hourly chunks. You could use it within the context of your own school to encourage teachers to consider the unfolding picture of learning.

CHAPTER 13

Moving on from planning[1]

Navigating new learning horizons with children at the helm

Teachers, like early explorers navigating the vast seas of curriculum, pedagogy and assessment, are guided by different stars that rise at different times. The government changes curriculum expectations or inspection focuses on a new dimension, and so our course changes. The move towards a 'knowledge-driven' curriculum, as promoted by Michael Gove, has led to pedagogy being dominated by formulaic approaches, particularly with respect to the way teachers *deliver* content.

Many schools have turned to the structures, methods and approaches espoused by researchers such as Barak Rosenshine, which have their roots in cognitive psychology.[2] There has been an emphasis on quizzing (as opposed to testing), which builds on the work of Henry Roediger and Andrew Butler,[3] which in turn emerges from

---

1   This chapter has been adapted from M. Waters, Navigating New Learning Horizons: With Children at the Helm, *APSE Bulletin*, Issue 22 (February 2021): 1–4. Available at: https://www.aspe-uk.eu/wp-content/uploads/2021/03/ASPE22_Feb_2021.pdf.

2   B. Rosenshine, Teaching Functions in Instructional Programs, *Elementary School Journal*, 83(4) (1983), 335–351.

3   H. L. Roediger III and A. C. Butler, The Critical Role of Retrieval Practice in Long-Term Retention, *Trends in Cognitive Sciences*, 15(1) (2011), 20–27.

Ebbinghaus' work on the forgetting curve.[4] More recently, as Ofsted has begun to focus on curriculum breadth and depth,[5] schools have been reviewing their intent.

While the techniques that grow from those mentioned above have validity for some aspects of the curriculum, others need a wider pedagogic base. In their study of educationalist Lawrence Stenhouse, John Elliott and Nigel Norris consider the quality of exchange in the classroom in terms of placing knowledge in a context and applying it to a wider construct.[6] John Hattie has always emphasised the importance of coherence in his analysis of effect.[7] It is the capacity to steer the path of learning to make the best use of all approaches to teaching in the context of learning intentions that is needed at the moment: a touch on the tiller.

Figure 13.1 might be useful in this regard. What teachers want and need to achieve is deep and purposeful learning where children get to grips with big ideas and big questions. At least, that is what we find most schools have produced in terms of their intent to satisfy a deep-diving inspector. At the same time, we know that the content emphasis in the national curriculum is on knowledge and facts. These ambitions are not mutually exclusive. What good teachers do is help children to make sense of the knowledge they acquire and to explore deep understandings rather than dwell on surface knowledge, which is usually insecure.

---

4   H. Ebbinghaus, *Memory: A Contribution to Experimental Psychology*, tr. H. A. Ruger and C. E. Bussenius (New York: Teachers College, Columbia University, 1913).

5   Ofsted, Education Inspection Framework (14 May 2019; updated 23 July 2021). Available at: https://www.gov.uk/government/publications/education-inspection-framework/education-inspection-framework.

6   J. Elliott and N. Norris (eds), *Curriculum, Pedagogy and Educational Research: The Work of Lawrence Stenhouse* (Abingdon and New York: Routledge, 2012).

7   J. Hattie, *Visible Learning: A Synthesis of Over 800 Meta-Analyses Relating to Achievement* (Abingdon and New York: Routledge, 2009).

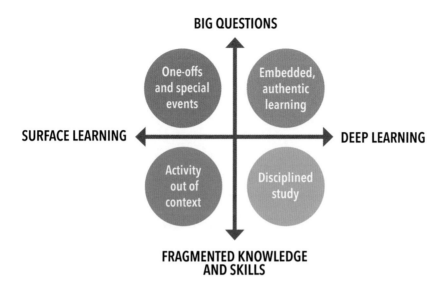

Figure 13.1. Implications of pedagogic intention

Figure 13.1 draws out children's learning experiences when it takes place consistently in a particular quadrant. Of course, the quadrants are not necessarily equal: we can move the horizontal and vertical axes to change the balance. In our work, we aimed to explore the upper-right quadrant – which is also, surely, the ambition of all schools and teachers as well as politicians.

In the lower-left quadrant, the learning experience is at the end of the continuum of 'putting the curriculum into the child'. The teacher delivers the learning with high levels of pupil compliance, which might be managed perfectly enjoyably through correctness and rewarded effort. Children and their families believe they are making progress because they receive high marks or stickers, proceed through obvious incremental levels or win positive regard from their teacher.

The upper-left quadrant sees surface learning being used to address big ideas through special events, often as a supplement to or break from the quadrant below. The rhythm of the exercise-driven approach of the lower-left quadrant is balanced by fleeting opportunities to engage with events such as an Eco Week, educational visit or artist in residence. The teacher now becomes an 'arranger': the children have memorable days to supplement their 'proper' work. These are comfortable experiences. While the experience is often worthy, too often it only fleetingly punctures the surface. Dressing up for World Book Day emphasises the joy to be gained from literature, but it is the spoonful of sugar that helps children swallow the medicine of reading schemes and phonics during the rest of the year. Learning to be a reader is about more than that.

The lower-right quadrant takes the child deeper: the teacher uses their expert knowledge of the subject discipline to provide intellectual challenge in a structured way, utilising the precise pedagogic techniques described by Rosenshine and others.[8] What develops in children, sometimes quite early on, is the concept of being good (or not) at history, geography, art, science or mathematics, based on their ability to grasp the content, especially abstract concepts. We know they are in the foothills of a subject discipline, but they believe they are on the lower rungs of a very long ladder of accomplishment. They are either climbing or stuck.

The upper-right quadrant is the one that brings us closest to immersing the child in the curriculum. It is here that we see children building intellectual coherence with an awareness of integrated subject disciplines because the teacher is the authoritative architect of experience. This quadrant is coming into clearer view after the discourse of the last few years: how do we make learning authentic rather than create engaging but undemanding experiences? How do we apply learning so that children develop their competence within disciplines that will help them to believe they are young historians, geographers, scientists, mathematicians or artists? How do we get children to grapple with big ideas and at the same time become more informed by delving deeply into detailed and

---

8   Rosenshine, Teaching Functions in Instructional Programs.

sometimes disputed knowledge domains and avoiding simplistic understanding? How do we help them to deal with contentious issues as maturing young people by involving them in conflicting or alternative versions of reality?

One way to address these questions is to teach children how to become researchers, scholars, performers, activists and inventors by helping them to manipulate the detail of the knowledge, facts and skills they learn and, in doing so, come to terms with complexity. This is what some educationalists refer to as promoting 'pupil agency', including Eduardo Briceño, who builds on the work of Albert Bandura and Carol Dweck.[9]

What most teachers need to do is to give one of those important touches on the tiller to shift the emphasis away from the teacher as the performer on the stage and towards the teacher as oiler of the machine of learning, which is what the classroom is. The pedagogy of instruction for 'standard' lessons, which has been honed over the last few years, becomes part of a pedagogic repertoire using the instruction element at the right moment and for the right purpose.

> The realisation that there was little point in asking a class of children to produce thirty of the same outcome dawned.
>
> *Will Ferris*

For children to exercise agency over their learning, the teacher needs to place before them the sorts of challenge that will take them further into the subject disciplines and to new levels in terms of embedded

---

9   See E. Briceño, Mindsets and Student Agency, *High Tech High Unboxed* (13 April 2013). Available at: https://hthunboxed.org/unboxed_posts/mindsets-and-student-agency. See also A. Bandura, *Social Foundations of Thought and Action: A Social Cognitive Theory* (Englewood Cliffs, NJ: Prentice Hall, 1986); and C. S. Dweck, *Mindset: The New Psychology of Success* (New York: Random House, 2006).

understandings. This requires real audiences and real purposes that enable the children to engage in authentic processes, such as making things, carrying out experiments, doing research, using artefacts or holding debates.

At the heart of this lie decisions, as the first step in planning, about what we want the children to learn, both in terms of specific concepts, knowledge and skills and also in terms of children's products and their behaviours as inventors, constructors, scholars or reporters. Once this has been decided, the teacher's task is to sequence the story of that learning into the time available: to build an organisational narrative of how learning will unfold through classroom activities.

The trick is to avoid breaking the content into one-hour performances of the standard lesson. If we want the children to develop agency as historians, for example, does a lesson on one teacher-selected explorer for six weeks with a class who produce thirty versions of the same thing help them to understand exploration? Or would pairs of children studying fifteen explorers build a wider collective and cumulative understanding?

Of course, the latter would be more effective but, typically, the limit on the availability of book resources doesn't allow for sufficient research and the children cannot all do this work at the same time without resorting to website copying as opposed to research. If we spread the paired research work over time, then the rest of the class can be the audience to a daily presentation as each pair reaches, say, day five of their study. For this to work, the teacher needs to set clear parameters and expectations for each pair, and instruct the class appropriately on, for instance, how to carry out effective research and how to present to an audience. Similarly, the children will become more adept at presenting their work through a continuing and well-managed reflection on the effectiveness of each presentation, which will exemplify the essentials of public speaking, managing questions, presenting an argument and illustrating points. Done well, this aspect of pedagogy (exposition) has the effect of lifting the outcome incrementally over time, as the children learn from the efforts of others.

At the end of four weeks, with a new pair of children starting daily on a five-day piece of research on their designated explorer, the class are familiar with fifteen different explorers and should have enough insight to build a class construct of the big ideas about exploration: venturing into unknown territory (physically or intellectually), making discoveries that add to previous thinking, and learning that some discovery is accidental and some intentional. Our organisational pedagogy will have enabled the children to flourish because of the scope of the examples provided. This is far into the top-right quadrant of Figure 13.1, as opposed to that which can be achieved through a weekly lesson about one explorer at a time, which would occur in the lower quadrants.

But, you might be asking, is the knowledge secure? This is where the skill of the teacher becomes central in drawing out key facts – perhaps by devising a weekly class quiz of five questions on each explorer, meaning a twenty-five question low-stakes quiz every week. The aim is to make it competitive, not between individuals but on a whole-class basis, with the challenge being to beat last week's class score. Watch the children collaborate and redo the same test to offer comparison, while also tackling the new week's questions. After five weeks, in a class of thirty children, the number of facts being tested will sit at 125, with a potential class total of 3,750. The children will know a lot! They will also have learned to research, memorise, speak to an audience, analyse questions and help each other.

The teacher's own mental narrative of the theme to be navigated identifies and clarifies the best way to organise people, time and other resources. A science experiment on the changing state of matter might be done best with a carefully briefed teaching assistant working on an experiment with a group of six children daily for

◀ p. 63

a week, perhaps investigating the changing state of substances when subjected to heat, dissolved in water or exposed to air over time: chocolate, jelly, ice, sand and clay. Learning about fair testing, control samples and the accurate recoding of mass, temperature or time, for example, are drawn out as the children build a results model to share with each other in an extended session for all groups led by the teacher the following week at a 'conference of scientists'.

Such examples of organisational pedagogic planning or micro pedagogy bring agency to the learner, and regard the classroom as more than a place where the teacher introduces a class lesson in each session of the day with an explanation of the objectives.[10] Such lessons are an important part of the repertoire of the good teacher, but the development of agency in children demands that other approaches are built into the planning through the use of a narrative that enables teachers and children to picture the learning unfolding.

 p. 212

We agreed to:

- Ask teachers to use narratives to build their confidence and competence in imagining the structure of a theme and the sequence of learning.

- Incorporate special events into themes so they would be embedded rather than happy days and a break from routine.

- We would keep emphasising that planning should focus on what the children need to learn rather than what we want to teach.

We needed to keep encouraging teachers to aim for the upper right-hand quadrant of Figure 13.1: the big questions and the deep learning in authentic embodied learning. We accepted that some learning activities would exhibit the characteristics of other quadrants, but that any activity in these quadrants should have a

---

10 For more on this see Brighouse and Waters, *About Our Schools.*

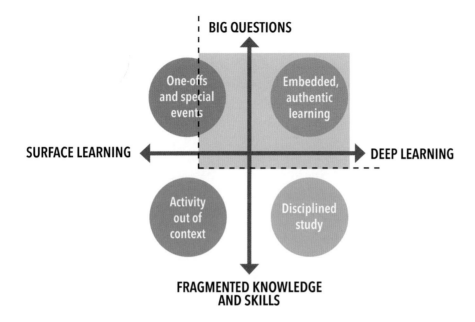

Figure 13.2. Implications of curriculum and pedagogy, revisited

secure purpose and be integrated into the upper-right quadrant. We have illustrated this in Figure 13.2.

These decisions were crucial in the drive towards quality and depth. We also had to build teachers' awareness of possibility and get examples underway in a spirit of collaboration across schools. While our conferences and meetings were important, we needed other mechanisms too. So, we also decided and agreed to:

- Use an interactive planning portal. While this was economic in terms of ensuring a common approach, its real benefit was in making planning a collaborative venture because everyone had access to everyone else's effort.

As teachers became more adept at planning effective learning opportunities, we saw an improvement in learning and attitude and some improvement in the quality of the children's products. What became apparent, however, was the extent to which the previous orthodoxies of teaching had sold children short in terms of some basic skills that stretch across the curriculum. In Chapter 12, on pedagogic repertoire, we discuss the need for both instruction and practice; our teachers realised that they needed to integrate these into their teaching with urgency.

Often, teachers and children were frustrated or disappointed with the outcome of a learning activity because they lacked some basic skills which had not been developed in the previous formulaic approach to lessons. We faced another snake: teachers found themselves seeing good learning foundering because the children did not know how to do the detail of the tasks behind the task. We had to look closely at what we called cross-curriculum skills.

CHAPTER 14

Thinking seriously about cross-curriculum skills

Getting the prerequisites in place to make learning successful

If we want our children to develop intrinsic learning skills and enact the whole range of approaches that bring learning alive in the subject disciplines, it takes more than ambition. We might want them to use research, work with archives, build models, carry out experiments and so on, but unless we teach them to do it, many of the worthwhile learning experiences we plan will founder.

When we want children to create a chart of results or record the results of an experiment using timers or scales, the whole thing will fall apart if they don't possess the necessary fundamental skills. They cannot acquire these alongside the learning. They need to be competent in the skills that act in a minor capacity to the major learning underway. If such skills are going to be practised and used in context to support the major learning, they first need to be learned as prerequisites to support all the major learning that can then continue unfettered.

The planning of a theme designed to secure the understanding of big ideas or deep knowledge will require the children to engage with the discipline of subjects. Learning becomes practical when teachers ask children to develop products that help them to dig below the surface, engage with the content and make the learning explicit. The teacher exploits the purpose in learning by providing authentic audiences for those products, which need to be of the highest quality. In doing so, the teacher illuminates for children the concepts, skills and knowledge being learned. This is what turns science into a discipline rather than a subject in an exercise book or a lesson on a Year 11 exam timetable.

This is different from making sure the work is neat and well-presented. It is about ensuring qualities such as accuracy and precision and skills such as cross-referencing and improvisation. It is about depth, organisation and polish. None of this can be achieved in passing. It is a case of planning ahead and teaching well.

In any planned sequence of learning, it is important to identify what prerequisites will be essential at what point; if neglected, this will signal a missed part of planning and frustration for teacher and children at the quality of the outcome. The astute teacher thinks ahead and spots the areas where the children's efforts may stumble. What will they need to be able to do to become the presenters, measurers, map-makers, recorders and inventors they need to be in order to work as geographers, scientists, historians and musicians?

p. 242

What are the prerequisites and how do we organise to teach them?

There are two main types of prerequisites:

1. Those that comprise a specific skill which, once learned, can be employed as needed because they have been mastered.

2. Those that can be learned and refined through continuous practice and open the door to a new set of opportunities.

The first type includes skills such as being able to use an encyclopaedia or the index of an atlas, read and create a periodic timeline, read the scale on a thermometer or a timer, read a map and use a compass. It also includes basics such as being able to use scissors, rulers and all manner of science equipment from pipettes to lenses. The second type includes skills such as using a pencil to draw or brush to paint, mixing colours, clear handwriting and writing for different purposes or audiences.

Both skill groups need to be mastered and both are improved with familiarity, but the second group will improve with practice that enables incremental improvements. These might be deemed cross-curriculum skills – skills that underpin learning in many subject disciplines and are transferable in their use and application.

How important is competence in cross-curriculum skills?

When we first raised the issue of children learning cross-curriculum skills with our curriculum leads and teaching and learning leads, it was met with one of those responses that suggested they thought, 'Of course – that's obvious.' Yet, the reality was that teachers' planning mostly involved them trying to teach the necessary skills immediately before they were needed or, worse, when lack of skill was spoiling their best-laid plans. There was a tolerance of what the children produced rather than a recognition that better teaching of prerequisites would improve outcomes and build pupil confidence. It was simply seen as one of the persistent problems of teaching – a fact of teaching life – that a significant proportion of the children would be unable to complete planned learning because certain skills were lacking. At worst, the teacher would sidestep the issue by producing printed sheets, doing the task for the children, giving them a lot of supervision or using one result for the whole class. It can become very limited and sterile.

One major benefit of the children developing a range of cross-curriculum skills is that teachers are less stressed and hassled when managing classroom learning and have more time to engage with the subject discipline in depth. Teaching children skills that will be employed regularly across the curriculum is one of the central levers for success.

What do we mean by cross-curriculum skills?

Most teachers recognise the scene: a theme on Egyptians is a perfect opportunity to teach about the maths of pyramids, so we ask the children to make some pyramids out of card. By breaktime, frustration reigns because so many children can't cut or fold paper or use glue. We get a few excellent examples, a few wobbly and sticky but passable efforts, and a whole array of rather curious-looking shapes that a pharaoh would not wish to be seen dead in. While the children are out at play, we decide to change the theme to lunar landscapes and shelve the pyramids for a different context.

Folding, cutting and gluing are the prerequisite skills that would have enabled the original piece of planning to come to reality as a learning experience – to achieve its intent. They can't be learned at the point of need because, as with any new skill, a bit of failure is to be anticipated as we embark on our first efforts (while we exercise and gain more practice). As we have seen, children need excellent instruction, exercise and practice over time.

◀ p. 212 In a sense, the geometric shape work doesn't matter in this instance because we can learn about pyramids without making one out of card. The real place for the folding and sticking is in a carefully managed series of sessions showing the children how to make a range of three-dimensional shapes as part of geometry in mathematics (such as cubes, cuboids, pyramids and tetrahedrons) followed by a range of other shapes (such as dodecahedrons and icosahedrons), which they will become fascinated with if it is well taught, especially if the teacher makes the link between geometry and the ancient Greeks.

Teaching skills like these requires precision in the teacher's skill of instruction: small steps are explained and demonstrated, with everyone watching closely, and then the children have a go in a step-by-step fashion. It is necessarily pedantic; this is not a creative or interpretive activity. It is about showing the children what to do. Of course, teachers provide the scaffolding. Our first cuboid is made using squared paper so it requires only cutting and folding. Measuring and drawing accurate lines comes at a later incremental stage.

However, the children still need to be instructed in how to fold paper carefully, how to use scissors effectively, and how to measure and draw a line with a ruler accurately. They need to have go, fail, just about manage and gradually become more capable. And when they are capable, they need to practise regularly and with concentration until they become proficient. Using scissors to cut accurately is a given and measuring accurately is to be mastered, as are drawing lines with a ruler and folding paper accurately.

Practice, another aspect on the curriculum–pedagogy axis, requires repetition to improve accuracy and speed coupled with feedback. Children can generate their own feedback as a form of assessment. They know whether their cuboid is regular and they are dissatisfied if it is distended or crumpled. This is called ipsative assessment.[1] They also require feedback which identifies where they need to be more precise and which helps them to get it right. Practice is not something we do one week and tick off in our planner. For children to become proficient in most basic cross-curriculum skills, ten minutes regularly generally beats a longer time infrequently. If we can find a context for

---

1   T. Isaacs, C. Zara, G. Herbert, S. J. Coombs and C. Smith, Ipsative Assessment. In *Key Concepts in Educational Assessment* (London: SAGE, 2013), ch. 26. http://dx.doi. org/10.4135/9781473915077.n26

practice, such as making it into a game or making it real, so much the better – but sometimes the game has to be 'getting better at this'.

Naturally, in terms of any of the manipulative skills, children's mastery is complicated by their growth. Some children may meet with frustration because their little hands are too clumsy, while others find it fun, but then those same children may reverse in dexterity as growth spurts alter their physical coordination.

Even with the few examples mentioned so far, there is the question of organisation. We can instruct a whole class on how to fold paper or use scissors, but watching to ensure they do it properly might mean working with smaller groups. It is hard to beat the silent concentration of a group of children with their tongues poking out the side of their mouths as they diligently fold a piece of paper as though the future of the planet hangs on its accuracy. But they will, if the instructions are sufficiently serious and being proficient is made to matter enough.

Of course, the teacher sometimes has a valuable resource available in the form of other adults in the room. The effective teaching assistant helps to secure success by acting as an observer while a whole class is being instructed and pinpointing those children experiencing difficulty, or coaching small groups and individuals later until the number of children who cannot do the procedure is nil. In our schools, due to funding constraints, teaching assistants are almost entirely allocated to support teachers with children with specific learning needs. This is different from some other primary schools where teaching assistants carry out general duties. Other adults can also include student teachers on placement, appropriate parent helpers, non-class-based staff including senior leaders and people beyond the school, such as the trust executive or the school inspector who often seems to be at a loose end. (That last example is a joke!)

The learning of these basic skills fits into the *how to* dimension and, mostly, is best addressed using a short-term drip approach. Children who practise for a few minutes each day will build competence and confidence in these cross-curriculum skills. The teacher's challenge is to set aside the time and increase the expectation for accuracy by varying the challenge: measuring different dimensions, cutting different lengths and shapes, folding nets to create a range of different shapes. Home learning is another useful vehicle. A set of regular challenges will develop incrementally into a set of skills that the children can employ when required across the curriculum. 'We can build a tetrahedron and a prism; now, let's build an obelisk!'

The teaching of competence in skills applies to any small area of mastery that can be utilised in context. Learning to use an index can begin with a class session with the teacher using exposition to show how to find a reference in an encyclopaedia or a location on a map in an atlas. Led through the steps by their teacher, many will get it first time. Others will come unstuck and need to repeat the experience until they catch on. Again, they will need short, regular drips of practice to become quicker and more accurate in the process.

The examples so far, and those in Table 14.1, are the sorts of skills which, once learned, can be applied with competence whenever needed. They are binary skills: we can do them or we can't. Being nearly good enough at measuring or folding or cutting is as good as being no good. We can't be quite good at locating a reference in an index or plotting coordinates on a map. Children without these skills do not have the prerequisites for behaving as developing historians, geographers or scientists.

Table 14.1. Prerequisite skills that children need to be taught

Age	Binary prerequisite skills
Year 1	Alphabetical order. Effective pencil grip. Select appropriate paintbrush to suit task. Make eye contact when in conversation. Speak with appropriate volume to an audience. Sit correct side for left- or right-handed writers. Cut along wavy and curved lines. Cut corners accurately. Use a ruler to draw a straight line. Appreciate and practise rhythms.
Year 2	Carry PE equipment safely, individually and as part of a team. Thread a needle. Organise work/table space to begin. Organise changing and sorting clothes for PE and swimming. Draw a length to a set measurement. Fold paper to specific instructions. Cut out a circle. Cut an interior space (e.g. inside a circle) without breaking the outer space. Cut without closing scissor-blade tips to produce a smooth edge. Use primary colours to make secondary colours.
Year 3	Use a paper cutter safely. Use a hole punch, lining up papers for uniformity. Search logically and quickly in a dictionary. Read a range of scales accurately (e.g. dials, thermometers, rulers). Construct a mathematical table. Read a mathematical table. Use tools safely (e.g. hacksaws, vices, hammers). Select and use appropriateness hardness of pencil for drawing.

Age	Binary prerequisite skills
Year 4	Use contents and indexes.
	Select and use the appropriate font to suit a task.
	Use a pair of compasses to draw a circle.
	Estimate various lengths.
	Estimate examples of mass, time and volume.
Year 5	Manage the basic Dewey Decimal System in libraries.
	Place a protractor accurately.
	Use a pair of compasses to draw a circle to a given measurement.
	Use a pair of compasses to draw a circle equally, inside and out.
	Draw and plot a line graph.
Year 6	Draw a pie chart with accuracy to represent data.
	Use coordinates to explain.
	Use six-figure Ordnance Survey grid references.
	Join two points accurately freehand to form a curve or straight line.

There are other cross-curriculum skills that children need to learn which are incremental in the sense that we all improve with regular practice – for example, sketching or mixing primary colours in paint. In these cases, the more we practise, the better. Our practice helps us to be more accurate or to create a more refined product. In respect of colour mixing or sketching, the best place to start is with the teacher employing exposition to show children, for example, how primary colours blend to form secondary colours. Instruction follows p. 212 next: closely observed small steps with the children mirroring what the teacher does. From there on, the children need regular practice with a series of stepped skills in order to become proficient. Perhaps a one-colour wash, then a wash of varying intensity, then a wash of mixed colours and so on until they can produce the colours found in an object or flower.

For sketching, the children need to be helped to understand how and why to use pencils with different degrees of hardness and a range of techniques to create shade, tone and texture. By using exposition and then instruction, the teacher can help them to build skills, competence and confidence. Practice will hone their skills and lead to incremental improvements over time. That practice needs to be regular and often. Every child needs a sketchbook they can turn to, in the same way as they would turn to a novel and get stuck in whenever there is a spare minute. The growing record of progress found in a sketchbook will be assessment enough and will show to the children the story of their own development.

Space prohibits the description of all the skills that need to be taught and then practised in an incremental way.

Addressing the issue of cross-curriculum skills was one of the pivotal points in our work to develop a successful curriculum and pedagogy. What appeared to be a snake became a ladder as teachers embraced the issue and saw the efforts of their labours. Previously, learning had stumbled because teachers were trying to develop knowledge through practical activities which the children could not manage. Now they saw them gaining knowledge through their competence and fluidity with these basic skills.

The snake we had to overcome to access the ladder: helping to build adult confidence and competence

Two other matters influence this key area of making the curriculum bear fruit. They both relate to the adults with whom the children work.

The first one is difficult to raise and concerns the competence of those adults. When we initially raised the issue of teaching the children specific cross-curriculum skills as prerequisites, the teachers

and teaching assistants nodded in agreement. What's more, they thought they already taught them. Indeed, many did, but usually only when they were needed for a specific task and usually as a standard formulaic lesson. Often, after a string of early failures, many had resorted to dodging the issue. For example, the classrooms were full of pots of green paint rather than yellow and blue being mixed with white to create a range of green shades. The green paint sat alongside pots of purple, pink, brown and orange, all of which reduced the children's need to mix colours for themselves.

Secondly, and more awkwardly, many teachers either didn't know how to do the skill themselves or, more likely, didn't know how to teach it. Most adults can fold paper or use scissors to cut along a straight line. The problem is that they do such things by routine and so, when instructing children, take too much for granted. For instance, we might demonstrate cutting with scissors by placing the paper in the jaws of the scissors, but if we are holding the paper in the air as we do so, and the children copy us, those with less developed wrists and fingers or less experience struggle. They need instruction with the elbows resting on a firm surface and the scissors pointing away from the holder, so they can see the line along which they are cutting. They also need to cut with one bold snip and then move the jaw to the end of the cut. Usually, children chibble with the scissor blades out of nervousness and concentration and make a mess. Precise instruction, closely observed, and practice are all vital: drip, drip, drip.

While the adults accepted this requirement, the next challenge for us was that many revealed that they hadn't considered how to approach teaching the skills on our list and had never been shown how to do so – and they wanted help. Hence, our conferences and workshops where trainers would take colleagues back to basics, not in a patronising way but to build confidence and show teachers (many of whom had never been taught previously) how to teach some of the skills they did instinctively. It was here where our conferences made a real difference. Spending time learning a range of techniques in art and design meant the teachers could understand the purpose and how to teach it, and across the school there were people with a range of techniques to share.

At this point, some readers may be identifying with our teachers' concerns about a lack of skills. While they could see the point of prerequisites, the emphasis on teaching skills through instruction and extended short-term practice aimed at increasing speed, mastery or accuracy made some of them uncomfortable. Weren't we supposed to be helping the children to be creative and to express themselves? Didn't this approach inhibit imagination and ideas and restrict the children's natural urge to experiment and explore? Our answer was that children are much more equipped to be creative and imaginative if we give them the tools they need to do the job. Without those tools, they are more likely to be frustrated and limited.

Elsewhere on the curriculum and pedagogy axis, we find discovery, problem-solving, role play and simulation, which all are valid approaches to aspects of theme-based learning and securing the KPIs. Our teachers and teaching assistants responded, worked on the p. 212 development of skills for themselves and the children, and saw the difference in terms of improved attitudes, such as perseverance and care for quality. They saw fewer wasted materials and significantly less preparation of 'ones I did earlier' among children who could not get past first base with drawings, modelling or research tasks. They also saw the quality of the children's products improve.

We agreed to:

- Emphasise the cross-curriculum skills with the children as important aspects of learning.

- Use this emphasis to further conversations on the teachers' pedagogic repertoire.

- Recognise improvement in cross-curriculum skills in situations such as assembly and the display of examples of improvement.

- See the skills as part of home learning.

- Ensure that cross-curriculum skill development for teachers and other adults was part of our conference programme.

At the right point in the development of curriculum, it is worth emphasising:

- The need to think explicitly about the teaching of cross-curricular skills.
- That anticipation of prerequisites is a necessary part of planning ahead through the narrative of the theme.
- Appreciating the notion of the major and minor focus for work in more than one discipline.
- Making sure we are clear about the need for explicitly taught and practised cross-curriculum skills.

CHAPTER 15

Let's talk about communication

How to get messages across, building common purpose and sharing understandings

In everything we have described so far, the issue of communication has been fundamental. We do have documentation, but we have ensured that our documents come alive through the way they encourage people to interact both within and beyond their schools.

Our trust-wide conferences have been an important pivot for development. We use them to set the scene and point the direction. Once our curriculum work had been underway for a year, we held a second conference with a central focus on what quality products look like. It began with a keynote speech from Mick on the importance of high-quality learning outcomes, including photographs of excellent children's products from the previous term. The staff were inspired by their own efforts and proud of what they had begun to achieve with the new curriculum.

This motivated them to want to learn more about what we meant by high-quality learning and how we secure it, especially in terms of the focus for the day, which was practical and creative art. To support this, we organised workshops for staff run by experts in the field, some delivered by external facilitators and some by secondary subject specialists. The staff had a morning and afternoon and could select two workshops that interested them. The aim was for them to learn what could be expected from young children in various subject areas, if we had high expectations and aspirations.

The choices were:

- Learn the importance of exploring clay with young children and how this develops their sensory needs.

- Outdoor cooking: how and why.

- Learn how to safely introduce creative woodwork to young children.

- Planning the perfect art project.

- How to teach poetry.

- The ethic of excellence – sketching.

- Using research to develop design criteria that lead to innovative, functional and appealing products.

We imagine you are wondering why these areas were chosen. Great question, and the answer is that they came out of lots of discussions with head teachers and curriculum leads about a good place to start in getting teachers and others to focus on their role. We could have begun with a spread of subject disciplines, but we risked overwhelming staff with having too large an area of focus and ending up with a scattergun approach to raising expectations. Like all good solutions, we began by asking ourselves what the problem was. We decided that the issue we were trying to address was that teachers had got caught up in planning single, stand-alone lessons. They were not thinking about a sequence of lessons with a very particular end point for the children. As a result, lessons were tokenistic and the children didn't have time to really immerse themselves in getting better at particular skills. This was our key challenge and the one with which we had to begin.

We decided that the arts was a great starting point because teachers could see how knowledge, skills and applications combine to achieve high-quality outcomes in the form of children's products. It also felt like an enjoyable and practical way to support teachers by offering help in a range of creative subject disciplines. They would be taught by experts on what substantive knowledge was needed in order to understand the disciplinary concept of the subject and why, and therefore be able to apply it as part of an interdisciplinary learning theme.

Initially, the staff were apprehensive, and in some cases reluctant, about taking part in the workshops. However, as the day progressed they grew in confidence and began to think about how they could use these new skills in the classroom. For the rest of that year, we saw a striking improvement in the quality of the teaching of these subject disciplines. This was a real example of how quality professional development with hands-on practical experience can improve and develop teachers' practice. Unless they become accustomed to the detail of teaching and organisation, as well as the skills and techniques required, there is likely to be little change in outcomes.

After the success of the second conference, we decided to retain the structure and format. The conference theme for the following year was subject leadership and subject disciplines. Again, the feedback from staff was enormously positive and we were reassured that our efforts at communication were convincing teachers that learning could be further developed. The day started again with a keynote from Mick, who refreshed our memories on the journey we had travelled and the distance we had come. We once again shared images of high-quality learning and the trust exhibitions we had curated. Staff were excited and proud of the work we had achieved collectively across the trust.

Teachers were now keen to work with their fellow subject leads and subject teams rather than simply with their own schools. The noticeable big step forward was that the subject discipline coordinators were exerting a collective influence on the content and approach of teaching in our Curious Curriculum. This would have been unimaginable a couple of years earlier when the role of the coordinator was limited and passive rather than there being a dynamic expectation for them in each school and collectively. During the conference, the coordinators led extended sessions with groups of teachers about the subject discipline they were leading.

Supported by external specialists, which included secondary school colleagues, the coordinators were tasked with discussing: how do we *seek* learning? How do we *track* learning? How do we *capture* learning? We had recognised that this language was enabling teachers to discern the links between our KLIs and the way we observe and articulate progress in children.

To enable the conversations, we asked the leads to focus on how their subject discipline could:

- Produce and write the subject specialist trust statement of intent. These would be the things we would be seeking.

- Discuss and determine excellence in the role of subject leadership. This is what we would be tracking. For example, what needs to be collated in the subject folder? How do we monitor progress?

- Identify the types of things we could collect and evidence in our subject floor books. These were our efforts to capture learning.

p. 70

The collective energy and enthusiasm from the subject groups was palpable. As most schools only have one subject discipline coordinator (some looking after more than one subject), the leads felt that they wanted to take ownership of the role, felt empowered and connected with the trust, and felt part of a wider team.

The takeaway learning on professional development for a multi-academy trust is to realise your collective power: the strength in numbers, your ability to organise and deliver training, and development at scale and depth. If you get the steps leading up to the provision and the structure of the message you are trying to give right, you will see the quality of teaching and learning improve exponentially.

Conferences, as we discussed earlier, can have a crucial influence on positive development, but they can also be a waste of resource, especially teachers' time. Conferences can also leave people feeling good about their school or role but make little difference in terms of impact on children's learning. For us, conferences have been ladders towards progress but, except for the introductory one, they have always had a specific curriculum development focus, addressing emerging and specific needs.

In thinking through large conferences, it is worth considering:

- How the focus of conferences builds gradually over time.
- How to use specialist support at the appropriate time.
- How to build a feeling of togetherness without losing individual commitment.
- How to group individuals to obtain maximum benefit from the conference.
- How to follow up and use the momentum created.

Communication works in many ways. We have found that involving people in conversations with each other has been vital, alongside the sort of communication that sets out to inform, explain, persuade and require. If we want our colleagues to develop their skills, they need opportunities to recognise progress and development. That is where our exhibitions came in – another of our ladders.

CHAPTER 16

The exhibition – gaining traction with children, staff and parents

Oiling the wheels of progress

We had reached a point where there were glimmerings of good practice in nearly every school. Staff were feeling buoyant about the progress being made and could see for themselves the difference in the children's achievements. But they were only glimmerings.

To keep up momentum, it was put to the head teacher group that it might be beneficial to hold an exhibition of children's work from all the schools. Approval was instant. Head teachers grasped the potential benefit of teachers viewing work from across the schools and of children feeling recognised and gaining an insight into the quality that could be achieved. Parents would appreciate the quality of the work and the children would have a real audience for their efforts.

This was October, and the exhibition was to be held in March, so there was plenty of time. These sorts of developments are a bit like the leadership task of risk management planning: we spend time considering what might be without really being convinced that it will happen. Red, amber or green; mitigation done and we get on with life. The reality hit when, with a month to go, we contacted the schools about the exhibition arrangements. There was the suggestion that we might push the exhibition back for a while.

Deferral is a serious issue for leaders at any level. For the head teacher, pulling back from a plan in the face of a lack of energy from staff might be well received initially, in that something is taken off the to-do list. On the other hand, it will also set a precedent for the future. For the classroom teacher, extending the deadline for children to finish work needs careful consideration.

With the exhibition, it was a case of discussing the best way forward and properly examining the reasons why it was creating pressure. Like so much leadership work – and so much work on developing learning in schools – it comes down to communication. The head teachers had mentioned the exhibition in their schools but, as most agreed later, only tentatively. With a month to go, they had not done any significant organisation. It had been agreed that the exhibition was going to be 'genuine' in that we would use children's products that had been generated naturally through the course of their learning. We were not expecting – indeed, we were actively discouraging – the production of specific work for the exhibition. In this way, the only demand on the school would be mounting the products, curating a good exhibition and managing the children during visits. Some head teachers anticipated that, towards the end of term, such a demand on some staff would be the last straw. They didn't necessarily know this to be true, they just imagined it might be, especially when they had given such slight indications of their expectations so far.

Of course, the two of us also realised our own failings. We had done the classic thing of seeing agreement as action, without setting the parameters that people were probably expecting. Hence, when it surfaced again, there was both uncertainty about what was required and the need to talk with staff about the 'new' expectation of an exhibition, along with that common concern of getting it wrong. We said that we would hold an exhibition, so we did, but in some cases with reluctance and with much of the work left to the poor soul who had the job of coordinating everything.

Of course, when it did happen it was great! The relatively small contributions from each participating school looked terrific when assembled, and the shared pride was there for all to see and feel. The secondary school hall was a hive of activity for two hours until 10am when the first guests would arrive. Suddenly, it was all worth it. Generally, the quality of the children's work was good, here and there it was very good and occasionally it was excellent.

The challenge was to emphasise what really mattered. There was an immediate interest from staff in the way each school had displayed

the work – for example, the colours and techniques, the use of lights or draped material to create a softer impression. As interesting as these details were, we wanted to stress the quality, technique and impact of the writing or artwork rather than the way it had been displayed. We also wanted to show the diversity of approaches to a similar theme in different schools. These niceties may have been important for focusing the attention of visiting teachers, who were rightly proud of their colleagues' hard work, pleased with level of achievement on show, delighted with the children's efforts and keen to find new ideas to use in their own setting. All of these feelings were valid, but we wanted to use the exhibition as a chance to push on development, which had been the initial intention.

The guests began to arrive: groups of children from each school were brought on a timetable to see the exhibition. Immediately, teachers realised there was more work to do. It was clear that many children had no idea what to do at an exhibition; if we were going to use school visits to museums, galleries or sites of interest productively in the future, the chances were that we would not gain maximum benefit unless we helped them to use this visit well. For many children, there was the excitement of seeing all the products. At the same time, their keenness to spot their own contribution or those of their friends took precedence over looking closely at the work on show and trying to learn from it. We concluded that next time (a significant anticipation!), we would try to shape the children's visits better – preparing them beforehand, perhaps providing a stimulus to encourage observation and organising hosts from each school to act as guides to their section.

The arrival of parents at the end of the school day was another learning point. Typically, those who attended were the parents of children with products on display, so naturally they made a beeline for their own child's work. However, we were keen to encourage them to study other exhibits from other schools and see the spread of learning.

As teachers from the schools arrived, the same natural tendency struck: their own school first and then the rest. Trying to get teachers below the surface features to see the elements that had been the focus of much of their own recent professional learning was crucial. Secondary phase teachers were another group of interest: fascinated first by exhibits relating to their own subject discipline, intrigued by quality and, in some cases, looking beyond features of presentation and digging deep into aspects of writing. Later on, there was a tendency to stand back and consider the breadth of the curriculum and the ways in which different subject disciplines inform and support one another.

Evaluation of the exhibition was thorough and all agreed that such efforts were worth it and could be a spur to further development, if done well. There had been learning points about establishing expectations, avoiding it being a competition and preparing visitors as well as the exhibition itself. The biannual exhibition highlighting the work of different pairs of year groups is now a well-established fixture, much anticipated by the children and staff. Some see it is as a culmination and others as an incentive to the next step of our developmental work.

We agreed to:

- Use the concept of an exhibition within each of our schools as part of our annual schedule and our routine work.

- Teach the children how to mount their work and present it at an exhibition, and how to use the event well.

- Develop the skills of using an exhibition well on appropriate educational visits to gain maximum benefit from the stimulus.

- Consider a nominated focus for future exhibitions that might include priority skill areas or themes and age groups of children.

Some issues to consider when planning exhibitions in schools:

- See the exhibiting of children's products as an important part of feedback, recognition and evaluation.
- Use displays of children's products as vehicles for staff consideration of quality. Hold staff meetings in different teachers' classrooms and organise part of the agenda around considerations of pupil progression, using the exhibited examples as a starting point.
- Allocate each class a space (e.g. four metres by two metres) and related table space. Teach the children how to guide people around the exhibition in readiness for parent visits.
- Make use of occasions such as informal parents' evenings.
- Agree some whole-school principles for how to display children's work. The quality of mounting and presenting can make a huge impression on visitors. Children are perfectly capable of preparing their own exhibitions from a young age - if we teach them how to do it.

Through all of our work, the head teacher has been vital to success. If you want to develop effective curriculum and pedagogy in your school, you will know that central and active engagement is the most important influence. Our work has also shown us how head teachers need to develop themselves, and how much they have been affected by the discourse of recent years, particularly the accountability agenda. There is no doubt in our minds that our head teachers have been examples of ladders in moving forward expectations for learning. In the next chapter, we describe the issues we think any head teacher or person supporting a school from outside needs to consider and address. As you read it, reflect on your own situation.

CHAPTER 17

The head teacher's role

The head teacher as lynchpin: keeping the focus on learning

We could have placed this chapter at the very beginning of our book because it is both important and almost a statement of the obvious. If head teachers want to see effective learning in their school, they need to engage with it and create the conditions that will encourage teachers to constantly seek to improve on their previous best. The professional challenge of headship is to work through others to build the quality of children's experience.

The last many years of increasing expectations on leadership has meant that many head teachers have struggled to manage their day. The demands of school organisation (short term and long term), the management of staff (teaching and non-teaching) and responding to the needs of parents and children (planned and immediate) have combined to create enormous complexity. Add to this their responsibility to the local authority or trust – in terms of engaging in developmental activity and preparing clerical returns, satisfying governors and dealing with all manner of external agencies, while also keeping a weather eye on national policy changes or inspection – and it is easy to see why the job starts to draw people away from the core purpose.

> I remember the first time that staff were able to generate theme ideas without the need for lots of input from heads, curriculum leads and other schools. It was a real breakthrough.
>
> *Matt Lankester*

Many primary schools now have a deputy head teacher who, in part or in whole, is not committed to a class of children, which in theory helps to share the load but in practice often creates different pressures because the deputy has to be shown the expectations. Worse still is when the head teacher and deputy find themselves meeting to talk about complexities and allowing these issues to take up a disproportionate amount of time. Too often, such meetings result in a list of yet more things that need to be done.

Once time out of classrooms is a natural routine for leadership, it becomes very hard to take the step back into them. Consequently, it becomes more difficult to spark and keep up momentum in conversations with staff about curriculum and teaching and learning, either formally or informally. When the 'distant' head teacher begins a discussion about these matters, many staff see it as another form of reference control – that is, the head teacher is only asking staff to think about certain practices because it is a new Ofsted requirement or there is some other compulsion.

After the initial phase of our work, during which head teachers hosted our visits and discussed their starting points in respect of the challenge ahead, there had been a burst of enthusiasm and energy. However, shortly after racing up the ladder of expectation and renewed aspiration, the schools faced a snake that could have dragged everything back down again. Head teachers began talking to us openly about the pressures they were feeling and their worries concerning how little time they were spending in classrooms. When we discussed this issue, they realised that this was one of those roundabouts that you have to get off or you are on board until the music stops.

It is to their enormous collective credit that head teachers raised the issue and felt so concerned about addressing it. Professional goodwill and trust were growing through the work they were doing together and the structured experiences through which they were learning together. We knew these head teachers were not unusual. Across the country, head teachers experience the sensation of being pulled in all directions, of wondering whether they are focusing on the right things, of seeing the work pile up however hard they try to shift it. Books and courses both empathise and implore senior leadership to follow the ubiquitous five or seven simple steps to success. They sound simple on the page or on the screen, but back in school they can become yet another burden.

As a first step, we explored some principles about how school leaders make a difference, day by day, to children's learning effectiveness. The head teachers were provided with some suggestions on how to manage their influence on the children's learning – the thing they most wanted to secure in their school.

Mick picked one of the assemblies he often uses with the children as a starting point for discussion. (If nothing else, the head teachers would get a new assembly.) Having spent much time living in towns that are famous for making shoes, the first slide is a picture of some shoemaking equipment – the 'last'. A last is used to shape the shoe and hence we get the term 'built to last'. Over time, the word has come to mean something that lasts a long time but the origin comes from shaping leather to fit the last. Next, he described some of the processes involved in shoemaking, particularly where waste leather is trimmed to fit the last, both to economise and also to make the stitching easier. This process of trimming waste is called 'skiving'. The word skiving has come to be used to indicate laziness or looking for a way out of hard work, but the original meaning of looking for

Built to last

Skiving

economy and cutting out waste is apt. In the assembly, Mick explores with the children how we can economise in the way we do our work or in the way we use school resources and facilities.

The children are always amused when it is suggested that skiving is sensible – and it is for head teachers too. So, what has skiving got to do with head teachers? It wasn't long before we were talking about all sorts of possibilities and came up with some essentials:

- Talk about the school and its children, then the data.

- Don't let the children become units.

- Don't get fixated on emails.

- Walk around the school twice daily – learning and environment.

- Discuss learning and teaching on the way.

- Plan good assemblies.

- Spend half an hour individually with every teacher and teaching assistant termly.

- Think of PPA as fruitful and effective time.

- Look seriously at movement around school – reduce crowds, lines and queues.

- Economise on marking and clerical planning.

- Think about the start and end of the school day.

- Water the plants and enjoy the flowers around the school.

None of these activities create work, but they do create a better climate for the work of the school and a positive tone for the work of the head teacher. They also focus on the sorts of things that make a school effective. All of them imply an attitude of mind. They are aspects of professional well-being for leadership, and at the same time they help head teachers to focus on what does matter and not get consumed by what doesn't. A useful read is David Gumbrell's book *Spin,* which contains 39 reflections on how to manage time and tasks in leadership.[1] Each one has an introduction which provides a background source for an assembly or a theme.

There wasn't a head teacher who disagreed with the list, and in truth it prompted a sense of guilt about not doing them enough, becoming desk-bound or worrying about whether these sorts of activities were 'allowed'. This led to another turning-point conversation during which head teachers were open with each other about how the pressure of the job was trapping them, and how feeding the machine was consuming their own enthusiasm for the very aspect of the job that mattered – affecting people to make a difference to children's learning.

---

1   D. Gumbrell, *Spin: Time and Task Management in Teaching* (St Albans: Critical Publishing, 2021).

All of this was important because it enabled the very people who were the engines of success for the children to articulate the difference between how they wanted to work and the reality of what their work had become. Extended discussions with the head teacher group led us all towards further commitments.

> Coming into the trust, it is about being strong enough to focus leadership on learning. We have all had experience of head teachers who are office-bound and produce priorities for others to enact.
>
> *Jen Wathan*

In terms of head teachers' leadership of their schools:

- We committed to reduce living by data and documents and increase living through dialogue.

- We committed to leading learning rather than organising, and to approach the task in the way described in our job interview.

- We were explicit about walking the walk, even though for a lot of us that might mean re-entering a sphere of activity that had become less practised.

- We recognised that we were often knocked off course by the relentlessness of the management agenda that comes with school leadership. The unexpected is likely to detain us and our inexperience may mean that we spend too much time on some tasks because we give them undue status.

- We committed to asking for advice on the best way to fulfil straightforward tasks economically rather than allow ourselves to spend time worrying.

These points were crucial: if head teachers could sort out the distracting and worrying pressures, the teaching and learning agenda would have a fighting chance. One thing that emerged as significant was the head teacher's year planner, which helped them to determine what to do when, how often and how long to take on managerial matters. It was working well until the pandemic; we hadn't anticipated that.

While Mick might have spurred debate and helped to build agreement and commitment to revised approaches, it was Claire who spent time in schools day after day reminding head teachers what they had agreed. She also organised leadership meetings with head teachers in different formats for different purposes. Between them, Claire and the head teachers decided that four types of meeting were required:

1. Briefing – exchanging information and feeding back.

2. Training – helping head teachers to get better at what they do (professional development).

3. Well-being – supporting each other and becoming a team.

4. Individual/one-to-one – school improvement in their setting; a balance of support and challenge.

Head teacher and leadership meetings have taken many forms over the years. We have tried meeting every week for a few hours, meeting every fortnight (for one briefing and one training session) and meeting for one hour-long briefing and then again later in the week to develop projects and improvement priorities. We have learned that the structure of the meeting depends on two factors: firstly, the leaders in the room and, secondly, what we were working on and the messages we were giving at that particular time.

For now, we have settled on a blend of meetings for all head teachers in the trust:

1. An email briefing of key information every Monday.

2. A two-hour meeting to discuss issues and bring queries, concerns and problems to the table.

3. A one-to-one hour-long meeting between Claire and each head teacher every fortnight about personal and school-specific matters.

4. A two-day school improvement visit every six to eight weeks, where the head teacher and Claire discuss how she can help to quality assure progress and also spend time supporting and developing leaders within the school.

5. An awayday once every six to eight weeks to spend some quality time developing ideas and thinking about the best way to take our school improvement direction forward. These might include an external contribution.

This combination will no doubt change again. This is irrelevant, though, as the point we are making is that support and challenge for head teachers is just as important as it is for staff. Within a school, staff need to feel part of a team and that they have an opportunity to share ideas, voice concerns and become vulnerable with colleagues. The same principle applies across a group of schools. We needed to get to a place where heads saw their head teacher colleagues as the trust's collaborative senior leadership team rather than as competition or a threat. We needed to believe that we were only as good as our lowest-performing school, and therefore be prepared to make sacrifices in our own school for the greater good of all the children. We also needed to believe that we were leaders serving the needs of all the children in the trust, and acting to a large extent (but not entirely) through our school community.

This took time, patience and emotional literacy. There were challenges along the way and not everyone agreed or believed in this approach. However, we now stand as a group of head teachers who support, admire and back one another. The group is willing to show professional humility and ask for support, and is also prepared to accept when someone else's idea or strategy is the right course of action.

Alongside the internal team-building structures and strategies, we knew we wanted to be outward facing too. We were lucky enough to be involved in a national initiative, fondly named 'The Triads', where multi-academy trusts and a group of schools in the West Midlands, Leicestershire and Devon, along with our own, took it in turns to visit each other's school in groups of three. Twice a year, we travelled to another part of the country to visit a group of schools and talk about quality learning. These structured triad visits were definitely not mini-Ofsted experiences; indeed, the framework was not used or allowed as a template. This was well prepared, formative and diagnostic analysis and conversation with trusted colleagues.

As the visits programme unfolded, more and more curriculum leads were able to take part. The benefits of these visits were multiple; testing out different curriculum approaches was one of them. Participants would discuss rationale, methods, products, quality, range, depth and more, all in a context of mutual respect. Some of the conversations were challenging (far more challenging than with inspectors), touching on fundamental philosophies and practices which demanded justification or change. They were also an opportunity for fellow professional colleagues to focus on two things: firstly, something head teachers were proud of and believed was strong and of high quality; and, secondly, something that was vexing them, that they had tried to improve but for some reason was missing the mark.

The carefully managed two-day residential triad visits were a pivotal point for us as a group of schools. Partly because they enabled us to gain an external view of our school in a way that you don't get from an Ofsted inspection, and partly because they enabled us to bond as a group of professionals – opening ourselves up to critique and feedback and making ourselves vulnerable. It was an enlightening experience for all involved.

As a head teacher or someone who encourages and supports head teachers, it might be worth considering:

- The extent to which the head teacher's approach mirrors what they said at interview.
- The extent to which the expectations on them mirror what they were asked about at interview.
- The extent to which a head teacher is focused on teaching and learning and whether the managerial aspects of leadership are claiming time and energy unduly.
- How to help head teachers feel part of a professional community.
- What links are available to colleagues beyond the immediate school community?
- How to help head teachers manage the day, week, term and school year in a way that is productive and professionally rewarding.

Next for that dose of realism which everyone knows about but rarely features in those 'how to' books about leadership and managing change. Schools are complicated places at the best of times and the path to progress is rarely clear. On top of that, challenges can come from any angle, sometimes anticipated and sometimes unexpected. You are invited to read the next chapter on our tangle of snakes and reflect on your own trials over the last five years in the course of developing your school. We have tried to describe some of the difficulties involved in the development of curriculum and pedagogy, which will affect most primary schools to some degree.

CHAPTER 18

Things happen

How even the best-laid plans can go awry

When we set off on a new pathway or with a new ambition, we usually do so in the belief that we will get to our destination. In this chapter, we explore the route we took towards our objective and some of the things that knocked us off course.

As teachers create the weather in their classroom, so the climate beyond will influence what they can do and what they believe they are allowed to do. We have had our share of problems in the course of developing our Curious Curriculum, and we think it is worth offering our thinking on some of the helpful and irritating influencing factors that can affect progress. They are unlikely to be the same as your own, as they are affected by time and circumstance, but they do tend to fit into a pattern: people, incidents and government policy (in any order), as well as the unexpected.

This is why leadership models are often frustrating. The ubiquitous 'seven steps' make perfect sense in theory, but in the harsh reality of normal life, climbing those steps is sometimes precarious – and sometimes it feels as if they are getting steeper as we climb. It is never long until the next book or the next course emerges offering a different set of enticing steps. In this chapter, we try to help you look at some of the influences and to think ahead – without suggesting we have all the answers.

Strategic planning and the twisting snake that made us lose our way

One aspect of schooling that is different from how it was twenty years ago is planning, particularly strategic planning. The attention paid to planning in leadership programmes, coupled with the growth of computer technology which has normalised spreadsheets and Gantt charts, has helped those leading development in schools to stay one step ahead and create a pathway to success for themselves, their teams and other partners.

This has been enormously useful in building leadership confidence and shaping awareness of the importance of longer term development, although human nature means that any divergence from the plan is often explained away rather than addressed. In a school, the consequences of an undelivered development programme are rarely measured, as they are in business, in terms of loss of revenue or profit or wasted investment. One of the features of the culture of schooling is that typically it rationalises unfulfilled plans and changes of direction.

> We have got past teacher performance. You have to get teachers to see past the Twitter clamour. What matters is getting teachers to think of their own development as professionals.
> *Sharon Clark*

This approach to failure is one of the examples of how schooling is different from other sectors. Over time, schools have been urged to mirror leadership practices in other arenas, such as sport. They have been encouraged to focus on marginal gains to improve performance or to adopt business strategies (even though most schools are bigger than most of the businesses in their area). The great management and leadership advance linked to Michael Barber's influence led to schools being exhorted to build teams and establish a 'go for it' or 'no excuses' culture.[1] Risk assessments, RAG (red, amber, green) ratings and mitigations become part of the process of managing change. Yet, too many developments in schools begin with a bang and end with a whimper.

However strong the plan, people often find a stronger reason to explain why it proceeded at a slower pace, delivered something different or changed direction. We are a tolerant profession that understands, makes allowances and adjusts.

> This was going to be a mammoth undertaking, a journey not a sprint, and everyone within the trust would need to be on board to make this happen.
>
> *Sarah Williams*

When we began our work on curriculum and pedagogy, we wanted a plan with a timeline. We believed this would help those driving the development to see the extent of what they were trying to achieve and recognise that it would take a long time. A plan would set some deadlines for action and responsibilities, which would also act as commitments.

At the same time, we were very aware that plans do not always come to fruition. Too tight a plan would set up the potential for shortfall.

---

1   M. Barber, *How to Run a Government So That Citizens Benefit and Taxpayers Don't Go Crazy* (London: Allen Lane, 2015).

We also appreciated that the staff we were working with, although full of enthusiasm, had little experience of the sort of effort needed to fundamentally change practice in pedagogy and curriculum. Most of our colleagues were attracted to the task ahead, its philosophy and purpose, but whether they shared the same vision of what was ahead was debatable.

For some senior staff, it was a case of 'willingness will be enough'. At the outset, there was an outlook of 'tell us what we need to do and we will do it'. A positive attitude comes naturally to a profession that has become more and more used to implementing new expectations, but our leaders didn't necessarily appreciate the effort that would be required.

We decided to explain the next steps at every stage, always describing the horizon as well as the nearest steps towards it. We hoped that this would make things feel achievable, and the togetherness would mean that nobody would go off on a tangent or be left too far behind because they had not grasped an imperative. We wanted people to understand that development in curriculum and pedagogy is not a start and finish activity, but something we should enjoy professionally as one of the central tenets of teaching.

The key question in planning is how to gain agreement, understanding and commitment to next steps and make sure everyone at each level in the team receives the same messages, not in the sense of transmission but in a spirit of collaboration. There were fewer spreadsheets and checklists, and when they were used it was only to enable awareness. There was more conversation, challenge and checking that we were doing what we said we would – for all involved.

The process has taught us that we were better off without a large-scale project plan. It meant that we could act quickly on possibility and opportunity and could differentiate for different people's variable

Shaping our Future

We have been learning to ha cross-hatch and shade.

progress. This was about building an ongoing conversation about how things were done rather than checking that things had been done. It was not about meeting a schedule of key milestones but ensuring that we reached each milestone, determining where we would go from a particular crossroads and making sure we avoided blind alleys. It was also about making sure people moved ahead together, helping one another and enjoying the journey.

As it happened, the lack of a detailed plan was helpful in allowing flexibility over time. It meant that the unexpected and unanticipated could be absorbed, coped with or capitalised on without causing us to take our attention away from the horizon. Looking back, it is fascinating to revisit the distractions and roadblocks as examples of how development can be affected by external factors. Reflecting on potential diversions enables us to think about how to handle similar external factors in other contexts.

Government policy – a ladder for building clarity entangled with snakes

When the government published the revised national curriculum in 2013, many schools re-examined their approach. It was partly as a result of the uncertainty which followed that Olympus Trust decided to address the curriculum.

What happened just after we began to look at curriculum and pedagogy together was that the government began to pursue a different approach to recording children's attainment in the core subjects. As with all things associated with SATs, concerns arose in schools as they tried to come to terms with new demands. The distraction of the concept of working 'at expected levels' or working at 'greater depth' was unsettling for both teachers and leaders when compared with previous practice. This could easily have caused the first hold-up on our curriculum effort.

We determined not to allow this to divert us, but to quickly embrace the concept and apply it in our consideration of the broader foundation curriculum. What was an expected level in art, geography or science, for example? How did we know whether a child was working at greater depth in the history of DT? We avoided resorting to descriptors and playing with words, but we did use meetings with teachers to look at children's efforts and moderate our judgements of what quality looked like in a range of subject disciplines – always aiming for excellence. In trying to describe what we needed to see as the outcome of our efforts, we developed our thinking around key performance indicators (KPIs).

Of course, amending the way children's attainment was assessed played into one of the biggest potential diversions of all: accountability.

Accountability – a snake with a nasty bite

The school system is in the thrall of accountability arrangements. The shadow of inspection hangs over every school, although those deemed outstanding know they have some breathing space to check the banners on their fence and the endorsements on their letterheads. For many years, the cat-and-mouse game of inspection has meant for most schools a serious pressure on any potential blemish.

At the beginning of our effort to transform curriculum and pedagogy, accountability acted as an anchor. On the one hand, the importance of SATs results meant a relentless leadership focus on literacy and numeracy, which had the effect of distorting teaching. Mornings were meaningful and intense to the extent that afternoons were seen as anything between less important and light relief.

For leaders, teaching observations were a morning commitment, so teachers could organise more 'fun' experiences in the afternoon.

However, even though there was a wider curriculum in the afternoon timetable, the children's experience was largely of literacy extension. Printed sheets abounded as teachers gathered evidence that they had 'covered' the curriculum; the children shaded in the phases of the moon, labelled skeletons or filled in dates on prepared timelines. There was some art and design and DT, although it was often done as home learning with family support. In describing the products of home learning, teachers would note the imagination, creativity and attention to detail, often with a touch of envy.

This is not to say that the children did not enjoy learning. The Great Fire of London provided opportunities for children to create Tudor buildings, either in 2D or 3D, with tissue-paper flames if they lacked the skills to mix paint. The *Titanic* sailed regularly, with the gap between rich and poor highlighted through the cabin decoration. *Horrible Histories* created a pathway for a term-long theme with the children learning to sing the catalogue of Henry VIII's wives' demise. The Roman 'tortoise' shield technique was practised (without meeting the Latin word *testudo*). Maps of the UK were annotated, with Eire left entirely blank because it was off limits.

The children had regular visits to places of interest: the zoo, a famous bridge, the coast, museums, galleries and religious buildings. These were good experiences in social and recreational terms but whether they were exploited in terms of the learning was doubtful. The pressure of SATs was skewing the whole curriculum. p. 37

On the other hand, with each attempt to extend the range of the children's experiences or increase the depth of learning, teachers would be hesitant – however much they appreciated the premise or saw the educative purpose – for fear of taking their eye off the ball or even appearing not to worship at the temple of results. Results day in the summer was distorting all the fine words in our vision statements and straplines. Any invitation to make teaching more purposeful and worthwhile was met with an image of Hilaire Belloc's cautionary words, 'Always keep a-hold of Nurse / For fear of finding something worse.'[2]

Of course, an even worse anchor was inspection. When we began our curriculum work, inspection was a trump card to be played by anyone who was uncertain or challenged. 'What would Ofsted say?' is usually a rhetorical question meaning, 'I don't want to talk about this any further.' The inspection framework at the time did make reference to foundation subjects but school reports were overwhelmingly about the core curriculum. Rumour, urban myth, stories from colleagues in other schools and accounts at a head teacher conference from one of their number who had trained as an inspector carried far more weight than the framework. Who could blame a head teacher for focusing on the essentials in the morning and giving a veneer of respectability to the afternoons – a sort of two-tone school?

Urgings to develop more productive foundation subject teaching were welcomed, with staff oddly talking about 'being given permission'. At the same time, those same people were quick to point out the potential folly, suggesting that 'we would have to be brave' to do this. Some head teachers portrayed themselves as courageous crusaders, urging a 'creative curriculum' or similar, almost as an antidote to the prevailing trend. The truth was, though, that the threat of inspection was real. The schools involved were looking over their shoulders, with some justification, but lifting standards is about more than doing a lot of literacy and numeracy. It is about doing it well.

In many cases, the managerial approach of recent years, and the emergence of the formulaic lesson, had resulted in pedestrian

---

2   The poem, 'Jim, Who Ran Away from His Nurse, and Was Eaten by a Lion' by Hilaire Belloc is a brilliant resource for choral speaking with a class of upper Key Stage 2 children. It can open up all sorts of conversations about risk as well as issues of Victorian and Edwardian childhood at the opposite end of the social scale from the oft-referenced match girls and chimney-sweeps. Belloc wrote several poems in this vein – see *Cautionary Tales for Children* (London: Eveleigh Nash, 1907). Available at: https://www.gutenberg.org/files/27424/27424-h/27424-h.htm.

teaching. It had also created well-meaning efforts at comprehensive planning for the purpose of showing the inspectors, almost with the idea that only the top line needed to be done. During inspection, the parts the teacher was confident about could be taught. Over time, the inspection cat would catch the schooling mouse, first with book scrutiny and then conversations with children to expose the gap between planning and practice.

Our outlook on all of this was straightforward. We were going to pursue the stated aims of the schools; phrases such as 'seeking potential', 'rounded learning' and 'broad curriculum' would need to become a reality. The straplines on the signs at the gates and the photographs in our brochures for parents would become routine rather than snapshot moments.

Whenever we heard the 'What would Ofsted say?' refrain, we would counter with something along the lines of, 'They would be positive.' We had good reason to think this: Ofsted had always recognised good teaching where knowledge, skills and dispositions are properly addressed. Inspectors have always, rightly, criticised superficial teaching with tenuous subject links and the trivial treatment of significant learning opportunities.

In 2019, a year into our work on curriculum and pedagogy, the tide suddenly turned. HMCI Amanda Spielman announced yet another new framework which would focus on the curriculum. In doing so, she criticised much of the practice that had emerged in previous years. The question, 'What would Ofsted say?' was suddenly about more than rhetoric.

Fortunately, the drift of Ofsted's new framework was in tune with the steps we had been taking: knowledge that matters, experiences that drive learning deeper, teachers interpreting the curriculum carefully. Spielman's comment in a conference speech mirrored our efforts over many months:

Our evaluation of the quality of a school's curriculum will reflect the quality of their practice, rather than their ability to use the 'right' curriculum language. Indeed we have also shown ... that we can quite quickly distinguish between those who have a genuinely good curriculum, implemented well across a school, and those who simply talk a good game.[3]

The framework brought with it pilot inspections. Our feedback from deep dives by scuba inspectors with flippers was positive and reinforced our developments.

The three 'I' words – intent, implementation and impact – played straight into our court. We had been using three key questions to shape our work, which mapped well onto Ofsted's indicators:

1. Intent: What are we trying to achieve?

2. Implementation: How will we best organise to secure what we seek to achieve?

3. Impact: How will we know whether we are successful?

Schools across the country were now engrossed in producing intent statements, while they waited for early inspection reports to confirm whether they were on the right lines. Our attitude was that we had already spelled out our intent, and what mattered was how we addressed it through bringing curriculum and pedagogy together – implementation.

Our approach was to dwell on three I's that would support the growth and effectiveness of learning and at the same time tune in with Ofsted's three I's. The first was *insight* – a key skill for head teachers, curriculum coordinators, teachers and teaching assistants. We need insight to know whether our children are learning what we

---

3   Ofsted and A. Spielman, Speech to the 'Wonder Years' Curriculum Conference (26 January 2019). Available at: https://www.gov.uk/government/speeches/amanda-spielman-at-the-wonder-years-curriculum-conference.

are intending. Is the impact good enough? Are the children investing in their learning? Are they engaged? Is the learning relevant to the children? Are their products of a good enough standard? Are they being challenged to extend the quality of what they produce? Are they building knowledge and mastering skills? Are their attitudes to learning appropriate? Are they self-initiating, self-organising, competent, seeking quality and collaborating well when necessary and being responsible with respect to the demands placed on them? Is necessary knowledge being embedded and used? Are they grappling with and using intellectual concepts? Are they relating abstract concepts to wider, real-world situations?

Insight is directly related to the intent. The big question is whether the learning is maintaining its *integrity* – our second 'I' word. This is the crucial one. Does our insight tell us whether the impact of our effort is maintaining the integrity of our intent? If the impact doesn't match the intention, our work has no integrity and one or the other

Figure 18.1. Leading the curriculum

has to change. Professionals strive to reach their intent, so the next challenge is our third 'I' word – *improve*. The watchword of our development in curriculum and pedagogy has been to improve, and to know that, however far we go, there is always more to enjoy.

Figure 18.1 shows the leadership imperative in terms of accountability. The three I's of Ofsted's inspection are valid, but how leadership interpret and use them is what ensures that the school is effective – and leadership ensure that.

Overall, our approach to the pressures of accountability has been to go with the developments positively and use them as a lever to support our ambitions. This is different from simply using accountability as a form of reference control – saying, in effect, 'We need to do this because someone else wants us to – sorry.' That has been the downfall of many schools.

Having said all that, we have included a few quotes from Ofsted reports on our schools below. We do so not to celebrate or advertise our own success, but to reassure those who wonder how the curriculum and pedagogy we are developing resonates with inspectors.

Even though this school was judged as requiring improvement very early on in our development, inspectors noted:

> *Leaders have ensured that pupils experience a broad and balanced curriculum. Leaders listen to pupils to ensure that their 'curious' curriculum inspires, motivates and engages pupils. Pupils who spoke with inspectors were unanimous in their views that the curriculum developed a wide range of knowledge, skills and understanding. For example, pupils in Year 5 were eager to share their strong knowledge of current world problems surrounding sustainability. The curriculum provides a wealth of extra-curricular activities which pupils also said help them develop a deeper understanding of their work. In Year 4, pupils were keen to recall*

how their visit to a Roman villa helped them understand life in the Roman era. This aligned with what inspectors found in pupils' work books.[4]

A subsequent section 8 inspection of the school judged:

School and trust leaders have established a programme of training for staff that has enabled them to revise the design of the curriculum and improve the quality of teaching and learning. Leaders frequently evaluate the impact of changes to the curriculum. Staff are positive about the school's development. They state that the school is improving and that they are well supported. ...

Leaders have designed a curriculum to ignite pupils' curiosity about the world they live in. Through well-planned themes, leaders intend for pupils to learn a range of subjects such as history, geography and art. However, there is some variation in the quality of the design of subjects other than English and mathematics. The art curriculum is well planned enabling pupils to apply their knowledge of sketching and painting in a range of contexts. However, the French curriculum has not yet been fully embedded across all year groups.[5]

A section 5 inspection, which judged good, observed, 'Leaders provide a well-organised and challenging curriculum and recognise the importance or widening pupils' vocabulary. The curriculum is carefully planned and based on what pupils need to learn, including in the early years.'[6]

---

4   Ofsted, School Report: Stoke Lodge Primary School (9–10 January 2019), pp. 3–4. Available at: https://files.ofsted.gov.uk/v1/file/50058229.

5   Ofsted, Monitoring Inspection Visit to Stoke Lodge Primary School (12 May 2021), pp. 2–3. Available at: https://files.ofsted.gov.uk/v1/file/50165559.

6   Ofsted, School Report: Inspection of Meadowbrook Primary School (12–13 October 2021), p. 2. Available at: https://files.ofsted.gov.uk/v1/file/50172978.

We are pleased that Ofsted recognises our work, yet they are but one voice and only one of our indicators of impact. We don't jump through hoops; we challenge ourselves with snakes and ladders.

> I think we have external pressure much more in perspective now.
> *Sharon Clark*

Staff changes – snakes and ladders

For all the usual reasons, the people working in our schools have changed. Having worked hard to devise an agreed agenda, with a shared understanding of what we are trying to do and why and building a collective commitment, the supposition might be that each new arrival takes us back to square one. Of course, that would never be tenable. As new staff join the school, therefore, it is vital that they understand the Olympus story so far. Once the coherent vision for our work is underway, newly appointed colleagues must be able to subscribe to it. However, while the next few chapters may have already been written, they should also have an opportunity to influence the chapters beyond.

To help people understand what they are subscribing to, clear and concise documentation is crucial. This is one of the benefits of the documentation we have produced during the development of our approach. New staff can read about the thinking behind our ways of working and tune into the fundamentals of planning and teaching and our expectations for children's learning.

Of course, new appointees bring fresh perspectives, different expertise, diverse experiences and unique talents. The challenge is to ensure that each new staff member knows they have chance to contribute to the school's thinking, whether they arrive as a head teacher, newly qualified teacher or teaching assistant. Good head teachers spot potential, engage with colleagues in ways that acknowledge their effort and enquire into their thinking and practice. They accumulate a fund of opportunities to explore either within their school or on a wider front. This is why appreciative inquiry is such an important leadership tool.

Bought-in published schemes – a ladder for some and a snake for others

We could have saved a lot of trouble if we had simply purchased one of the published schemes of work that are available. We probably would have created a lot of trouble for ourselves too.

When the new national curriculum was introduced in 2013, several publishers modified their previous offer and some newer companies sprang up offering schools a ready-made solution. Many of these providers are very good, offering structured learning to cover all content and attractive, high-quality resources for teachers, children or both. Schools can adopt the published schemes, secure in the knowledge that they have invested in something that does the heavy lifting for them. For publishers, a few schools judged outstanding who use the approach will attract others locally.

Why didn't we use one of these approaches? At the outset, we decided that the issue we faced was the long-term deskilling of teachers, as the emphasis on a core curriculum had left them uncertain about how to approach planning of the wider foundation curriculum. The deskilling also extended to the pedagogy they employed. This meant that, even if the best resources were available to teachers, they would still need support to make it work. It doesn't matter how good, comprehensive, attractive, interactive and well-organised a resource is, if a teacher doesn't know how to use it, the result will be less than satisfactory.

Earlier in this book, we outlined the intricacies of pedagogy and the need for a detailed understanding of planning processes. We weren't convinced that these issues would be addressed by buying an off-the-shelf solution. For other schools, a bought-in commercial curriculum might be just the right thing at just the right time. For us, the key question is always whether the pedagogy can match the curriculum intent. Improving the curriculum does not on its own improve teaching.

◀ p. 212

Old practices linger on – a sleeping snake coming back to bite us

With any development, letting go of the old is always a challenge. It must have been the same for Columbus when his crew watched the European mainland drop below the horizon and saw nothing ahead. Teachers, like all of us, want to hang on to what they know – just in case. There are very few instances of new developments being adopted swiftly and irreversibly; the Fosbury Flop is one exception.

We had the problem of teachers trying the new but overtly or secretly persevering with the old. It is a case of holding your nerve, recognising and talking about the new, and turning a blind eye and giving no recognition or credence to that which needs to be left behind.

We had a similar challenge with leadership approaches. Some head teachers had become deskilled at being in classrooms, absorbing what was happening and talking about it. An increasingly managerial outlook, in conjunction with an accountability regime, meant that most leaders saw visits to classrooms as a formal opportunity to carry out an observation. These might have to continue to keep the inspection wolf from the door, but if our development was going to work, leaders needed to be close to the action and, where possible, taking part. We wanted head teachers and curriculum leads to engage in a continuing conversation about curriculum and pedagogy.

Parent outlooks – extending ladders

We had very few issues with parents' outlooks. In fact, their interest and enthusiasm reflected their children's growing awareness of the wider curriculum.

One of our parents provided us with this endorsement:

I have been to some fantastic exhibitions of primary learners' work hosted at the secondary schools. This has been an exciting development, showcasing the very best of the Curious Curriculum work, and a chance to demonstrate progression and excellence in the standards of work produced. Some of the children whose work was on display were also at the exhibitions and spoke eloquently and confidently about their work.

My son, who recently progressed to an Olympus trust secondary school, said, 'I feel inspired by this new learning curriculum and I am happy to have participated in it. I have enjoyed the experience of creating new and interesting work such as painting Hokusai's wave and writing stories about cave children. It has been a fun change to my ordinary schoolwork and I am happy to have experienced it.'

Another parent valued the fact that the curriculum develops the whole child, not just their academic side:

Linking the Curious Curriculum Unleashed to the UN Sustainable Development Goals means that my child is also learning for life and the world around him when he leaves school. He is able to develop his personality and interests in a fun and engaging way. I love that my son is able to learn academically through topics which really interest him and that he is passionate about. He regularly comes home and shares his learning with me because he enjoys it so much.

Of course, the exhibitions helped as much as publications and regular updates from the school.

The key message of always doing things well with parents is vital. For a long while, schools have held 'celebration assemblies' to which groups of parents are invited. These are valuable opportunities for transmitting the purpose and success of curriculum and pedagogic practice. On some occasions, such assemblies resemble an audience-participation television show, with the acclaim of the child more important than the reason they are being acclaimed. It is good for children to feel celebrated and special, but it is better that they are celebrated because of real and tangible achievements.

Too often, the head teacher leading such assemblies is little more than the master or mistress of ceremonies – a figurehead. Occasionally, they appear lost as the assembly happens around them, uttering phrases that befit Young Mr Grace in *Are You Being Served?* who tells everyone he meets, 'You've all done very well!' while not having a clue what is happening.

Well used and managed, celebratory assemblies are a chance for the head teacher to effectively lead a staff meeting with the children and parents present: a judiciously collected selection, linking children's products from different age groups, will create an image of progression. Similarly, examples of KPIs and consideration of knowledge or skill provide opportunities to acknowledge the child and, with subtlety, thank the teachers and teaching assistants. It also shows that the head teacher notices the pedagogy going on around the school during the week.

Transition to secondary schools – the perennial snake

Those involved in primary schooling have worried for decades about what happens to children's progress when they move to secondary school. As children leave primary schools in the summer and head off to different secondary schools, they are cast to the four winds and arrive after the summer in different secondary schools. Likewise, secondary schools begin the autumn term taking in children blown in by the four winds from any number of primary schools. And yet we talk of continuity … It is an incredibly complex challenge.

Many children enjoy the transition, finding themselves in a new environment at just the right moment for them, and they adapt and thrive. For others, it is like the feeling we get when we step on an escalator that is going slightly faster than we anticipated; they stumble and recover but it can take a long time. For those who have struggled in primary school, the new environment may represent a fresh start and they flourish, but for others it can be the start of a downward spiral in many aspects of their life.

In our schools, we have been working hard on transition with regard to curriculum and pedagogy. It is difficult terrain. There is every will to address the issues that we all recognise affect children: the size of the school, the change in routine, the number of teachers, the new community and the demands of pupil work. At the same time, both secondary and primary sectors have their own agendas, which always seem to push transition away from the top. The leadership world is full of failed transition programmes built on good intentions.

Olympus Trust has four secondary schools which have been working on curriculum and pedagogy in parallel and using the same principles of intent as the primary schools. Transition work between primaries and secondaries in the trust is successful, but each year over half of the children leave our primaries for other schools and over half of the new secondary intake arrive from primaries outside the trust.

We decided to begin within our own trust and to explore the idea of a theme that would extend across different subject disciplines, which could begin in Year 6 and continue during the early part of Year 7.

The secondary schools were prepared to consider an interdisciplinary approach following a pilot in one of our secondaries the previous year. Secondary staff had reported increased engagement and quality of work from the children who had been able to make links between content in different subject disciplines.

The problem for the secondary schools was greater than for the primaries because they received children from outside the trust who had not completed the first phase. The challenge was to use the learning of one group and add further teaching to extend the learning of all.

The theme we chose was 'Identity'. It is one of those catch-all titles, but it tuned into the idea of a child needing to re-find themselves in a new context in their lives. Teachers from Year 6 and Year 7 spent time planning, first content and then the pedagogic approach, building a narrative that would carry the theme through the time span. Anticipation was high. Once the groundwork was underway, we were ready to ask other local schools whether they wished to be involved in the work. Then we had a pandemic.

The pandemic – a long snake

And then there was COVID-19. The lockdowns changed the agenda for everybody; we haven't recorded every detail in this section because each school has its own tale to tell. However, we have shared some of our reflections that demonstrate our outlook and described some of the steps we took to keep improving against the odds.

In March 2020, we decided that our approach would not fall into a state of suspended animation, but that we would keep the momentum going. We had already worked up some ideas for our transition programme, so we decided to see whether we could make them work in a different context. We set about designing some activities for children to do at home across the curriculum range.

We developed a Transition Challenge for all children joining our secondary schools in September 2021. The idea was that challenges would be sent to each child from their future secondary school, and they would take the products to their new school to work on in the autumn term. We devised tasks that, according to our evaluation, the children really enjoyed. We extended them, while also making sure that they would be manageable at home, regardless of circumstances (which parents appreciated). These tasks will have traction way beyond COVID times.

Our staff sessions also moved online. We decided that we would try to keep going with staff development, so we set up remote meetings for teachers to engage in their year-group sessions. Mick produced filmed segments of CPD to support the next part of our planning, which focused on pedagogic quality, and the schools used them to suit their own circumstances. It wasn't ideal, but we kept making progress.

The Olympus Academy Trust

LEARNING CHALLENGE 2 | People, Places and Me

The Maths of Me

This is about gathering data about yourself which we can compare with all the other children in your class when you come to school.

Measuring
Measure in centimetres (cm) as accurately as you can and write down the results clearly on a chart. For some of these, you will need someone to help you.

1. Your height (no shoes)
2. The circumference of your head, 1cm above your eyebrow
3. The distance between you thumb and furthest finger
4. The distance from your big toe to your heel
5. The length of your arm from finger-tip to shoulder
6. Your waist
7. The length of your stride from toe to heel.
8. The width of your mouth from one edge of your lips to the other.
9. The length of your ear from top to lowest point (the end of the lobe).
10. The length from shoulder to shoulder in a straight line.
11. How high you can jump from a standing position.
12. How high you can hop from a standing position.
13. Stand with both feet together on a line on the floor, maybe a tile or where the flooring changes in a doorway. Jump, with your feet together and measure how far you leap.
14. Touch the highest point that you can reach up a wall with one hand (don't jump). Measure from there to the ground.
15. Stand sideways by the wall. Crouch and spring up and touch the wall. How high is it from where you finger touches to the floor?

How big are your lungs?

How big are your lungs?

Do this over a sink or in the garden
Fill a Coke tin to the very top with water. Get a drinking straw and put it in the hole and blow for as long as you can. Water will come out of the top as the air goes in. When you run out of puff, STOP.
Pour what water is left into a cup or mug. If you have a measuring jug, pour the water into that and measure how many millilitres (ml) it is. Take that number away from (subtract it from) the number on the side of the Coke tin to find how many millilitres of air you have blown out of your lungs.
Write down the amount and bring it with you in your folder.

Olympus Transition Challenges : Y6

Page : 1

LEARNING CHALLENGE 1 | People, Places and Me

Reading and Geography Challenges

Under the Skin- by Catherine Macphail

This is an inspiring story of a young asylum seeker's struggle to build a new life with his family in Britain. At last Omar's family have a safe place to live. But life on the estate isn't easy, despite him suggesting in the opening chapter that his new home is idyllic. His supposed 'best friend' Sam is always there - in Omar's tower block, in his class, and in his face. Sam wants to push Omar around, but Omar's pushing back. They're worlds apart - and too close for comfort. While the book has moments exploring Omar's sadness, there are many humorous moments, especially when Omar explores the English culture and unpicks our odd turns of phrase.

Reading challenge

Read the book, identifying unfamiliar words and finding the definition as you go. K... of these words and bring them back to school in September
Now answer the following questions- you may represent your answers in any form... thought map, diary entry or even through a bullet journal. It can be colourful or bla... white. You will be sharing your answers back at school.

- What do you understand by the term asylum seeker or refugee?
- In the opening chapter Omar writes a letter, suggesting his new home is idyllic wh... really. Why do you think he does this?
- How do you think Omar felt arriving in Britain, think about what he left behind an... feeling, looking forwards? Use the text to support your answers.

We know the text you have been sent is likely to be easier than books that you mig... to but the content will probably be more challenging. The book explores a differen... period in history that you might be less familiar with. You might have to research a... particular culture or period to understand what you are reading. Take time to und... characters and the decisions they make as you read the book.

Olympus Transition Challenges | Y6

LEARNING CHALLENGE 6 | People, Places and Me

Artistic Me

This challenge asks you to enjoy producing a creative design.

First, we would like you to find an object in your home that has a firm base. It could be a tin, a solid box or an ornament. The base has to be no more than 15 centimetres across at any point. You have a tape measure in your pack to check.

You will need a piece of plain white paper. One of the A4 papers in the pack is fine but if you have something bigger such as the back of a sheet of wrapping paper, that would be fine and you can choose how big to do your design.

You will also need a pencil.

Now you are ready to start.

Put your object near the centre of your paper and, holding it still, draw around the base.

Next lift up the object and move it so that it now overlaps the original outline … and draw around it again.

Repeat this at least five more times until you have seven outlines overlapping. You can continue if you wish to either fill your paper or to create a better design. It doesn't matter if one of your outlines go over the side of the page…but your design is your decision.

Next, you need to shade or colour the design. You might like to use paint or crayons, if you have at home. If not, a pencil will be great if you use it well.

Very carefully, you should colour each segment of the design so that the shade or colour changes wherever two lines cross.

If you are using a pencil, you can shade with lots of different tones of grey or black. You might choose to create patterns with your pencil…dots, stripes, small circle, hatching, curvy lines.

You need to choose no more than six colours or six pencil patterns or six pencil shades.

The challenge is to colour or shade your design without any two touching segments being the same. It is not as easy as it sounds and you might need to have a couple of practices. Try to be as neat as you can be and, if using shading or patterns, try to keep the shades and patterns consistent.

When you have finished, save your finished product. Don't forget to do your learning review.

When you bring your design to school, we will exhibit every effort produced by all our new children and learn about famous artists who have worked and designed in this sort of style.

Let's get designing!

Olympus Transition Challenges | Y6

Page : 1

The pandemic continued ...

The year that followed was no less challenging. We could develop a survive mentality or we could focus our energies on thriving. With a combination of working remotely and in person, we set about our usual school improvement cycle of reviewing the previous year's progress and adapting and adjusting the school improvement implementation plan. The portal became a repository for our recovery curriculum (although we felt that 'rebound' was better adjective). It included not only the key elements of the English and mathematics curriculum that needed to be retaught, but it also had a sharp focus on social and emotional learning, which we felt was essential.

Mick ran a series of online sessions for year groups of teachers focusing on the next phase of our curriculum development. He helped them to build a narrative within the context of the theme that we would run later in the year. These were filmed and the staff were able to use them in their own schools when considering their plans.

Teachers were keen to keep the momentum going and didn't want to let the pandemic stunt progress. Inevitably, however, it did. Staff turnover and the lack of opportunities to work as practically as before all meant that teachers were adapting their planning and finding PowerPoint printed sheets a more convenient mode of delivery.

Our continued focus on developing subject leader expertise was a welcome break from talking about 'bubbles' and the consistency of the best hand sanitiser. Our May 2021 INSET saw staff enthused about the subject they were leading and animated when supporting their colleagues with the latest thinking and resources from professional associations.

Staffing challenges aside, we were growing and developing all the time. September 2021 confirmed this when, once again, staff INSET training on the disciplinary concepts in teaching history reinvigorated everyone to stop thinking about what we couldn't do and focus more on what we could do. We started the new school year with renewed energy and enthusiasm, praising ourselves for our resilience and the resigned acknowledgement that this was going to be our 'new normal' for some time to come.

Yet, in spite of all our efforts, as we reached early summer 2022, we knew that we were at the limit of that resilience. Our schools were flagging and some of the best practice was starting to slip. We saw that we would need to act to reinvigorate the ethos and culture of high expectations ready for the new school year in the autumn. We recognised why some of our work was stalling and previous less successful practice was re-emerging:

- Even over the course of just two years, there had been a significant change of leadership within the trust's schools. All but one of the headship changes had seen people move within the trust, but those settling into new schools were also now working with …

- A significant change in personnel, with many experienced staff having left and been replaced often by early career teachers. These individuals had not been part of the gradual development of the Curious Curriculum.

- Furthermore, their initial teacher education experience had been truncated, disrupted and limited in scope. Several new members of staff in each of our schools were coming to terms with teaching itself, so the Curious Curriculum was but one thing on their agenda.

- The support that would normally be provided through curriculum leads was less apparent than before the pandemic. Our curriculum leads and subject leads had reshuffled or moved to promotions beyond the trust and newly appointed colleagues were finding their feet.

- We also suspect that many staff had become used to the 'command and control' outlook during the staggered return to school. The bubbles, distancing and routines necessarily demanded an approach that discouraged personal initiative.

All this meant we were again seeing some of the features that we had set out to remove previously: one-off lessons, downloaded lesson plans, perfunctory learning activities, teachers deciding what they wanted to teach rather than what we needed the children to learn. All of this sent us back to first principles: the why and how of the Curious Curriculum.

Whereas our first drive for development drew the whole community together in establishing practice, our current approach is much more differentiated, not between staff with different abilities but between staff with different knowledge and experience of what we are trying to achieve. Hence, head teachers have a quadruple role in respect of the Curious Curriculum. They have a role to play with regard to their whole staff, another with their curriculum and subject leads, a further role in 'coaching' new staff to the school or trust and, of course, their collective work with one another.

Planning for the unpredictable

We have outlined some of the bigger challenges we have grappled with – or tried to dodge – in order to keep our work moving forward. One of the benefits of not having a highly detailed plan is that adjustment doesn't mean failing to achieve objectives. On the other hand, adjustment must not become a rationalisation for lowered ambition.

In terms of planning ahead, it might be worth considering:

- How far is the school prone to being knocked off course? You could think about the way previous plans have come to fruition easily or with difficulty or tailed off into quiet failure.
- What are the sorts of factors that can be anticipated as potential challenges or threats to progress? What are the potential mitigations?
- To what extent is the school cognisant of Ofsted and inspection, and how far does any change in framework send a jolt through the school? Good schools are 'inspection confident'. We wanted our teachers to own and use the Curious Curriculum, to engage with it and to talk confidently about it with anyone who wanted to discuss it with them.
- Are we adept enough to recognise when things are starting to slip in order to address the problem within our community? Are we open enough to devise a plan of action to take us forward again? Early success will develop a good school culture, but it has to be sustainable through difficult times as well as positive times.
- Is strategic planning flexible enough to take account of unexpected influences and, at the same time, secure enough to hold people to progress? A feature of our work on the Curious Curriculum is that planning has always remained an important priority, but it has never dominated urgent agendas in schools.

The impact of impact

As this book tells the story of how we have implemented our intended curriculum, it might be reasonable to ask where the important word 'impact' features.

The three watchwords of Ofsted's approach have become embedded in the language of schooling. Part One of our book describes how we implemented our curriculum to achieve our learning ambitions for children. In this part, we explain how we set about establishing our shared outlook: revisiting our intent and some of our challenges with implementation. For school leaders, it is important to keep the notion of impact high on the agenda.

Our view is that observing and checking impact is not an event but an attitude. Impact is inherent in all the work we do (the use of the word in this sentence is the fifty-sixth so far in the book). From the outset, we have been using our insight to consider whether the impact of the curriculum is what we seek. It was there at the beginning when we looked at the practice in our schools and asked ourselves whether this was what we wanted. It has been there at the times when we checked whether the practices we were promoting were being implemented in the way we anticipated and whether they were achieving our intention. When our insight suggested they were we asked ourselves how to maintain progress and build further, and when they weren't we needed to reconsider. These were what we came to see as our snakes-and-ladders experiences in curriculum development.

Over the course of the last five years, we have evaluated impact many times and acted on what we have found. Some occasions were planned, scheduled and structured (see Table 18.1) and others took place because it is what we do all the time as a natural part of leadership. It is our belief that looking at impact is a continuous part of our job: teachers, teaching assistants and leadership at every level. By taking multiple snapshots of learning, we eventually have enough to put them together to create a video (or zoetrope). By using our insight, we can check the integrity of reality against intent.

Table 18.1. The head teacher's year

	Weekly	Monthly	Three times a year
Analysis of results	Formative analysis to inform planning and next steps.		Teacher assessment. Summative data collected through PiXL papers.[7]
Internal feedback: **Meetings with director of education** **Support from teaching and learning lead** **Trust reviews**	Weekly meeting with director of education as a leadership team to bring forward current issues. Weekly briefing from director of education on things to be aware of.		
External feedback: Ofsted **Triads** **External visitors**			
Conference			
Exhibitions			School exhibitions take place at the end of each theme.
Subject staff meetings **Year group staff meetings**			Subject leaders and year group teachers get together across the trust to discuss how their subject or year group is progressing in their school.
Moderation: **Subject leads** **Year teacher leads**	Moderation of all writing during PPA sessions between class teachers.		Whole-school writing moderation. This is then followed up by senior leadership team to check accuracy. Subject leads moderate outcomes to ensure each curriculum area is progressive across the school by ensuring detailed monitoring takes place. This is captured through floor books.
Networks			
Parent feedback		Schools gather parent voice through parent forum.	Schools gather feedback from parents during parent–teacher consultations.
Pupil views	Head teachers gather pupil voice weekly with Hot Chocolate Friday and junior leadership meetings or pupil council.		

---

7   See https://www.pixl.org.uk.

Six times a year	Biannually	Annually	External schedule
Through governance in our local governors' meetings. Across the trust in our trust school improvement board meetings.		External data such as SATs.	
Termly support in school used to support quality assurance and progress against school improvement plan.	The trust conducts a review twice a year to monitor progress and support improvement.		
External visitors support the trust at least six times a year with training.			External agencies, e.g. Ofsted and our academy triad work, are used every eighteen months for four years.
		An annual Olympus conference supports professional development and takes place in one of our secondary schools.	
	Trust exhibitions take place twice a year in one of our secondary schools.		
	Writing moderation across the trust facilitated by the local authority and trust teaching and lead.	Curriculum subject leads moderate learning across all subject areas across the trust.	External writing moderation with local authority three times a year for Year 6 and Year 2, and twice a year for EYFS and Years 1, 3, 4 and 5.
Curriculum leader network meetings.			
Schools gather parent feedback during exhibitions and at the end of each term.			
Head teachers gather pupil views every term from learning and reviews.			

CHAPTER 19

Impact

As we reach the five-year mark in our development of curriculum and pedagogy, what impact have we had?

The teaching profession is notoriously self-effacing in talking about its own achievements, reticent about blowing its own trumpet and quick to point out failings and blemishes in practice. We are no different and prefer a modestly positive analysis to overbearing certainty. We can honestly say, though, that teaching, learning, standards and outcomes at Olympus Academy Trust are much improved on where they were. We can say that the curriculum is fit for purpose in a way that was not the case when we began. We can say that most teachers enjoy teaching the Curious Curriculum and find it stimulating professionally and less taxing to manage. We know that, in the main, parents see the value and purpose of the curriculum and support it to a greater extent than they did. We know that our governors and trustees believe in what we are doing and want us to further develop our work.

> Sometimes you don't realise how much you've shifted practice, until you see examples of what we used to do.
>
> *Sharon Clark*

> The changes and improvements have been very exciting.
> The Curious Curriculum has been aligned across the primaries
> in order to facilitate a consistent approach, which engages our
> learners and stimulates their imagination – and produces results.
>
> *Kate Sheldon*

Not everything is as we would want it to be and work remains to
be done. We know that we need to do more to extend the links
between our children's Curious Curriculum experiences and
their mathematics learning, in the way we have with English; it is
developing but we need to make it more secure. We need to extend
the children's agency in devising scientific experiments that build
from the stimulus we offer. We need to further develop their capacity
to research, collate and present findings and strengthen the notion
of learning communities.

We are getting there, but we know we will never truly arrive. We are
near the very top of our snakes-and-ladders board, but we know
we won't reach the last square and finish. As we hit the final straight,
we will extend the board. The idea of improving on previous best
is the most helpful target in education, and it extends professional
enjoyment and expertise too.

Where next?

As we have tried to stress throughout this book, our agenda changes
as we travel. While many children have been negatively affected
by their COVID-19 experiences and have slipped back in terms of
some aspects of their development, most have come back to school
ready to learn and enjoying the challenges on offer. Our bounceback
efforts are important, but perhaps more so are our renewed efforts to
invigorate learning and develop curriculum and teaching. Established

routines are back in place after the pandemic, but, like many schools, we need to rebuild the children's agency in their learning. Mostly, children are eager to return to their schooling, but it is taking time to progress from the PowerPoint-led teacher-questioner and children-responder experiences of much online learning.

While we seek to build again learning relationships with our children, we have the delightful new challenge of building learning relationships with new children. In the last year, we have seen an influx of families from Hong Kong settling in the neighbourhoods of schools within our trust. All schools have received some, and in a couple of schools we are now receiving several new children every week, to the extent that we are having to reconfigure class arrangements. Our school communities are already a mixture of young people with different heritages, and our new arrivals only add to the opportunity for children to appreciate the richness of the world in which they live. One good thing, and a real fillip, is that their parents express a delight in the curriculum and teaching that their children enjoy. Our challenge is to look again at our Curious Curriculum *through the eyes of the child* and make sure that it resonates with their world.

Our ambition over the next few months is to explore ways to ensure that our pedagogy takes learning deeper. We are looking closely at how we move the learning experience and take the children's achievements to more profound levels. We are also revisiting the curriculum/pedagogy axis to look at how children can be engaged in enquiring, innovating, debating, discussing, making links, applying, inventing and questioning – all intentions that are set out in our original pedagogic principles.

We are looking again at teachers' questions – at which modes of questions work best with which pedagogic approach and encouraging teachers to expand their repertoire of questioning techniques. We are also considering which sorts of children's writing relate best to which pedagogic approach and building breadth of children's experience into our planning. We are trying to take learning to a greater depth than ever before. We want our children to dive deep into our Curious Curriculum.

That is our story so far: the twists and turns of our snakes and the steps we have taken on our ladders – many successfully. We have tried to be realistic and describe a very complicated series of developments in a way that will help you to consider the elements that are most important to you within your own setting. Like any story, some bits have been left out, others have been embellished and some understated. In order to capture the essence, we have collated our learning into some key pieces of advice from which you might choose to select the most apposite or tick off those that you take for granted. As you read the suggestions in Part Three, you should be able to identify where it comes from in the account you have just read.

PART THREE

Twenty-five pieces of advice to change learning in your school

If we were asked to offer some advice to carry schools through the process of building a new approach to learning, our reflections would boil down to twenty-five core messages. These represent a clear picture of what lies ahead, as well as being a resource to turn to regularly in order to revisit principles and support you to make progress.

1. Ensure that leadership is an active pursuit: head teachers have to be involved in pedagogic and curriculum dialogue

Is this too obvious a starting point? The term 'head teacher' is very symbolic. The purpose of schools is to enhance children's learning through the best pedagogy to secure the curriculum outcomes that are sought.

If teachers create the learning weather in their classroom,[1] then the head teacher creates the climate. As leadership has become more managerial over the last couple of decades, there has been less of a focus on the core purpose of schools: the learning agenda. Naturally, some of the early leadership programmes covered those elements of the job that were previously lacking or contemporary urgencies: finance, staffing, premises, safeguarding and the like. These are all vital for the effectiveness of a school, of course, but nothing should usurp the learning agenda.

A good leadership team knows that it is the driving force of curriculum and pedagogy, and therefore that delegating overall responsibility is a folly. This goes further than scheduled and periodic lesson observations to fulfil perceived inspection criteria. It goes further than regular meetings to review planning or to scrutinise and

---

1   See H. G. Ginott, *Teacher and Child: A Book for Parents and Teachers* (New York: Macmillan, 1972), pp. 15–16.

evaluate children's books. The best schools – those that experience real development in curriculum and pedagogy – know that, alongside the learning in the classrooms, the presence of the head teacher is fundamental to progress and improvement.

> Senior leaders, trustees and governors supported the financial investment required to make our new approach happen through release time, ongoing CPD for all staff, staff conferences, external support and publication of documents.
>
> **Sarah Williams**

If we want to develop learning, we have to be close to it – and often. That means being in classrooms every day for no other reason than to see what is going on and talk about it with teachers, teaching assistants and children. The quality of that conversation is crucially important. A leader who asks how a development has taken place and considers where next will have more impact than someone who simply approves or disapproves. A leader who relates what they are seeing to another colleague in school will have more impact than someone who simply notes their observation and moves on.

These conversations should be about the core principles, the vision and the practice. It all comes back to expectation and coherence: the head teacher is the touchstone for what the school is trying to achieve.

2. See curriculum as going hand in hand with pedagogy and learning outcomes

Curriculum and pedagogy are inextricably linked. Too many schools try to address them 'in order'. The best way forward is to stay broad when building a rationale and determining the processes you will follow. It doesn't take longer and staff will understand more fully how their work will unfold. Once the momentum builds, the excitement is tangible.

3. Decide on who will challenge and push your thinking

You will need someone external to offer an objective point of view. Who will be the stone in the shoe? It needs to be someone you trust and who will be dispassionate enough to hold a line, while at the same time being aware of the pressures that affect schools so that developments are timed and adjusted in order to manage progress. It needs to be someone who can be relied upon to bring a wide perspective, experience of several schools and settings, research awareness and an appreciation of ongoing debates. This should include, but not be overly influenced by, an understanding of inspection framework changes. We should always have trust that inspectors will recognise the fundamentals of good practice.

4. Think long term

Any school that decides to develop curriculum and pedagogy needs to recognise that they are embarking on a long-term process. Many schools make the mistake of thinking that producing a policy means the job is done. Filing cabinets, real and virtual, are full of policies in a continuum of conditions from pristine to dog-eared. The only policy that matters is the one that meets the children. Too often, policies are produced to satisfy others – inspectors, local authority, trust or governors – when what a policy should do is support the teachers and others who work with the children to enable effective practice. While a policy might spell out minimum expectations, the ambition for learning should surely be greater than that. The policy should contain an unfolding description of a horizon to aim towards on an intriguing professional journey.

It might be that curriculum and pedagogy are top priorities for a while and then other aspects of schooling might step into the limelight. Good leadership ensures that priorities dovetail rather than allowing the inference that some aspects have reduced importance. While behaviour or special educational needs and disabilities might need to be a focus for consideration, they are enmeshed with curriculum and pedagogy rather than separate. Good schools never let curriculum and pedagogy fall from the agenda.

5. Aim for excellence

No matter where we start, we need to aim for excellence and seek the highest of standards. Teachers, teaching assistants and children need to be shown high-quality examples and we need to be explicit about the merits of the work.

A piece of writing might be termed good because of its correct grammar or its use of appropriate vocabulary, but it will be excellent if it meets its purpose and has an appropriate effect on the audience. A piece of artwork or dance will be excellent when the techniques employed communicate the intended message. A classroom discussion will be excellent when all engage and when contributions continuously move forward the thinking of the group as a whole. A song will be sung excellently when attention is paid to the quality of the sound rather than just the volume.

This means establishing early expectations of each other. What types of work will be displayed in classrooms? What will we talk about? What we will value? If we have a growing and shared view of excellence, we can start to plan for it in terms of learning experiences, resources and time. This affects our planning and anticipation of each day in a classroom setting, whether at school, on a residential visit or at the swimming pool. Our search for excellence for the children starts with our belief in the excellence of our own work.

6. Work out who the decision-makers are

In theory, we want everyone to make decisions, but the reality is that different decisions are made by different people depending on their level of responsibility and the nature of the task. This means thinking really hard about delegation, and when someone is given responsibility, really meaning it.

Anyone involved in a working group must be capable of being a decision-maker. People cannot keep going back to their department, head teacher or phase leader to ask permission or check out the next step. Likewise, staff at every level should expect to be advised, supported, guided, helped and challenged. This is called a collegial outlook, and work on curriculum and pedagogy is a good place to build it. Get the right people in the room – and always make sure that you know your own place in the room. How far do you want to drive and support? How far do you want to influence?

7. Start with where you are

Get everyone on board with identifying what needs to change, stay or be ditched. Without being open about the starting point, it will be hard to make progress. Getting people to see the issues we are trying to address without seeming to know it all or being ultra-critical is a serious leadership challenge. It needs to be done, though, and done with care. A full-on critique can work, but it isn't advisable very often.

Straight-talking – being honest and allowing the truth to be heard – is important. However, it should always be the practice or provision that is at fault or in need of improvement, not the individual. At the same time, it is important to recognise good practice, areas where there are opportunities to build upon and the efforts that people are making, especially when that effort could be more richly rewarding and satisfying.

8. Remember that at every stage the 'why' is vital!

Why are we doing this work? Why have we decided to start here? Why have we chosen to move thinking and practice in this direction? Why are we looking at this now? Why is this important for leadership, staff and children? Do the parents understand why we are stressing certain aspects of our work? A focus on reason and purpose must underpin all development; it cannot be overstated. The more we talk about reason and purpose, the more we will hear others talking about it.

9. Make sure that communication is disseminated

Too often, developments stumble because only a few people are privy to the important information. This leads to others potentially feeling disengaged and disenfranchised. What matters is keeping the conversation about curriculum and pedagogy alive. Constant dialogue is better than big announcements at long intervals. People need to keep thinking and talking about the issues under the microscope.

Communication comes in many forms, so take every opportunity to keep staff, including teaching assistants, in the loop. CPD events, such as conferences on school closure days, are important in terms of setting a compass direction or using a mirror to reflect on progress, but an online portal can provide an ongoing and interactive forum that keeps the momentum going. Handbooks are useful, although they can imply that issues are 'finished' or 'signed off'. It is a good idea to call any policy or supportive documentation a 'draft' and set a date for review and updating in the light of developing experience and thinking.

The most effective communication is always the low-key and regular consideration of developments as and when they happen. The good leader uses the incidental: being close to the learning as it happens, making conversations real and tangible, putting policy into context and bringing a teacher's impact into sharp relief.

10. Remember that collective confidence will grow as progress is made and good developments unfold

Some of the tensions that might have existed at the beginning will begin to dissolve as you move forward. As new staff arrive, it will be important to ensure that they are properly inducted. They need to know the expectations and working practices and be told the story so far in terms of developments to date. This revisit is a vital opportunity for the staff involved to retrace their steps and recognise the achievements they have made.

Keep revisiting your own thinking too: be fixed on your principles and the rationale for practice, and talk about the steps taken without harking backwards. Others might do so, but try not to imply that the staff were waiting to be led. Encourage people to give the credit for progress to each other. Leadership means constantly being ready to state why we work as we do and looking for the right moment to nudge people towards the next steps on this ambitious professional learning expedition (we aim for greater than a journey!). Talk about what is working, use appreciative inquiry and exhibit professional curiosity.

11. Keep doubling back to issues that have been worked on previously

Over the last twenty-five years, there has been a more systematic approach to leadership in schools. The development of National Professional Qualification for Headship programmes was much needed and helped the profession to see that leadership can be learned and cultivated. What such programmes have offered, extending to many other national professional qualifications, is a course that sets out the key components of school leadership and insights into ways to approach it. Most of the programmes have an implicit assumption that participants will be in the role for a finite time before moving on, either to a new level or another role. As the syllabus unfolds, it rarely repeats sections, giving rise to the suggestion that there is a step-by-step approach to the job. If only it were that simple!

What we all know, and what we have recognised so often in our work in developing the Curious Curriculum, is that very little happens quickly. Innovation can happen overnight but it rarely does. Sometimes, a new approach takes off with a flurry of excitement, but shortly afterwards it founders as people get stuck at second base. More often, new practices take time to become rooted and embedded.

When we first encouraged teachers to develop their teaching of art, for example, they were introduced to observational drawing and the use of pencils of different hardness to create tone and texture. The teachers were keen, made an effort and were buoyed by the children's response, who were focused and produced good drawings. The problem was that although the teachers were keen and willing, they didn't know how to extend the work, what techniques should come next or what to use as a stimulus.

The challenge for us was to use the first step to make progress and restate the principles, which was about more than simply covering techniques but also an emphasis on quality, excellence, appropriate materials and equipment, a good stimulus for learning and the best use of time. All of this applied to observational drawing, but to so many other aspects of the pedagogy we were trying to develop as well.

Similarly, when we encouraged teachers to extend the range of their pedagogic repertoire, they did so initially and then fell back into old habits. The challenge of leadership is to keep doubling back in a spirit of constantly making progress rather than criticising. Just as with children, corrections feel different and overload is avoided when we build on what is working, and so it is with colleagues too.

12. Recognise that people think they want answers when what they really need is to be guided towards developing their own solutions

Teachers, by nature, want to do well by the children they teach. They are usually willing to do as they are asked, and more than willing if they have been involved in developing the outlook and policy. Sadly, events in the recent past have reduced the extent to which teachers feel ownership of the work they do. If we want good curriculum and pedagogy, they need to feel they are working on an agenda that they have helped to create.

When asked to develop thinking and practice, there is the tendency in many teachers to ask (and be told) what the finished requirement should be. The temptation to provide an off-the-shelf plan or a ready-prepared solution. While this approach can occasionally bring benefits and save time, it usually requires much more support than is anticipated in terms of addressing misinterpretation, misapplication or misuse.

Energy is more often better spent in engaging people in developing the approach they are going to adopt, so they understand the essentials, know the thinking behind it and can influence its shape. In short, they have ownership. That doesn't mean we don't help; what it does require is a subtle and well-thought-out infusion of thinking and example at the right time – and a constant reminder of purposes and principles.

13. Work out how to integrate aspects of work that are high quality into the developing framework for learning

When all of this different practice starts and new horizons are being offered, many people want to revert back to when they felt comfortable, but moving forward doesn't mean severing ties with every aspect of current practice. One of the challenges is to work out what approaches fit with the new curriculum but may need to be developed and, most importantly, to explain why.

The practice, when done well, must fit with the aims and values of the curriculum and pedagogy. We don't keep a practice because we like it or because a lot of staff or children enjoy it. It is not about what we like but what we need; people like sweets but they need teeth! We might believe that forest schools, Philosophy for Children or Mantle of the Expert, for example, fit with our basic tenets for learning. That means we develop them and do them well. Indeed, we can seek to build other learning around these thriving aspects of our school and use them to drive into new learning territory.

14. Accept that developing practice is more complex than using maxims, acronyms and buzzwords in classrooms

Teachers seem to love mnemonics such as KISS (keep it simple, stupid). Try to avoid the situation where classrooms become a shimmering mass of laminated posters, many too high up to read, which are rarely referred to in teaching. Too many mnemonics, acronyms, maxims and aide-memoires simply become an empty vehicle for teachers to show they have taken seriously the new policy of the school. We all know them, and they have some value, but good development in pedagogy is about more than using the latest buzzwords. It is about more than having a RUCSAC (read, understand, choose, solve, answer and check) of taxonomies, including VCOP (vocabulary, connectives, openers and punctuation) and two stars and wish[2] for a WAGOLL.

If people in your school use too many of them, tell them to SUMO (shut up, move on)![3]

15. Develop the use of appreciative inquiry: recognise progress and use it as a spur to the next step

Appreciative inquiry should always take people deeper by extending the conversation and their insight into the reason why things are working as they are. Good exponents of appreciative inquiry encourage more focused consideration of the details, which helps teachers to see the subtleties of their work and the impact they are making. It also nudges them towards a realisation of what the next steps might be.

This is different from balancing support and challenge and it is different from never being satisfied. Appreciative inquiry should be used with challenge in a mix of about four to one to encourage the right sort of atmosphere and ethos in school. Never being satisfied is debilitating both for ourselves and others. We need to recognise

---

2 Two stars and a wish solicits two stars (areas where the children's work excelled) and one wish (an area where there can be some level of improvement).

3 See P. McGee, *S.U.M.O. (Shut Up, Move On): The Straight-Talking Guide to Succeeding in Life* (Chichester: Capstone, 2015).

progress and be satisfied with our efforts, using it to prompt consideration of what could be possible.

16. Welcome new staff to the moving staircase of development

The appointment of new staff brings all sorts of opportunities. Firstly, any vacancy offers the chance to incorporate relevant experience and skills. We should seek to appoint teachers or teaching assistants who can add to the expertise the team already possesses rather than someone who simply fits in. The arrival of a new colleague should create a dynamic spark and fresh energy.

At the same time, we need to ensure that any new arrival is quickly and fully up to date with the direction of curriculum and pedagogy in the school. Key messages can so easily get lost in translation. Importantly, the 'why' has to be central to avoid the risk of backward steps. A good induction is essential, with an emphasis on aspects such as quality and progression, so new staff need to experience the whole school, from the youngest to the oldest children.

Documents are valuable, and so are examples of pupil products and photographs of key moments in development. Devoting attention to setting the tone with new staff reaps benefit in terms of inviting innovative suggestions and avoiding missed steps and trips because they were ill-informed.

17. Use the children's enthusiasm for improvement and progress

The children are the first to see and appreciate improvement and progress – and they usually want more. One thing we learned very quickly was that the children will carry the momentum once we can get it going. They are quick to notice change, they spot that the teacher is trying to do something different, they sense a renewed emphasis and they realise there is a different urgency or focus.

The challenge is to seize on their interest for all the right reasons. Rather than just congratulating them on their product or appreciating their effort (both of which are important), we also need to engage them in consideration of their learning. It is part of the metacognition agenda: do they realise how a new approach to learning is helping them to go further, think deeper, make connections, take responsibility, aim for quality and achieve well? This is about more than saying, 'Well done'. As the children see the improved quality of what they produce, they will want more.

18. Help teachers to develop techniques through professional dialogue as well as training

Professional dialogue is vital for teachers. It is only though dialogue that a teacher can explore, wonder aloud, understand, check, grasp and articulate the thinking that will move their practice forward. Training works when showing teachers how, for example, to use new equipment or resources, to develop a new technique to add to their repertoire or to use a new school-wide system properly. If we want teachers to relate practice to broad principles and develop their pedagogic repertoire, then training and showing them how will only get you so far. Teachers need a chance to make sense of things, express their concerns and hear what others have tried.

On any closure day, the balance between exhortation, training and dialogue should be about equal in terms of time. Too much of any one can lead to a blurred focus. Whole-staff meetings can be useful, although teachers and teaching assistants need to be organised into the right groupings and solve the right problems. Good leadership ensures that each person talks with appropriate colleagues with a focus on, say, age cohorts, subject disciplines or school policy issues. This will help them to relate their discussion to their own experience. The challenge is then to connect the outcome to the whole-school approach.

19. Work out how to use government policy and inspection to help you without becoming a hostage to them

The trick is to utilise external influences rather than allow them to call the tune. By all means keep a weather eye on Ofsted and avoid being caught out by new government expectations, but schools need to avoid making constant adjustments to expectations because of pressure from elsewhere.

Teachers who hear justifications for new practice as being somewhere or someone else's expectation get used to this reference control. They begin to feel like cogs in a wheel and lose their own professional impetus. If we believe that our efforts in curriculum and pedagogy are for our children in our school and our community, then we should have enough confidence in what we have planned to be able to absorb external expectations with a touch on the tiller.

At times, we can use a new directive from central government or a revised inspection framework as an impetus for reconsideration or review, especially when the focus is on an aspect that enables us to refresh a previously untouched part of our plan or one that is not as strong as we would wish it to be. Mostly, though, a school pushing for quality in terms of curriculum and pedagogy will be in front of the curve when new developments unfold, and this should create a quiet confidence as we wait for the external agenda to catch up.

20. Anticipate and utilise parents' interest and enthusiasm

Most parents want the best for their children, and most parents are quick to notice enthusiasm in their children as a starting point for success. The judicious involvement of parents in their children's learning will build their confidence in the school and their own enthusiasm for the sort of learning we seek to encourage.

It is worth considering what constitutes quality home learning. Home learning that reinforces images of what the school sees as vital will foster parents' commitment, especially when coupled with the opportunity to attend events in school. At these events, it is vital that parents are reminded regularly about why the learning is as it is. Too often, we give the impression that the parents' role is to clap and be proud, when what we really want is for them to understand the core principles, help their child and extend what we offer in school. We need to help parents understand that to produce what they have seen has demanded teamwork, organisation, concentration, determination, knowledge, skill and effort.

21. Keep governors involved at all times

Whether we work through a local governing board or a directly to a trust, it is crucial to engage fully with governance. The better informed and conversant with curriculum and pedagogic thinking governors are, the greater the chance of success. People involved in governance need to know the school's philosophy and rationale in order to inform their expenditure agreements and set the parameters for appropriate monitoring. Advocacy results from being convinced, and that comes from positive progress.

22. Keep checking for impact

Make sure that impact is a constant touchstone for the effectiveness of development. Impact is not simply a formal endpoint but a blend of formal and informal approaches that are built into everyone's responsibility. That means we are all keeping a weather eye on our own satisfaction with what we actually achieve set against what we say we want to achieve. Spotting impact helps with evaluation and tells us whether we are on a snake or a ladder.

23. Build a shared evidence base

Plan for all teachers and teaching assistants to be closely engaged with literature, theory and research and to share their insights. Be cautious about becoming too wedded to any particular school of thought or becoming unwittingly carried away as a group on a wave of excitement about a new-found silver bullet. Enjoy rich professional debate about the best practice and challenge each other from a basis of deep engagement with the profession. Evidence-informed practice is an important concept; evidence-challenged practice is even more important. We need a curious approach to our own professional learning.

24. Look outwards, share and learn from others

No matter how good we are and how well development is going, we can always improve. We can all learn from others, especially teachers. Judith Little's observation that you know a good school because it is a place where teachers engage in *talk* about teaching practice; *observe* each other teaching; *plan*, *organise* and *evaluate* their teaching together; and *teach each other* is worth revisiting.[4] Providing

---

4   J. W. Little, The Power of Organizational Setting: School Norms and Staff Development. Paper presented at the annual meeting of the American Educational Research Association, Los Angeles, CA, April 1981, pp. 12–13. Available at: https://files.eric.ed.gov/fulltext/ED221918.pdf.

opportunities for teachers to work with one another is an important facet of development and should be part of the way schools operate.

Visits to other schools can be blended with the natural sharing within a school which brings together teachers of different and similar age groups and phases. But these interactions need to be moderated by leadership, which channels the discourse, nudges conversation and enables conclusion. Practice that develops from observing a colleague elsewhere needs professional justification, challenge and discernment.

25. Use public demonstrations of progress – assemblies, exhibitions and teachers showing each other what they are doing

One thing that will always engage children and teachers is seeing good examples. The best schools have worked out how to use assembly really well. There is the world of difference between a celebration assembly – a parade of examples from each class to be applauded – and an assembly where the person leading it uses children's products from around the school as an opportunity to talk about quality, technique or commitment to learning. The clever leader selects products from different age groups that relate to one another and emphasises progression or skills extension, or uses products to illustrate links in knowledge fields or the inter-related nature of subject disciplines. The successful assembly should be a professional learning opportunity for staff, as well as an image for children of their learning pathway, with a reminder of the road travelled and a vision of the journey ahead.

The challenge for leadership is to encourage shared outlooks in teachers, so they use similar techniques in the classroom to articulate to children the way in which their collective effort is developing and promoting greater awareness of learning. This is called responding to

children's effort, and it will be as powerful as any marking scheme in fostering progress

One of the key stepping stones in our story has been the exhibitions we have organised, both in individual schools and collectively across schools. While the idea of the exhibition was greeted with enthusiasm, the practicalities were a challenge at first. By assembling the few, but very good, examples of quality products from each school, we could achieve many steps forward from the same event.

Not only do the exhibitions provide a chance for the children to see each other's products, but their inclusion tells them that these things are valued and they are proud to be a representative of their school. For teachers, the exhibitions are an occasion to be part of something bigger and a subtle opportunity to see how their school's expectations and outcomes match others in the trust. Feedback from parents has been immensely positive, as has the response from secondary school teachers in the schools where exhibitions have been held. All these possibilities for public recognition exist within schools.

The important point about exhibitions is to recognise the developments in curriculum and pedagogy as well as valuing children's and teachers' contributions. The conversations need to be about reason and purpose: why did we do this? What did we achieve? How do we use the experience to move children's learning to new heights? How do we become yet more proficient professionals?

We asked ourselves these same questions throughout the process of developing our Curious Curriculum. Why did we do this? Because we wanted the best for every child. What did we achieve? We believe we have achieved a lot in terms of improved outcomes and learning outlooks for children, teacher confidence and competence, and leadership fulfilment. How do we use the experience? We keep building, looking for new possibilities and using research productively. How do we become more proficient professionals? That is the perennial question. We can keep coming up with answers, but we doubt we will ever think we have finished. That is the joy of teaching: always improving and always knowing there is more to be done.

> Realising our work was high quality because other schools beyond the trust were asking questions about how we get children to do it – that was a telling moment.
>
> *Nicola Bailey*

Afterword
by Dave Baker

If a multi-academy trust is to make a real difference to people's lives, it needs to have a shared purpose and values rather than just being a school leaders' friendship club. Since the inception of Olympus Academy Trust at the start of 2012, the trust vision has been about working together in our local communities to bring about improvement – we talk about collaboration, excellence and opportunity. We have developed a reputation for strong ethos and culture and for our moral purpose in welcoming schools in challenging circumstances and in need of support and change.

It became clear at a relatively early stage that Olympus needed to develop and articulate a clear educational philosophy and trust-wide school improvement strategy in order to facilitate change. It took slightly longer to come to a shared view that an alignment of curriculum and pedagogy would be essential in order to maximise our potential as a group of schools working together. The concept of the Olympus Way emerged and gained full support from the trust board, which recognised the importance of all learners in the trust having access to what already existed in the highest performing schools but also saw the importance of taking the strongest schools further. Trustees accepted that this would take time, that it would need proper resourcing and that it would require support through key central roles in the trust. Input would also be needed from external experts, along with time to focus on training and development. For Olympus, this included an ongoing commitment to eight staff training days each year (rather than five), devoted to collaborative curriculum development work across the trust.

Momentum gathered first around primary curriculum and pedagogy. Key staff established a set of principles, which fitted with agreed trust values, and started to develop a curriculum framework that would become crucial in transforming engagement, participation, progress and quality of outcomes. Significant investment went into staff training – this was vital in getting buy-in. After a slow start, the production of a suite of Olympus Way supporting publications, the creation of an online staff portal for sharing planning and resources, as well as network groups for collaborative working, led to a momentum shift. Staff began to realise the huge benefit for staff workload and well-being and learners became passionate about their curriculum and learning experiences. Inevitably, this tipping point was significant and was backed up by positive feedback from parents/carers, visitors and Ofsted inspection teams when they came calling (remotely and in person). However, this is not about Ofsted – this is about what makes better learning for young people.

From the perspective of the trust's executive team and the board of trustees, there has been a seismic shift in attitudes and outcomes across the Olympus primary settings. Visitors to Olympus primary schools cannot fail to notice that the environment is learning focused and vibrant. Children are encouraged to take pride in themselves and their work, and have bought into the concept of polished products as the normal endpoint for themed learning. The quality of trust-wide exhibitions at the end of a learning theme has increased year on year. It is not competitive between schools, teachers and children – but it is!

We are at a particular point on the Olympus journey. A huge amount of effort has gone into the development of both curriculum and teaching and learning. Progress has been significant but it has created a desire for more, bigger and better. Confidence has increased massively and enjoyment levels are high, but the team is determined that there is more to come. I am excited to see what that will look like, but I know that our values will determine our next steps as we work together to plan them.

Dave Baker, CEO, Olympus Academy Trust

Appendix

List of subject associations

With grateful thanks to the Council for Subject Associations (www.subjectassociations.org.uk), which endeavours to promote and support communities of interest in many subject disciplines.

We hope this list is helpful; please excuse any unintentional omissions.

Subject	Association name	Web address
Art and design	Council for Higher Education in Art & Design (CHEAD)	https://chead.ac.uk
Art and design	National Society for Education in Art and Design (NSEAD)	https://www.nsead.org
Citizenship	Amnesty International UK	https://www.amnesty.org.uk/education-resources
Citizenship	Association for Citizenship Teaching (ACT)	https://www.teachingcitizenship.org.uk
Citizenship	Community	https://community-tu.org
Citizenship	Compassionate Education Foundation (CoED)	https://www.coedfoundation.org.uk
Citizenship	Equality and Human Rights Commission	https://www.equalityhumanrights.com/en/lesson-plan-ideas
Citizenship	UK Parliament	https://learning.parliament.uk/en
Citizenship	Young Citizens	https://www.youngcitizens.org

Subject	Association name	Web address
Classics	Classical Association	https://classicalassociation.org
Computing	Computing at School (CAS)	https://www.computingatschool.org.uk
Design and technology	Design and Technology Association (DATA)	https://www.data.org.uk
Design and technology	National Association for Education Technology (NAACE)	https://www.naace.org.uk
Design and technology	Technology, Pedagogy and Education Association (TPEA)	https://tpea.ac.uk
English	English Association (EA)	https://englishassociation.ac.uk
English	National Association for the Teaching of English (NATE)	https://www.nate.org.uk
English	National Association of Writers in Education (NAWE)	https://www.nawe.co.uk
English	United Kingdom Literacy Association (UKLA)	https://ukla.org
Geography	Geographical Association (GA)	https://www.geography.org.uk
Geography	Royal Geographical Society (with Institute of British Geographers) (RGS)	https://www.rgs.org
History	British Library	https://www.bl.uk
History	Historical Association (HA)	https://www.history.org.uk
History	National Archives	https://www.nationalarchives.gov.uk
Languages	Association for Language Learning (ALL)	https://www.all-languages.org.uk
Mathematics	Association of Mathematics Education Teachers (AMET)	https://www.ametonline.org.uk
Mathematics	Association of Teachers of Mathematics (ATM)	https://www.atm.org.uk
Mathematics	Joint Mathematical Council of the United Kingdom (JMC)	https://www.jmc.org.uk
Mathematics	Mathematical Association (MA)	https://www.m-a.org.uk
Mathematics	National Association for Numeracy and Mathematics in Colleges (NANAMIC)	https://www.nanamic.org.uk
Mathematics	National Numeracy	https://www.nationalnumeracy.org.uk
Mathematics	STEM Learning	https://www.stem.org.uk
Music, drama and dance	Incorporated Society of Musicians (ISM)	https://www.ism.org

Subject	Association name	Web address
Music, drama and dance	Music Mark	https://www.musicmark.org.uk
Music, drama and dance	National Drama (ND)	https://www.nationaldrama.org.uk
Music, drama and dance	One Dance UK	https://www.onedanceuk.org
Physical education	Association for Physical Education (afPE)	https://www.afpe.org.uk/physical-education
Personal, social, health and economic education	Association for the Teaching of Psychology (ATP)	https://www.theatp.uk
Personal, social, health and economic education	Philosophy for Children (P4C)	https://p4c.com
Personal, social, health and economic education	PSHE Association	https://pshe-association.org.uk
Religious education	National Association of Teachers of Religious Education (NATRE)	https://www.natre.org.uk
Religious education	RE Today	https://www.retoday.org.uk
Religious education	Religious Education Council of England and Wales	https://www.religiouseducationcouncil.org.uk
Science	Association for Science Education (ASE)	https://www.ase.org.uk
Science	British Science Association (BSA)	https://www.britishscienceassociation.org
Science	Primary Science Teaching Trust (PSTT)	https://pstt.org.uk
Science	Royal Society	https://royalsociety.org
Science	Royal Society of Biology	https://www.rsb.org.uk
Science	Royal Society of Chemistry	https://www.rsc.org
Special educational needs and disabilities	Association for All Speech Impaired Children (AFASIC)	https://afasic.org.uk

Subject	Association name	Web address
Special educational needs and disabilities	Independent Provider of Special Education Advice (IPSEA)	https://www.ipsea.org.uk
Special educational needs and disabilities	National Association for Special Educational Needs (NASEN)	https://www.nasen.org.uk
Special educational needs and disabilities	National Autistic Society	https://www.autism.org.uk
Special educational needs and disabilities	Mind	https://www.mind.org.uk
Special educational needs and disabilities	Professional Association of Teachers of Students with Specific Learning Difficulties (Patoss)	https://www.patoss-dyslexia.org
Additional support	Association for Achievement and Improvement through Assessment (AAIA)	https://www.aaia.org.uk
Additional support	Association for Learning Technology (ALT)	https://www.alt.ac.uk
Additional support	Association for the Study of Primary Education (APSE)	https://www.aspe-uk.eu
Additional support	Association of School and College Leaders (ASCL)	https://www.ascl.org.uk
Additional support	British Association for Early Childhood Education	https://early-education.org.uk
Additional support	British Educational Research Association (BERA)	https://www.bera.ac.uk
Additional support	Chartered College of Teaching	https://chartered.college
Additional support	Chartered Institute of Educational Assessors (CIEA)	https://www.herts.ac.uk/ciea
Additional support	Curriculum Foundation	https://www.curriculumfoundation.org
Additional support	Early Education	https://early-education.org.uk
Additional support	Forest School Association (FSA)	https://forestschoolassociation.org
Additional support	Mantle of the Expert (MoE)	https://www.mantleoftheexpert.com
Additional support	National Association for Primary Education (NAPE)	https://www.nape.org.uk
Additional support	National Association of Environmental Education (NAEE)	https://naee.org.uk

Subject	Association name	Web address
Additional support	National Association of Head Teachers (NAHT)	https://naht.org.uk
Additional support	National Association of School-Based Teacher Trainers (NASBTT)	https://www.nasbtt.org.uk
Additional support	National Governance Association (NGA)	https://www.nga.org.uk
Additional support	National Primary Teacher Education Council (NaPTEC)	https://www.naptec.org.uk
Additional support	National Subject Association for English as an Additional Language (NALDIC)	https://naldic.org.uk
Additional support	Partners in Excellence (PiXL)	https://www.pixl.org.uk
Additional support	Researching, Advancing and Inspiring Student Engagement (RAISE)	https://www.raise-network.com
Additional support	Social, Emotional and Behavioural Difficulties Association (SEBDA)	https://www.sebda.org
Additional support	Staff and Educational Development Association (SEDA)	https://www.seda.ac.uk
Additional support	Universities' Council for the Education of Teachers (UCET)	https://www.ucet.ac.uk
Additional support	Values-based Education (VbE)	https://valuesbasededucation.com

Bibliography

Alexander, R. (2008) *Towards Dialogic Teaching: Rethinking Classroom Talk*. New York: Dorchester Publishing Company.

Auld, R. and Inner London Education Authority (1976) *The William Tyndale Junior and Infants Schools: Report of the Public Inquiry* [Auld Report]. London: Inner London Education Authority.

Bandura, A. (1986) *Social Foundations of Thought and Action: A Social Cognitive Theory*. Englewood Cliffs, NJ: Prentice Hall.

Barber, M. (2015) *How to Run a Government So That Citizens Benefit and Taxpayers Don't Go Crazy*. London: Allen Lane.

Belloc, H. (1907) *Cautionary Tales for Children*. London: Eveleigh Nash. Available at: https://www.gutenberg.org/files/27424/27424-h/27424-h.htm.

Bennett, N. (1976) *Teaching Styles and Pupil Progress*. London: Open Books.

Berger, R. (2003) *An Ethic of Excellence: Building a Culture of Craftsmanship with Students*. Portsmouth, NH: Heinemann.

Berger, R. (2012) Austin's Butterfly: Building Excellence in Student Work [video], *Models of Excellence – EL Education*. Available at: https://modelsofexcellence.eleducation.org/resources/austins-butterfly.

Briceño, E. (2013) Mindsets and Student Agency, *High Tech High Unboxed* (13 April). Available at: https://hthunboxed.org/unboxed_posts/mindsets-and-student-agency.

Brighouse, T. and Waters, M. (2022) *About Our Schools: Improving on Previous Best*. Carmarthen: Crown House Publishing.

Callaghan, J. (1976) A Rational Debate Based on the Facts. Speech delivered at Ruskin College, Oxford, 18 October. Available at: http://www.educationengland.org.uk/documents/speeches/1976ruskin.html.

Cooperrider, D. L. and Whitney, D. (1999) Appreciative Inquiry: A Positive Revolution in Change. In P. Holman and T. Devane (eds), *The Change Handbook: Group Methods for Shaping the Future*. San Francisco, CA: Berrett-Koehler, pp. 275–289.

Counsell, C. (2012) Wrestling with Enquiry Questions: Linking Content and Concept in Medium Term Planning [blog]. Available at: https://andallthatweb.files.wordpress.com/2012/07/wrestling-with-enquiry-questions.pdf.

Counsell, C. (2018) Taking Curriculum Seriously, *Impact: Journal of the Chartered College of Teaching*, 4 (autumn). Available at: https://impact.chartered.college/article/taking-curriculum-seriously.

Cox, D. (2020) Curricular Enquiry Questions in RE – Blog 1, *Missdcoxblog* [blog] (14 May). Available at: https://missdcoxblog.wordpress.com/2020/05/14/curricular-enquiry-questions-in-re-blog-1.

Davis, J. (2002) The Inner London Education Authority and the William Tyndale Junior School Affair, 1974–1976, *Oxford Review of Education*, 28(2/3), 275–298.

Dearing, R. (1994) *The National Curriculum and its Assessment: Final Report* [Dearing Review]. London: School Curriculum and Assessment Authority. Available at: http://www.educationengland.org.uk/documents/dearing1994/dearing1994.html.

Department for Education (2011) *The National Strategies 1997–2011: A Brief Summary of the Impact and Effectiveness of the National Strategies*. Available at: https://assets.publishing.service.gov.uk/government/uploads/system/uploads/attachment_data/file/175408/DFE-00032-2011.pdf.

Department for Education (2013) National Curriculum (14 October; updated 16 July 2014). Available at: https://www.gov.uk/government/collections/national-curriculum.

Department for Education (2020) *Development Matters: Non-Statutory Curriculum Guidance for the Early Years Foundation Stage* (rev. July 2021). Available at: https://www.gov.uk/government/publications/development-matters--2.

Department for Education (2021a) Early Years Foundation Stage (EYFS) Statutory Framework (March). Available at: https://www.gov.uk/government/publications/early-years-foundation-stage-framework--2.

Department for Education (2021b) *Sustainability & Climate Change: A Draft Strategy for the Education & Children's Services Systems* (November). Available at: https://assets.publishing.service.gov.uk/government/uploads/system/uploads/attachment_data/file/1031454/SCC_DRAFT_Strategy.pdf.

Department for Education and Nash, Lord (2014) Guidance on Promoting British Values in Schools Published [press release] (27 November). Available at: https://www.gov.uk/government/news/guidance-on-promoting-british-values-in-schools-published.

Department for Education and Skills (2003) *Excellence and Enjoyment: A Strategy for Primary Schools*. Nottingham: DfES. Available at: http://dera.ioe.ac.uk/id/eprint/4817.

Department of Education and Science (1978) *Primary Education in England: A Survey by HM Inspectors of Schools*. London: HMSO. Available at: http://www.educationengland.org.uk/documents/hmi-primary/hmi-primary.html.

Department of Education and Science (1984–1989) *Curriculum Matters. An HMI Series*. London: HMSO. Available at: http://www.educationengland.org.uk/documents/hmi-curricmatters/index.html.

Dudley, P. (n.d.) The 'Lesson Study' Model of Classroom Enquiry, *Teaching Expertise*. Available at: https://www.teachingexpertise.com/articles/the-lesson-study-model-of-classroom-enquiry.

Durand, S. (2016) Engage Your Early Learners Using Provocations, *Educa* (29 June). Available at: https://www.geteduca.com/blog/engage-early-learners-using-provocations.

Dweck, C. S. (2006) *Mindset: The New Psychology of Success*. New York: Random House.

Ebbinghaus, H. (1913) *Memory: A Contribution to Experimental Psychology*, tr. H. A. Ruger and C. E. Bussenius. New York: Teachers College, Columbia University.

Elliott, J. and Norris, N. (eds) (2012) *Curriculum, Pedagogy and Educational Research: The Work of Lawrence Stenhouse*. Abingdon and New York: Routledge.

Fiorella, L. and Mayer, R. (2015) *Learning as a Generative Activity: Eight Learning Strategies That Promote Understanding*. New York: Cambridge University Press.

Fisher, R. (2003) *Teaching Thinking*, 2nd edn. London and New York: Bloomsbury Academic.

Ginott, H. G. (1972) *Teacher and Child: A Book for Parents and Teachers*. New York: Macmillan.

Gumbrell, D. (2021) *Spin: Time and Task Management in Teaching*. St Albans: Critical Publishing.

Hattie, J. (2009) *Visible Learning: A Synthesis of Over 800 Meta-Analyses Relating to Achievement*. Abingdon and New York: Routledge.

Hattie, J. and Donoghue, G. (2016) Learning Strategies: A Synthesis and Conceptual Model, *NPJ Science of Learning*, 1. Available at: http://www.nature.com/articles/npjscilearn201613.

HM Treasury (2003) *Every Child Matters*. Norwich: TSO. Available at: https://www.gov.uk/government/publications/every-child-matters.

Isaacs, T., Zara, C., Herbert, G., Coombs, S. J. and Smith, C. (2013) Ipsative Assessment. In *Key Concepts in Educational Assessment*. London: SAGE, ch. 26. http://dx.doi.org/10.4135/9781473915077.n26

Jennings, A. (2019) *Vocabulary Ninja: Mastering Vocabulary – Activities to Unlock the World of Words*. London: Bloomsbury Education.

Kidd, D. (2020) *A Curriculum of Hope: As Rich in Humanity as in Knowledge*. Carmarthen: Independent Thinking Press.

Kirby, J. (2015) Knowledge Organisers, *Pragmatic Reform* [blog] (28 March). Available at: https://pragmaticreform.wordpress.com/2015/03/28/knowledge-organisers.

Kotter, J. P., Akhtar, V. and Gupta, G. (2021) *Change: How Organizations Achieve Hard to Imagine Results in Uncertain and Volatile Times*. Chichester: John Wiley.

Lad, N. (2021) *Shimamura's MARGE Model of Learning in Action*. Woodbridge: John Catt Educational.

Little, J. W. (1981) The Power of Organizational Setting: School Norms and Staff Development. Paper presented at the annual meeting of the American Educational Research Association, Los Angeles, CA, April. Available at: https://files.eric.ed.gov/fulltext/ED221918.pdf.

McGee, P. (2015) *S.U.M.O (Shut Up, Move On): The Straight-Talking Guide to Succeeding in Life*. Chichester: Capstone.

McLennan, N. (1999) *Awesome Purpose*. Aldershot: Gower Publishing.

McLeod, S. (2020) Piaget's Stages of Cognitive Development: Background and Key Concepts of Piaget's Theory, *Simply Psychology* (7 December). Available at: https://www.simplypsychology.org/piaget.html.

Middleton, C., Gubbay, J. and Ballard, C. (eds) (1997) *The Student's Companion to Sociology*. St Malden, MA: Blackwell.

Miller, M. (2018) Organising Knowledge: The Purpose and Pedagogy of Knowledge Organisers, *Impact: Journal of the Chartered College of Teaching*, 4 (autumn). Available at: https://my.chartered.college/impact_article/organising-knowledge-the-purpose-and-pedagogy-of-knowledge-organisers.

Myatt, M. (2018) *The Curriculum: Gallimaufry to Coherence*. Woodbridge: John Catt Educational.

Myatt, M. (2020) *Back on Track: Fewer Things, Greater Depth*. Woodbridge: John Catt Educational.

Myatt, M. and Tomsett, J. (2021) *Huh: Curriculum Conversations Between Subject and Senior Leaders*. Woodbridge: John Catt Educational.

Oates, T. (2014) National Curriculum: Tim Oates on Assessment [video] (22 May). Available at: https://www.youtube.com/watch?v=-q5vrBXFpm0.

Ofsted (2019a) Education Inspection Framework (14 May; updated 23 July 2021). Available at: https://www.gov.uk/government/publications/education-inspection-framework/education-inspection-framework.

Ofsted (2019b) School Report: Stoke Lodge Primary School (9–10 January). Available at: https://files.ofsted.gov.uk/v1/file/50058229.

Ofsted (2021a) Monitoring Inspection Visit to Stoke Lodge Primary School (12 May). Available at: https://files.ofsted.gov.uk/v1/file/50165559.

Ofsted (2021b) Research Review Series: Religious Education (12 May). Available at: https://www.gov.uk/government/publications/research-review-series-religious-education/research-review-series-religious-education.

Ofsted (2021c) School Report: Inspection of Meadowbrook Primary School (12–13 October). Available at: https://files.ofsted.gov.uk/v1/file/50172978.

Ofsted and Spielman, A. (2018) Amanda Spielman's Speech at the Wellington Festival of Education (22 June). Available at: https://www.gov.uk/government/speeches/amanda-spielmans-speech-at-the-wellington-festival-of-education.

Ofsted and Spielman, A. (2019) Speech to the 'Wonder Years' Curriculum Conference (26 January). Available at: https://www.gov.uk/government/speeches/amanda-spielman-at-the-wonder-years-curriculum-conference.

Parsons, S. and Branagan, A. (2013) *Word Aware 1: Teaching Vocabulary Across the Day, Across the Curriculum*. Abingdon and New York: Routledge.

Plowden, B. (1967) *Children and their Primary Schools* [Plowden Report]. London: HMSO. Available at: http://www.educationengland.org.uk/documents/plowden/plowden1967-1.html.

Quigley, A. (2018) *Closing the Vocabulary Gap*. Abingdon and New York: Routledge.

Reid, A. (2020) Cultural Capital, Critical Theory and Curriculum. In C. Sealy and T. Bennett (eds), *The researchED Guide to the Curriculum: An Evidence-Informed Guide for Teachers*. Woodbridge: John Catt Educational, pp. 41–48.

Robinson, M. (2013) *Trivium 21c: Preparing Young People for the Future with Lessons from the Past*. Carmarthen: Independent Thinking Press.

Roediger III, H. L. and Butler, A. C. (2011) The Critical Role of Retrieval Practice on Long-Term Retention, *Trends in Cognitive Sciences*, 15(1), 20–27.

Rose, J. (2009) *Independent Review of the Primary Curriculum: Final Report* [Rose Review]. Nottingham: Department for Children, Schools and Families. Available at: http://www.educationengland.org.uk/documents/pdfs/2009-IRPC-final-report.pdf.

Rosenshine, B. (1983) Teaching Functions in Instructional Programs, *Elementary School Journal*, 83(4), 335–351.

Rosenshine, B. (2012) Principles of Instruction: Research-Based Strategies That All Teachers Should Know, *American Educator* (spring), 12–19, 39. Available at: https://www.aft.org/sites/default/files/periodicals/Rosenshine.pdf.

Schwab, J. J. (1962) The Concept of the Structure of a Discipline, *Educational Record*, 43, 197–205.

Shavelson, R., Ruiz-Primo, M. A. and Wiley, E. (2005) Windows into the Mind, *Higher Education*, 49(4), 413–430. doi:10.1007/s10734-004-9448-9

Staricoff, M. (2021) *The Joy of Not Knowing: A Philosophy of Education Transforming Teaching, Thinking, Learning and Leadership in Schools*. Abingdon and New York: Routledge.

Sullivan, R. (2018) DfE Clarifies Reference to Enquiry-Based Learning, *Historical Association* (8 August). Available at: https://www.history.org.uk/ha-news/categories/455/news/3613/dfe-clarifies-reference-to-enquiry-based-learning.

Sumpter, O. (2022) Using Vocabulary Tiers to Improve Literacy, *Bedrock Learning* [blog] (8 March). Available at: https://bedrocklearning.org/blog/using-vocabulary-tiers-to-improve-literacy.

Sweller, J. (1988) Cognitive Load During Problem Solving: Effects on Learning, *Cognitive Science*, 12(2), 257–285. doi:10.1207/s15516709cog1202_4

Twiselton, S., Randall V. and Lane, S. (2018) Developing Effective Teachers: Perspectives and Approaches, *Impact: Journal of the Chartered College of Teaching*, 3 (summer). Available at: https://my.chartered.college/impact_article/developing-effective-teachers-perspectives-and-approaches.

UNICEF (1989) *The United Nations Convention on the Rights of the Child*. Available at: https://downloads.unicef.org.uk/wp-content/

uploads/2010/05/UNCRC_united_nations_convention_on_the_rights_of_the_child.pdf.

Waters, M. (2013) *Thinking Allowed: On Schooling*. Carmarthen: Independent Thinking Press.

Waters, M. (2021) Navigating New Learning Horizons: With Children at the Helm, *APSE Bulletin*, Issue 22 (February): 1–4. Available at: https://www.aspe-uk.eu/wp-content/uploads/2021/03/ASPE22_Feb_2021.pdf.

Willingham, D. T. (2010) *Why Don't Students Like School? A Cognitive Scientist Answers Questions About How the Mind Works and What It Means for the Classroom*. San Francisco, CA: John Wiley & Sons.

Young, M. (2018) A Knowledge-Led Curriculum: Pitfalls and Possibilities, *Impact: Journal of the Chartered College of Teaching*, 4 (autumn). Available at: https://discovery.ucl.ac.uk/id/eprint/10060317/1/Young_FINAL.pdf.

Young, M. (2020) The Curriculum. In C. Sealy and T. Bennett (eds), *The researchED Guide to the Curriculum: An Evidence-Informed Guide for Teachers*. Woodbridge: John Catt Educational, pp. 19–29.

About the authors

Mick Waters has been a teacher and head teacher before working as chief education officer for the city of Manchester. He also worked at a national level with the Qualifications and Curriculum Authority where he was director of curriculum. Over several years, he has been asked to work in countries across the globe either with national governments or directly with schools to develop revised policy and practice for leadership, governance and classroom teaching. While experienced in higher education, Mick believes in being close to teachers, children and schools, and is often to be found in the classroom working with children. He is passionate about the role of education in improving life chances for children and enjoys asking adults to look at learning through the eyes of a child.

Claire Banks started her teaching career in Devon. It took her around the UK where she taught in Scotland, Hereford and Worcester. Returning to the South West, she became a deputy head teacher and then head teacher in Bristol, before becoming director of education for the Olympus Academy Trust, a cross-phase multi-academy trust in North Bristol. Her work around personal, social, health and economic education and female genital mutilation has led to her involvement at national conferences. Claire's MBA in international educational leadership, and her interest in understanding her own school community, led her to develop leadership exchanges around the world, including Africa and South Asia, being fortunate enough to have developed strong links when visiting Pakistan and India. Claire has worked with head teachers on curriculum design and school improvement in a system leadership capacity, offering school-to-school support to school trusts. She contributes to executive leaders courses and her passion for succession planning for the profession has led to her coaching and mentoring on Aspiring Heads and Women in Leadership programmes.